NATO
AFTER THIRTY YEARS

"During those 31 years there has been more stability in Europe than that Continent has experienced in over a century."

From remarks made by General Lyman L. Lemnitzer, Supreme Allied Commander Europe, 1964–69, at Conference on NATO after Thirty Years, 16 April 1980, Center for NATO Studies, Kent State University.

NATO
AFTER THIRTY YEARS

Edited by
Lawrence S. Kaplan
and
Robert W. Clawson

 Scholarly Resources Inc.
Wilmington, Delaware

© 1981 by Scholarly Resources Inc.
All rights reserved
First published 1981
Printed and bound in the United States of America

Scholarly Resources Inc.
104 Greenhill Avenue
Wilmington, Delaware 19805

Distributed in the United Kingdom and Commonwealth
by George Prior Associated Publishers Ltd.
37-41 Bedford Row, London WC1R 4JH, England

Library of Congress Cataloging in Publication Data
Main entry under title:

NATO after thirty years.

   Includes index.
   1. North Atlantic Treaty Organization—Addresses,
essays, lectures.   I. Kaplan, Lawrence S.   II. Clawson,
Robert W.
   UA646.3.N227   355'.031'091821   80-53885
   ISBN 0-8420-2172-8
   ISBN 0-8420-2184-1 (pbk.)

CONTENTS

81-1186

PREFACE

This volume grew out of a conference entitled "NATO after Thirty Years," held on 16–17 April 1980 in Kent, Ohio, and sponsored by the Center for NATO Studies at Kent State University with the support of the NATO Information Service. In addition to the papers presented by the authors of the individual chapters, former Ambassadors Theodore C. Achilles and Robert Strausz-Hupé of the United States, and Escott Reid of Canada gave special addresses for the occasion and contributed their views to the proceedings. Further remarks were offered by General Lyman L. Lemnitzer, former Supreme Allied Commander Europe and a patron of the center.

Scholars and government officials knowledgeable in NATO studies served as commentators on the papers: James G. Banks of the Cuyahoga Community College; Albert H. Bowman of the University of Tennessee at Chattanooga; James Bruce of the National War College; Andreas Dorpalen of Ohio State University; Alfred Goldberg, historian, Office of the Secretary of Defense; Richard F. Grimmett of the Congressional Research Service at the Library of Congress; Alonzo L. Hamby of Ohio University; Morrell Heald of Case Western Reserve University; Ronald Hoffman of the University of Maryland; Warren F. Kuehl, director of the Center of Peace Studies, University of Akron; Joseph May of Youngstown State University; Stephen M. Millett and Robert L. Norman of the Batelle Institute; Arnold Offner of Boston University; Manfred von Nordheim, director of the Konrad-Adenauer-Stiftung, Washington, DC; Marvin Zahniser of Ohio State University; and Benedict K. Zobrist, director of the Harry S Truman Library, Independence, Missouri.

To these members of the conference the authors wish to express their appreciation for comments on and criticisms of their respective papers. Many of these remarks have been incorporated into this volume.

At Kent State University we received valuable assistance from colleagues and from members of the staff of the Center for NATO Studies. The following in particular deserve special recognition: Tim Fleshman, Roger Freeman, Mike Hicks, Wilda Lunsford, Mark Rubin, and Don Theiss. Margorie Evans, who typed and retyped the manuscript, provided energetic and skilled assistance. James Carlton played a key role in both conference management and preparation of the manuscript.

Lawrence S. Kaplan and Robert W. Clawson
Kent State University

INTRODUCTION

There is no dearth of literature on NATO. Every year symposia, conferences, and colloquia examine the problems of the organization and frequently come up with useful analyses of current issues. Books emphasizing the present and future also have dominated the corporate ventures of scholars and analysts working in schools of international studies, or policy think tanks, or government offices. NATO's decennial years in particular have been occasions for bursts of new thoughts on the Atlantic Alliance.

This volume seeks to open new paths by looking back to the origins of NATO and to relationships within and without the alliance that have been relatively neglected by scholars. The contributors are interested not only in where the organization stands after thirty years but also how and why it reached the place it has in the course of its first generation. Only in the last few years have historians been in a position to examine the workings of policymakers as they drafted an alliance out of the disparate traditions of Western European and American nations. The archives of Canada, the United Kingdom, and the United States are open to 1950, through the critical formative period of NATO. Even where the official records remained closed, memoirs and private papers of diplomats and statesmen of the member nations have yielded information regarding NATO's past that permits scholars to better understand the origins of the alliance where a decade ago this was not possible.

With this newly available information the Center for NATO Studies at Kent State University brought together historians and political scientists to examine the record from an historical perspective. For the most part, American historians have not yet turned their attention to the alliance. But as presidential libraries and Department of State and Defense records become more visible in the National Archives, the alliance can become a rich source of knowledge about the workings of alliance politics, military organization, and new institutions—international and supranational—created by NATO. The contributors to the volume arrange the chapters under three large rubrics, dealing sequentially with NATO's political history, particularly the relationships among its members; NATO's role in the world at large and its intersection with other organizations and nations; and NATO's military record, the primary function of its first generation.

NATO IN HISTORY

In an overview that attempts to locate change and continuity in the first generation and a half of NATO's history, Lawrence Kaplan finds both to have been present in abundance. Changes have been frequent and sometimes dramatic: witness the establishment of the Supreme Headquarters Allied Powers Europe (SHAPE) in the 1950s, the departure of France in the 1960s from the organization, and the proliferation of new bureaucracies in the 1970s. The image throughout its history has been that of disarray. And as the problems of the alliance became identified in the 1970s with the Third World, American leadership appeared either too self-centered under Nixon or too indecisive under Carter. But continuity is equally identifiable. What stands out over thirty years is the position of the Soviet Union as the reluctant unifying presence, and the role of the United States, despite the diminution of its authority, power, and reputation, as a critical factor in the effectiveness of the organization.

The domination of the United States over the alliance was most evident in the first generation of NATO's history. Norman Graebner makes a strong case for the years 1953 to 1969 as a coherent unit for historical analysis. The American commitment to NATO halted Communist expansionism, dissolved Communist subversion, and restored Europe to economic and political health. The Eisenhower administration both underscored the continuity of the United States in NATO and fostered growth of European reaction against American leadership. As Europe prospered, it identified containment with conditions for détente; the United States in turn regarded containment as a step toward liberation of Eastern Europe. This difference increased in the 1960s even though the Kennedy administration attempted to create a genuine trans-Atlantic partnership. The attempt foundered on American refusal to share nuclear weaponry and on Europe's suspicion that a Soviet-American standoff in nuclear power could jeopardize their security. In practice, however, Graebner points out that the United States accepted a de facto division of Europe and that Europe recognized American nuclear power as the fundamental deterrent force of NATO. Nonetheless, the absence of mutually defined goals portended troubles for the alliance in the 1970s and beyond.

In Colin Gordon's examination of the larger European states and NATO, he observed that their relationship is as much with the United States as with each other. For Great Britain, this included a trans-Atlantic "special relationship" nourished by the experience of World War II. French fears of a revived Germany in NATO prevailed over resentment of American leadership, at least until the 1960s. France's concern for its own freedom to maneuver among the superpowers as much as its doubts about the nuclear guarantee protection of the United States accounted for its defection from the military arm of NATO. Of the three large powers, Germany was the most dependent on NATO, even for its formation as a nation. While it benefited from the allies' needs for German manpower, territory, and resources, it remained closer to the United States than any of the others. The failure of unification bound Germany to the alliance and yet made *Ostpolitik,* with its economic and social investment in a good relationship with the East, increasingly important. On balance the alliance has served the national interests of their members. At the same time NATO has succeeded so far in "containing" France, rehabilitating Germany, and incorporating Britain into the European framework.

Nikolaj Petersen demonstrates that national interests also govern small power considerations of NATO. A major difficulty in analyzing the smaller nations is in identifying common themes to link disparate groups with no single national interest to unite them. Petersen resolves this by using the cases of the northern nations—the Low Countries and the Scandinavian members—where greater coherence can be found, and generalizations would be more operative than with the Mediterranean member nations. Basically, the small nations' concerns involved two issues: local balance of power and the particular security problems they pose to the nation involved. Denmark and Norway were more worried about security than Belgium and Holland, since the former were closer to the Soviet Union and unshielded by larger allies. Petersen notes that, given the absence of responsibility for the burdens of the alliance, the smaller nations could afford to emphasize the rhetoric of moralism and anti-colonialism in their relations with the larger powers. Although criticisms along these lines would include the role of the United States in Vietnam, the Nordic and Low Countries have been more willing to accept U.S. leadership in Europe than the larger countries. They value multilateral consultation but willingly have left the nuclear deterrent to the United States rather than have it spread among the members.

NATO IN THE WORLD

There is a tendency among those involved in an organization as complex as NATO has become to look inward for problems and for solutions. Yet, it was the outside world that brought the Atlantic powers together, and it is the outside world that continues to set the course of the alliance. Of all the external institutions related to NATO, the Warsaw Pact inevitably ranks foremost. Whether or not it is a mirror image of NATO's posture, the Soviet Union always has regarded NATO as a provocation. The Warsaw Pact in its own estimation was simply a reaction to the aggressive incorporation of West Germany into the alliance. Whatever lip service the bloc may give to imminent dissolution of NATO over the years, it generally has attributed a "worst case" behavior to NATO. The Soviet Union has gained nuclear parity and conventional superiority in arms on the continent, it has rationalized the existence of a permanent federal republic; but it continues to see in NATO an enduring symbol of American imperial domination. In the account of Robert Clawson and Glee Wilson, NATO by definition is dangerous to the Communist world and hence justifies mobilization of the Warsaw Pact.

NATO's relationship with the United Nations, in its own way, has been almost as sensitive as its relations with the Warsaw Pact. Much has been made of the incompatibility between NATO and the world organization, of NATO's potential for undermining the peace-keeping role of the United Nations. But Thomas Campbell submits that NATO has served rather than hindered the development of the United Nations. Despite the arguments of isolationists and internationalists who wished to use the United Nations to defeat the treaty, the roots of regionalism are found in the charter itself (articles 52 and 59). Rather than destroying the organization, the Atlantic Alliance created a supplemental security framework that permitted the bitter passions of Soviet-American rivalry in the Cold War to be removed from Lake Success. In part, the United Nations survived and grew because NATO and the Warsaw Pact conducted their contest outside the world organization.

With less confidence, NATO confronted another issue that was as sensitive as its connections with the United Nations; namely, the legacy of European colonialism. The United States, as Scott Bills clarifies, had to balance its self-image of traditional opposition to colonialism against the danger that excessive anticolonial zeal might weaken European allies. Urging gradual decolonialization upon the Europeans, the United States attempted to dampen the issue as much as possible. This tactic failed when France insisted that Algeria, as an integral part of France, must be included within the geographical scope of the alliance. While the question of the colonies of Britain and the Netherlands did not disturb the alliance to the same degree, the fact that other colonial empires were embraced in the NATO structure did affect the debate over the alliance in the United States; isolationists and internationalists could unite in deploring the linkage of America to European colonial claims. Bills concludes that subsequent troubles in U.S.-Third World relations were inherent in the Eurocentric decision of American policymakers. When the United States was forced to choose between the aspirations of dependent peoples and European concerns, the primacy of the Communist threat usually served the colonialist against the colony. Colonial unrest could be part of the Soviet design against the West, weakening the European partner and subverting the overseas territories.

Walter Lipgens addresses still another relationship. It is the Atlantic Alliance as protector, partner, and rival of the European Community in its midst. As he points out, throughout the first fifteen years of NATO's history there was little contradiction between the two; they were complementary. NATO provided the frame within which a European community could grow. The United States, from Truman to Kennedy, was devoted to European unity, on the assumption that a strong Europe would both lend its weight to the credibility of the alliance and would allow some reduction of American costs and efforts. In the second fifteen years, this spirit has soured as Americans resented European independence and Europeans resented American claims to authority it no longer seemed to possess. But Lipgens observes that despite all the mutual aggravations of the 1970s, interdependence is still a fact. The United States must recognize the value of European integration; a progressively uniting Europe rather than a fragmented Europe will promote a stronger alliance.

NATO IN ARMS

The military dimension of NATO appropriately occupies a considerable portion of the book. Insecurity brought the alliance into existence and the continuing need for defense has kept it together over the years.

Perhaps the most difficult of all military arrangements among the NATO allies lay in the implications of "integration." The term itself is elliptical, as André Kaspi points out, evoking images that ranged from cooperation among national armies to fusion of forces. Its implementation is as difficult to manage as to imagine. Desirable as a single NATO military organization would be, an extreme application would be fatal to any alliance; national pride alone would stand in the way of implementation. Kaspi contrasts the primitive ideas of integration prevalent in World War I when France sought to incorporate American troops into French units with the less drastic intentions of the Western Union of 1948. Fusion had failed in 1917; the American Expeditionary Force emerged as a separate entity. Fusion was not tried in 1948. Such success as the Western Union had would equate integration with common policies and common commands. The erosion of sovereignty would have to be gradual and national sensibilities respected. The failure of the European Defense Community (EDC) and the success of SHAPE in the 1950s seem to reflect the approaches of 1917 and 1948 respectively.

How to improve the military credibility of NATO forces has been an ongoing preoccupation of military planners. One of the oldest solutions, as pointed out in the introductory essay, is standardization of weapons. James Carlton observes the difficulties over the past thirty years in translating their goal into reality. The need for common weaponry has grown rather than dwindled over the years as conventional defense capabilities have become an increasingly significant part of the deterrent. Yet the movement toward standardization remains as troublesome as in the early years of the alliance. The sacrifice required by one nation to accept the other nation's plane, tank, or gun at the expense of its own industrial plants or at the expense of its perceived national interest usually has been too heavy to bear, if not economically then politically. Carlton sees limited hope for the future in the erosion of the American tendency to make its products the standard of NATO, and even more hope in the substitution of "interoperability" for "standardization."

While arms control understandably was not a vital concern of the alliance in the early years, according to Luc Crollen, it assumed increasing importance from the mid-1950s onward to the test ban and nonproliferation treaties of the 1960s and beyond to the SALT process of the 1970s. As a military equilibrium appeared to have been achieved between East and West, the European allies joined the United States in support of arms control measures even while they expressed uneasiness that nuclear conversations between the Americans and the Russians could reach agreement over arms restraint at the expense of their security. The Harmel exercise of 1967 led NATO to emphasize in the 1970s the complementary relationship between defense and détente and to make new initiative in arms control, particularly in the Mutual Balanced Force Reductions (MBFR) negotiations. At the same time Crollen observes that in this area—in contrast to that of standardization—NATO has worked out machinery for consultation and cooperation well adapted to NATO problems. He also expresses hope that this new consultative framework might serve the alliance equally well should far-reaching arms control plans materialize between the antagonists.

The changing military relationship between the United States and the Soviet Union has given rise, as Thomas Etzold points out, to many of NATO's second generation problems. Most notably, superiority in nuclear weapons has marked the military character of NATO from its beginnings. But strategy that was successful in the 1950s when the United States held a nuclear advantage over the Soviet bloc required significant changes in the 1960s and 1970s if deterrence would be maintained. Whether these have kept pace with the Warsaw Pact organization's military gains of recent years is moot though not trivial. The military power of NATO has not been tested, which may of itself be a measure of success; it may also be a source of uneasiness if lack of confidence in the American ally now prevades the alliance. Whatever its future, Etzold contends that NATO strategy has been and is a function of U.S. strategy; with all its current restiveness Europe has not removed itself from dependence upon American nuclear power.

The authors' conclusions reflect the richness and the variety of materials yielded by the history of the Atlantic Alliance. None of them is intended to serve as an apologia for the organization, or to engage in special pleading for one function over another, or for one country over another in the alliance. But each in its way reminds the reader of the roles played by NATO over the past thirty years as a vehicle for America's departure from isolationism and as a stabilizing force behind the economic and political achievements of Western Europe. By surviving more than a generation without losing its relevance to the member nations, new forms of international and transnational institutions have developed that merit historical analysis. Many of them are treated in the following chapters.

At the same time the authors recognize that their efforts have not produced a full history of NATO. The record is incomplete; the psychological, if not temporal, distance from even the earliest events is still too short. Both the perspective and the documents are insufficient.

Still a beginning can be made, as the authors have shown. Their contributions among other results point to lacunae that may be filled in the near future. Given the archival resources becoming available a thorough examination of the earliest years of NATO, particularly the years 1948–50, can be provided for "NATO in History." The place of the Mediterranean members of NATO deserves special attention. In "NATO in the World," the potential importance of China or Japan for the organization raises the issue of a relationship that the founding fathers of the organization could not have anticipated. As for "NATO in Arms," both the aborted EDC and SHAPE under General Eisenhower are important areas of research for the military historian. In the meantime, this volume offers its particular approaches to understanding NATO in the expectation that whatever old questions about the alliance that it seeks to answer will be replaced by challenging new questions.

CONTRIBUTORS

SCOTT L. BILLS is a recent Ph.D. graduate from Kent State University. He has served as a research assistant for the Foreign Affairs and National Defense Division of the Congressional Research Service, Library of Congress, where he authored a short essay for the committee print *Congress and Foreign Policy—1978.* He has been executive editor (1978–80) of the journal *Left Review,* in which he has published several articles on contemporary political themes.

THOMAS M. CAMPBELL, JR., has been a member of the history department at Florida State University since 1963 and professor of history since 1977. His special interest is in the diplomacy of World War II. He served as visiting professor at the University of Virginia in 1978–79. He was coeditor of the diaries of Secretary of State Edward Stettinius and the author of *Masquerade Peace: America's UN Policy, 1944–1954* (1973). He is currently examining the role of the United Nations in American diplomacy after World War II.

JAMES R. CARLTON is a research associate with the Center for NATO Studies at Kent State University. He served with U.S. forces in Europe in an 8th Infantry Division Armor Battalion, mainly in Germany. He is currently engaged in a long-term research project focusing on decision making in NATO weapons systems acquisition.

ROBERT W. CLAWSON is associate professor of political science, director of the Center for International and Comparative Programs, and administrative coordinator of the Center for NATO Studies at Kent State University. He has been an exchange scholar at the State University of Moscow and has traveled widely in Eastern Europe and the USSR. Author of articles on Soviet-sponsored international organizations as well as on Soviet domestic politics, he is now working on an analysis of the development and evolution of the Warsaw Pact.

LUC CROLLEN has been a member of Belgium's diplomatic service since 1975. He is presently at the NATO desk of the ministry of foreign affairs. Prior to that time he was a research and teaching assistant at the Catholic University of Louvain while completing his doctoral studies. He was a lecturer at the College of Europe in Bruges in 1971–72 and studied at the Johns Hopkins University, both in Bologna and Washington, DC.

Among his publications is a book entitled *Portugal, the United States and NATO* (1973).

THOMAS H. ETZOLD is professor of strategy at the United States Naval War College. He taught at both Yale University and Miami University (Ohio) before joining the faculty of the War College in 1974. He is the author of *The Conduct of American Foreign Relations: The Other Side of Diplomacy* (1977) and has coauthored, edited, and coedited other volumes on American foreign affairs. His latest work is a book-length study of the American military in the 1980s.

COLIN GORDON graduated from University College, Oxford, in 1953 and after six years working with Procter and Gamble (UK) left industry and joined the University of Salford. Specializing in international relations since World War II with special reference to European defense, he was a NATO research fellow in 1970 and is a member of the International Institute for Strategic Studies. Editor of *The Atlantic Alliance: A Bibliography,* he has published in journals and lectured in academic and military institutions on both sides of the Atlantic.

NORMAN A. GRAEBNER has been Edward R. Stettinius professor of modern American history at the University of Virginia since 1967. He taught at Iowa State University and the University of Illinois as well as serving as visiting professor at Stanford, University of London, and University of Queensland. His books and articles have ranged over the spectrum of American diplomatic history, with special contributions to the mid-nineteenth century and post-World War II periods. *Cold War Diplomacy* (1962, 1977) and *Ideas and Diplomacy* (1964) are among his major works.

LAWRENCE S. KAPLAN is university professor of history and director of the Center for NATO Studies at Kent State University. Prior to coming to Kent State in 1954 he was with the Historical Office, Office of the Secretary of Defense. He has written numerous monographs on U.S. diplomatic history and NATO affairs, including *A Community of Interests: NATO and the Military Assistance Program, 1948–1951* (1980).

ANDRÉ KASPI holds a professorship at the Sorbonne, where he is currently teaching American history and international relations in the twentieth century. He previously taught American history at the University of Lille. He has published a book on Jean Monnet's mission in Algiers entitled *La mission de Jean Monnet à Alger en 1943* (1971), and his doctoral dissertation was written on Franco-American relations in the first World War, *Le temps des Américains* (1976).

WALTER LIPGENS is professor of modern history at the University of the Saarland. Before coming to Saarbrücken in 1967, he taught at the Universities of Münster, Bonn, and Heidelberg. Additionally, he has been a visiting professor at the Institute of Advanced Study in Princeton, the University of Missouri, and the European University Institute in Florence. Author of numerous books and articles in eighteenth-century European history, he pioneered in historical studies of European political integration. The first volume of his *Die Anfänge der Europäischen Einigungspolitik, 1945–1950* appeared in 1977; an English version was published in 1980.

NIKOLAJ PETERSEN has been associate professor at the Institute of Political Science, University of Aarhus, since 1976. He was executive secretary of the Danish Foreign Policy Institute from 1967 to 1971 and editor (1976–79) of *Cooperation and Conflict: Nordic Journal in International Politics.* He is the author of numerous articles and monographs on comparative foreign policy, Danish defense, and strategic problems. He is currently preparing monographs on the origins of NATO, with particular reference to the role of the Scandinavian members.

GLEE E. WILSON is associate professor of history and coordinator of Romanian studies at Kent State University. Prior to coming to Kent State University, he taught at Oklahoma State University. His fields are ancient Greece and Byzantium. As a result of research activity in Romania, he recently has ventured into certain contemporary aspects of that country.

ABBREVIATIONS

ABC	atomic, biological, and chemical weapons
ACE	Allied Command Europe
AEF	American Expeditionary Force
AHG	NATO Ad Hoc Group
ANF	Atlantic Nuclear Force
ATGMs	antitank-guided missiles
BAOR	British Army of the Rhine
CBMs	Confidence-Building Measures
CDE	Conference on Disarmament in Europe
CENTO	Central Treaty Organization
CIA	Central Intelligence Agency
CNAD	Conference of National Armaments Directors
CSCE	Conference on Security and Cooperation in Europe
DPC	NATO Defense Production Committee
EDC	European Defense Community
EEC	European Economic Community
ENDC	Eighteen Nation Disarmament Committee
EPC	European Political Cooperation
ERP	European Recovery Program
GLCM	ground-launched cruise missiles
LRTNF	long-range theater nuclear force
LTDP	NATO Long-Term Defense Program
MAP	Military Assistance Program
MAS	NATO Military Agency for Standardization
MBFR	Mutual Balanced Force Reductions
MLF	multilateral force
NATO	North Atlantic Treaty Organization
NBMR	NATO Basic Military Requirement procedure
NDAC	Nuclear Defense Affairs Committee
NPG	Nuclear Planning Group
OEEC	Organization for European Economic Cooperation
OPEC	Organization of Petroleum Exporting Countries
PGMs	precision-guided missiles
POLADS	NATO Committee of Political Advisers
SACEUR	Supreme Allied Commander Europe
SALT	Strategic Arms Limitations Talks
SANACC	State-Army-Navy-Air Force Coordinating Committee
SEATO	Southeast Asia Treaty Organization
SHAPE	Supreme Headquarters Allied Powers Europe

SLCM	sea-launched cruise missiles
SPC	NATO Senior Political Committee
STANAV	Standing Naval Forces North Atlantic
TNF	Theater Nuclear Force
UN	United Nations
WEU	Western European Union
WU	Western Union
WUCOS	Western Union Chiefs of Staff

NATO IN HISTORY

NATO: The Second Generation*

LAWRENCE S. KAPLAN

"Plus ça change, plus c'est la même chose" seems to have a particular relevance to the history of the North Atlantic Treaty Organization. For over thirty years the organization that developed from the Treaty of Washington in 1949 has been beleaguered by apparently insoluble problems. Some of them appear under different names, but others bear the same labels in 1980 as they had worn in 1950.

The military necessity for standardization of the allied weaponry is as much a divisive question within NATO as it had been when the treaty was framed.[1] The ideal of a single weapons system used interchangeably by the member nations is still unrealized. Quarrels over issues such as enlistment time for servicemen, equitable percentage of national incomes devoted to defense expenditures, or the commitment of an appropriate number of divisions to the common effort racked NATO in the wake of the Korean War. These arguments remain volatile even as members recognize their own growing military vulnerability in a world increasingly dominated by rising Soviet power as well as by the natural resources of the Third World.

The political problems of the second generation of NATO are equally familiar. American attitudes toward European unification are as ambivalent toward the European Economic Community of the 1980s as they had been toward the Common Market of the 1950s. A European monetary system, with its implied threat to the American dollar, was regarded at the end of the 1970s with some of the suspicion that greeted

---

*Portions of this chapter have appeared in *Orbis* 24 (Spring 1980): 149–64 as "NATO and the Nixon Doctrine: Ten Years Later," and in "NATO in the Second Generation," *NATO Review* 28 (October 1980): 1–7.

[1] As early as July 1948 the Joint Chiefs of Staff raised the issue of standardization, identifying it as a major objective and assuming it to mean standardization with U.S. equipment. See memorandum by the director of the Joint Chiefs of Staff (Gruenther) to the director of the Office of European Affairs (Hickerson), 16 July 1948, in U.S., Department of State, *Foreign Relations of the United States 1948* (Washington, DC: Government Printing Office, 1974), 3: 190–91.

the apparent success of Eurocommunism in the middle of the decade. The strains developing from conflicting visions of Atlantic versus European communities were not simply a French device to assert themselves at American expense. They were built into an alliance that aspired to save Western Europe from communism, to secure it as America's junior economic partner, and to build a European polity and economy as an independent force of its own. Consensus between America and Europe on such an explosive issue as the sharing of nuclear weapons has not improved significantly since the demise of the Multilateral Force in 1964. Article 2 of the treaty, with its intention of encouraging "economic collaboration between any and all" of the members is still just a pious hope. Even new problems that emerged from recent circumstances seem, in retrospect, to have revived old arguments among the allies or renewed attention to old fissures rather than presented genuinely new configurations to the alliance.

THE NIXON DOCTRINE

There are identifiable milestones, however, that mark stages of NATO's growth, and the one that most clearly stamps the end of one generation and the beginning of another was the election of Richard Nixon and the ushering in of a Nixon-Kissinger era in American foreign policy. Major changes seemed to flow from the return of the Republicans to power in 1969 and from the Nixon Doctrine that accompanied it. Although the Kennedy-Johnson years witnessed some softening of the rigidities of the Dulles stewardship, the military structure of NATO continued intact, and the strident tones of anticommunism rang more loudly under Kennedy than they had under Eisenhower. During the Johnson administration, NATO was consigned to a form of limbo to be attended to when the Vietnam War ended. Since the war never ended for Kennedy or for Johnson, inattention to NATO was one of the consequences.

The Truman Doctrine had provided a frame for NATO in its first generation. The doctrine itself in the 1950s and 1960s appeared to have been etched in stone, a permanent part of America's political life, with the United States assuming the endless burden of containing an ever aggressive communism. In this scheme NATO was the foremost part of a "Grand Design," in the parlance of the Kennedy years. All the other treaties, including the Rio Pact with its historic link to the Monroe Doctrine, appeared artificial by contrast. The upheavals in the Middle East from Suez in 1956 to the Six-Day War in 1967 made CENTO appear either impotent or irrelevant, while the Vietnam War was the ultimate exposé of the hollowness of SEATO. NATO lived on, struggling with a defecting but not quite departed France and patching up various rents made by divisions among other uneasy allies.

No nation departed from membership voluntarily; no Communist action forced an involuntary departure. Although the Brezhnev Doctrine, applied quickly and ruthlessly in Czechoslovakia in 1968, exposed NATO's inability to extend the values of the treaty's preamble to the Soviet zone of control, Soviet intervention pointedly refrained from threatening gestures against the Western allies. The survival of NATO equated then with the reconstruction of Western Europe, much as the Truman Doctrine had hoped, and "no revisionism," according to Uwe Nerlich, "will undo the fact that this reconstruction of the old continent was a historical achievement of American foreign policy."[2]

The Nixon Doctrine was introduced as a new direction in American foreign policy in 1969, and inevitably NATO would be touched by it even if its message was intended primarily for Asia. Containment was redefined. On the one hand, it was to reflect an idea raised by Denis Brogan in 1950 during the Korean War; namely, that there were limits to American power, that the way to effecting success lay in the realignment of objectives to resources.[3] The failure of policy in Vietnam in a war that seemed to make a mockery of containment was the price of ignoring this wisdom. The Nixon Doctrine would retreat from apparently limitless support for anti-Communist regimes everywhere. On the other hand, the United States would identify priorities of attention, with the recognition that some parts of the world are of greater concern than others. Through this new weltanschauung there could be disengagement from East Asia as a place of lesser priority. The Vietnamese would have to defend themselves, although with the continued blessing and material support of the United States. The Nixon Doctrine is mingled purposely with the conception of Vietnamization, as Kissinger expressed it in *Foreign Affairs* before entering government service in 1969 as presidential adviser. It was rephrased in the president's visit to Guam in the spring of that year.[4]

The Nixon Doctrine signaled the end of the Vietnam War and the end of the diversion of American energies and resources from the European arena. It should have been well received in Europe and in

---

[2]Uwe Nerlich, "Europe's Relations with the United States," *Daedalus* 8 (Winter 1979): 87.

[3]Denis Brogan, "The Illusion of American Omnipotence," *Harper's Magazine* 205 (December 1952): 21–28.

[4]Henry A. Kissinger, "The Viet Nam Negotiations," *Foreign Affairs* 47 (January 1969): 211–34; "Informal Remarks on Guam with Newsmen," 25 July 1969, *Public Papers of the President, Richard Nixon, 1969* (Washington, DC: Government Printing Office, 1971), pp. 544ff.

NATO as the first priority in American foreign policy. In the view of the new administration, it should have been welcomed as a means of reinvigorating the alliance as well as of responding to pleas raised by the Europeans over the previous decade. Indeed, presidential candidate Nixon had lashed out at the Johnson administration the year before for ignoring NATO, particularly for making no mention of it in his State of the Union Message of 1968. According to Nixon, "actions have been taken by the United States which vitally affected the security of our European partners, without even the courtesy of prior consultation. . . . It's time we began paying Europe more attention. And if our ideals of Atlantic interdependence are to mean anything in practice, it's time we began lecturing our European partners less and listening to them more."[5]

As president, Nixon made a point of visiting Europe a month after his inauguration to dramatize his desire for "genuine consultation." Beyond this spirit of cooperation he promised to present a plan to move "from crisis management to crisis prevention" as East and West emerge from a period of confrontation into an "era of negotiation."[6] This commitment applied not only to relations within the alliance but also to relations with the Soviet bloc.

Kissinger himself had a long record of absorption in European issues, from his doctoral dissertation on the Congress of Vienna to his perceptive book, *Troubled Partnership,* published in 1965. In this work he considered a common Atlantic partnership with Europe to be vital for the success of NATO. He further advanced the importance of European unity as a prerequisite to internal harmony and urged the United States to accept and even to support a supranational Europe without recoiling from its consequences.[7]

Repeatedly over the next two years the Nixon administration gave evidence of its concern for NATO in ways that should have been unmistakable to Europeans. The most critical support derived from its stand on the Mansfield resolution (Senate Resolution 292) on 1 December 1969, calling for "a substantial reduction of U.S. forces permanently stationed in Europe."[8] This actually was repeating a resolution that the senator had proposed in 1967 as the Vietnam crisis worsened. The Mansfield arguments were numerous and weighty: 315,000 men, along

---

[5]Radio address, 13 October 1968, "The Time to Save NATO," in *Atlantic Community Quarterly* 6 (Winter 1968–69): 481–82.

[6]Remarks to the North Atlantic Council in Brussels, 24 February 1969, *Public Papers of the Presidents* (1969), p. 106.

[7]Henry A. Kissinger, *The Troubled Partnership: Reappraisal of the Atlantic Alliance* (New York: McGraw-Hill, 1965). See also John G. Stoessinger, *Henry Kissinger: The Anguish of Power* (New York: W. W. Norton & Co., 1976), pp. 137ff.

[8]U.S., Congress, Senate, *Congressional Record,* 91st Cong., 1st sess., 1969, 115:36147, 36167.

with 235,000 dependents and 14,000 civilian employees created the dollar gap in foreign exchange to the extent of $1.5 billion a year. The intention of the resolution, according to Mansfield, was to induce the allies to make a larger and fairer contribution to NATO, rather than indicate that the NATO military structure was overbuilt. In the event of an emergency, American troops could be flown back to Europe in minimal time. Nothing traumatic was anticipated, he claimed; the size of the American contribution would be reduced "without adversely affecting either our resolve or ability to meet our commitment under the North Atlantic Treaty."[9]

The greatest temptation to reduce costs through troop reduction occurred in the early part of the decade. Inevitably, the national mood of disillusionment with the military investment in Southeast Asia found some resonance in the NATO arena. Not only could costs be pared but also American anger over Europe's insensitivity to America's agony in Vietnam would be drained. Europe could and should do more for the common defense, particularly as the dollar weakened at a time when the economies of the Western allies flourished and their currencies strengthened at American expense.

The Nixon administration held firm, claiming that the United States would not reduce its forces unless there were reciprocal action by the Soviet Union. Any unilateral action would create a military imbalance that might induce the Soviet bloc to risk provocations it would otherwise avoid, and would generate doubts among allies about the steadfastness of American commitments in Europe.[10] The doubts were unavoidable as talk concerning neoisolationism flourished. If the United States could withdraw unilaterally from Asia, would there not be a precedent that might apply to Europe, no matter what the message of the Nixon Doctrine specifically announced?

The Nixon position was not simply a gesture of NATO solidarity. It was tested in 1971 when Senator Mansfield mounted his most powerful challenge in the form of an amendment to a bill extending the Selective Service Act.[11] It required that U.S. forces in Europe be halved to 150,000 men. To cope wih the popularity of this amendment, the administration mobilized former NATO Commanders Alfred M. Gruenther, Lauris Norstad, and Lyman L. Lemnitzer, along with such veteran Democrats as former Secretaries of State George Ball and Dean Acheson, to express their opposition to Mansfield's plan. Nixon also won the endorsement of former President Johnson who agreed that the drastic

---

[9]Ibid., pp. 36147–149.

[10]Wilfrid Kohl, "The Nixon-Kissinger Foreign Policy System and U.S. European Relations: Patterns of Policy Making," *World Politics* 28 (October 1975): 28.

[11]U.S., Congress, Senate, *Congressional Record,* 92d Cong., 1st sess., 1971, 117: 14397-99.

reduction of troop strength would have dangerous consequences for the alliance.[12] The amendment was defeated in the Senate on 19 May 1971 by a vote of 61 to 36.[13]

At the same time that it was averting the Mansfield threat, the Nixon administration served Europe in another fashion by maintaining, as Raymond Aron has called it, "a low profile" on matters that in the past the American voice would have been loudly raised. Aron observed "the ostentatious silence" of Americans on the British candidacy since 1969 for entry into the Common Market, in contrast to their heavy-handed advocacy of British membership during the de Gaulle years.[14] Moreover, the United States chose not to speak out against the *Ostpolitik* of Chancellor Willy Brandt despite serious reservations about the terms that the Soviet Union might demand in return for improved relations with the Federal Republic of Germany. The United States confined its public concerns to negotiations over the section of the German accords with the Soviet Union that related directly to its own position in Berlin. This discreet behavior appeared to fulfill the Nixon Doctrine's resolution to allow Europeans responsibility for managing their own affairs in ways they regard appropriate without American interference.

In retrospect, Nixon and Kissinger won little credit from the European allies for their pointed abstention from interfering in internal European affairs or even for their firm championship of the American military presence on the continent. Some of the reasons for the ingratitude emerged from the ambiguities within the Nixon Doctrine itself. The new "era of negotiations" the president welcomed in his State of the World Message of 1970 meant no denigration of Europe's role in America's future, but the priority of the European partnership was interpreted to be subsumed under other unstated objectives. Implicit in the structure of the Nixon-Kissinger vision of the 1970s was a détente with the Soviet Union, a sentiment Europeans had valued in the 1950s and 1960s but in the light of the Vietnam retreat was an object of suspicion. To many Europeans a unilateral détente with the Soviet Union seemed to be a consequence of reducing American commitments abroad, which out of necessity would include Europe as well as Asia. A drive for a new modus vivendi with the Soviet Union was an admission of inferiority in the competition of East and West. To build the new "structure of peace," Americans might sacrifice the interests of the European allies.

Fears of American weakness permeated Europe's perception of all aspects of the Nixon Doctrine. If the United States and the Soviet Union managed mutual restraint over strategic nuclear arms, the result also might

---

[12]*New York Times,* 13, 16 May 1971.
[13]*Congressional Record,* 92d Cong., 1st sess., 1971, 117:15960.
[14]Raymond Aron, "Richard Nixon and the Future of American Foreign Policy," *Daedalus* 101 (Fall 1972):18.

subvert American nuclear protection of Europeans. De Gaulle may have departed by the 1970s, but his cry that America would not sacrifice its own security for the sake of Europe continued to be heard. Within this context the call to Europeans to do more for themselves, rather than rely on American initiatives, seemed to have evolved less from American respect for their sensibilities or for their equality in the alliance than from a repressed wish to minimize American responsibilities for their commitments abroad. No matter what the guise might be, retreat from Asia could lead to retreat from Europe. The logic of the Nixon Doctrine was applicable everywhere in the world. "Its purpose," in the words of James Chace and Earl Ravenel, "was to assuage domestic opposition to costly interventionist wars through a limited military retrenchment, yet at the same time remain politically engaged throughout the globe."[15]

The message dispatched from its NATO allies was distrust in America's ability to maintain such a delicate balance. Partial disengagement in one area of the world only concealed a weakness that would be felt in other parts. Thus the American push for SALT I, or the Kissinger opening to China in the first Nixon administration, symbolized not détente but a serious loss of confidence that was damaging to NATO's sense of security.

Europe could point to other actions that eroded the credibility of the doctrine and also American relations with NATO, in general, at the same time that Nixon and Kissinger were congratulating themselves in turning aside congressional challenges. American economic policy could not be separated from the rest of foreign policy, and it was in this area that Europeans manifested their major concern. As the dollar weakened, Nixon followed the advice of Secretary of the Treasury John Connally and suspended the convertibility of the dollar in August 1971.[16] Moreover, a 10 percent surcharge was imposed on all imports. These acts shocked Europe, partly by their unilateral nature and partly because of the confessed weakness they demonstrated in what had been a bastion of stability for a generation.

The American justification for its defense of the dollar was not negligible; the dollar gap grew out of the massive American military expenses in Europe as well as from the burden of Vietnam and an underdeveloped export trade. The result was the devaluation of the dollar and the apparent end of the older policy of trade liberalization, as protectionist sentiment burgeoned in the United States. The impact on European economies of a cheaper dollar was sharp and immediate, and the European Economic Community was no help in mitigating its force or in mediating with the United States. Indeed, a major focus of Secretary

---

[15]James Chace and Earl C. Ravenel, *Atlantis Lost: U.S.-European Relations after the Cold War* (New York: New York University Press, 1976), p. 52.
[16]*New York Times,* 15 August 1971.

Connally's animus was the preferential trade agreements, especially over agricultural products that discriminated against American interests.

The Connally initiative was short-lived. A Smithsonian agreement in December 1971 created an essentially floating exchange rate system that helped to restore a temporary equilibrium to the monetary system.[17] The surcharge was lifted, American troop level was not lowered, and no major changes took place in Europe's own military contributions to NATO. However, the psychological damage could not be undone. Four years of the Nixon Doctrine had left Europeans as suspicious of American policy in 1973 as they had been in 1969.

THE "YEAR OF EUROPE"

The continuing drain of mutual recriminations accounted for the special exertions on both sides of the Atlantic to repair differences within the organization. The European Community opened the way for a new direction in its communique of October 1972, when it called for a "constructive dialogue" with the United States.[18] With the Vietnam War behind them, Americans responded to this outreach with at least a rhetorical concern for what Nixon labeled in 1973 the "Year of Europe."[19] Earlier in the year former Secretary of Commerce Peter Peterson led an explanatory mission to Europe and Japan, after which he reported on economic and political problems that he felt must be addressed as early as possible.

Kissinger's proposal for a new Atlantic Charter, a rededication of the Atlantic Alliance, followed in a major address on 23 April 1973. Phrases such as "fresh act of creation" and "a revitalized Atlantic partnership" punctuated his speech.[20] Europe's reaction was cynical. Despite the American avowals, the Kissinger overture contained many of the elements that originally contributed to the malaise. Laced with arrogance, the speech was drawn up without significant consultation either at home or abroad. Not even Secretary of State William Rogers had advance notice of Kissinger's terms. The message was: "The United States has global interests and responsibilities. Our European allies have

---

[17]Text of communique, Smithsonian Agreement, 18 December 1971, in Department of State *Bulletin* 66 (10 January 1972): 32–34.

[18]European Community communique, 21 October 1972, in *Keesings Contemporary Archives,* 18:25542.

[19]News conference, 31 January 1973, *Public Papers of the Presidents* (1973), p. 57.

[20]Henry Kissinger, "A New Atlantic Charter," Address delivered to Associated Press Editors' Annual Meeting, New York, 23 April 1973, Department of State *Bulletin* 68 (14 May 1973): 593–98.

regional interests." The style, characterized by Wilfred Kohl as "the royal-court model of foreign policy making," combined with the tone, could only grate upon European sensibilities.[21] This language accentuated the separation of Europe and America, and, by implication, the new and potentially dangerous bilateral relationship between the United States and the Soviet Union.

However, a source of continuing discord deeper than the lordly manner of Kissinger's presentation involved still another by-product of the Nixon Doctrine; namely, Europe's position in making greater sacrifices than it had in the past in building the military strength of NATO and improving its financial infrastructure. Kissinger's new overture, inspired in part by the stirrings of the European Community, assumed a unity among a majority of its members that could make burden-sharing a reality. President Nixon's expression of this assumption appeared in his May 1973 State of the World Address, with its emphasis on the European allies redressing the American balance of payments problem in Europe. The assumption greatly exaggerated the reality of European unity.[22]

It was not surprising then that the United States was now prepared to accept Europe as a coherent and potentially effective unit, capable of carrying greater weight in the alliance. West Germany was able to conduct its *Ostpolitik* with the Soviet Union with reasonable success, defusing in the early 1970s the burning issues of a divided Germany.[23] The United Kingdom, for its part, finally brought its strength to bear in an enlarged European Community in 1973, marking, as Michael Howard has claimed, "the final transformation of a Western Europe from a collection of weak and frightened clients of the United States into America's most formidable adversary."[24] The appearance was impressive. The population of the Europe of Nine was 260 million in 1973, as opposed to 210 million in the United States and 249 million in the Soviet Union. Its gross domestic product was \$1.0614 billion, almost twice that of the Soviet Union, although approximately \$250 billion less than the gross national product of the United States.[25]

The United States, however, did not recognize that Europe's strength lay in a "United States of Europe" that currently did not exist. There was no simple way for Europeans to act within a Europe that could not

---

[21]Kohl, "Nixon-Kissinger Foreign Policy," p. 18.

[22]Fourth annual report to the Congress on U.S. foreign policy, *Public Papers of the Presidents* (1973), pp. 402–4.

[23]Geoffrey Pridham, *Christian Democracy in Western Germany: the CDU/SCU in Government and Opposition, 1945–1976* (New York: St. Martin's Press, 1977), pp. 207–8; 228–29.

[24]Michael Howard, "NATO and the Year of Europe," *Survival* 16 (January/February 1974): 21.

[25]*Yearbook of National Accounts Statistics* (1974), International Tables (New York: United Nations, 1975), 3:5, 7.

raise troop levels or increase taxes for defense in the manner of the United States. For all the vocal opposition to many American policies in the early and mid-1970s and for all the potential equality, the foregoing figures suggest Europe could neither respond to American demands nor do without American aid. Kissinger frightened as much as annoyed Europeans with his call for equality from the NATO allies.

Given this disarray among Europeans they had no choice but to respect the continuing discontent in the Congress over the heavy costs that the alliance was imposing on Americans. The Mansfield resolution may have been contained and deflected in Nixon's first administration, but with the Vietnam War over, the administration was worried about neoisolationism arising from the disillusionment with foreign affairs. Since détente with the Soviet Union was in the air and since Europeans continued to complain without responding to American needs, Congress might have accepted the Senate plan in September 1973 to cut American forces in Europe in two slices: first by 40 percent and then by an additional 23 percent. Only a belated recognition that a similar unilateral initiative would undermine current negotiations for a mutually balanced reduction of forces stayed the legislators' hand.[26]

The European allies felt obligated to give at least lip service to American thinking and therefore accepted in place of Kissinger's new Atlantic Charter an affirmation of Atlantic principles.[27] Such a public celebration of European-American solidarity in the summer of 1973 was all the more important in light of the Nixon-Brezhnev accords of June 1973, in which the superpowers pledged to avert confrontations that would lead to nuclear war. The allies speculated that behind the high-minded words lay a Soviet-American nuclear standoff that could exacerbate Europe's vulnerability to Soviet political pressures. But Europe's words were grudging, its mood suspicious, and its spirit resentful. The term "West-West" dialogue conveyed a message that Europe and America were as far apart in mutual trust as they had ever been in the past.[28]

The impact of the October War in the Middle East best illustrates NATO's plight in 1973. Former Assistant Secretary of State Eugene V. Rostow called the Arab attack against Israel "the most basic thrust against the Atlantic alliance since 1945, far more serious than earlier crises over peripheral points like Cuba, Berlin, and Korea."[29] Whether or not the Berlin tensions were unfairly trivialized or whether the Arab assault was indeed a "fundamental Soviet thrust" intended to outflank the

---

[26]James Reston, *New York Times,* 28 September 1973; debate on troop reduction in U.S., Congress, Senate, *Congressional Record,* 93d Cong., 1st sess., 26 September 1973, 119:31507ff. Senator Kennedy, a former supporter of Mansfield, joined Senators Tower and Dole in warning about its effect upon MBFR.

[27]Final communique of North Atlantic Council, 15 June 1973, *Atlantic Community Quarterly* 11 (Fall 1973): 387; *New York Times,* 6 August 1973.

[28]*New York Times,* 5 August 1973.

[29]Eugene V. Rostow, ibid., 21 October 1973.

allied forces in central Europe and drive the United States out of the Mediterranean is immaterial. If the concerted Arab plan had succeeded, the Soviet Union would have been a prime beneficiary of its success. As it was the psychological, if not military, Arab victory yielded important dividends to the Communist bloc by forcing into the open differences within the alliance over the most appropriate response to the war.

The European Economic Community rushed to issue a declaration at Brussels endorsing the Arab interpretation of Security Council Resolution 242 of 1967, and in so doing implicitly legitimized the attack on Israel.[30] At the height of the war, Germany demanded that the United States cease shipping arms and supplies to Israel from West German ports. And when the United States ordered a state of alert as it appeared to challenge Soviet troop movements to the Middle East, the NATO partners, with the exception of Portugal and the Netherlands, shrank in dismay rather than applauded American support for a beleaguered nation.

The explanation for Europe's behavior in the crisis and its apparent repudiation of its responsibilities in the alliance lay not in its failure to comprehend the implications of the war for NATO's fortunes in the Middle East but in its fears for NATO in Western Europe itself. The power of Middle East oil dictated most of the responses and intensified emotions. American activity on behalf of Israel was seen as a complete disregard for European concerns.

This was not a view shared by most Americans. According to Irving Kristol in the *Wall Street Journal,* "the plain fact was that the United States found itself on the brink of a confrontation with the Soviet Union, and in this circumstance our European allies deserted us."[31] In this heated atmosphere it is hardly surprising that an American riposte would be made. The Jackson-Nunn amendment, a rider to a vital military appropriations bill, was the immediate reaction. Public Law 93-155, sec. 812 required the president to reduce U.S. forces in Europe by the same percentage as Europeans failed to offset costs in the balance of payment of American troops in Europe for fiscal year 1974.[32] For fear that a veto would trigger other more drastic congressional legislation, the administration accepted the amendment despite misgivings over the pall it would cast on negotiations with allies.

Officially, NATO had no alternative but to accede to American demands. At its December meeting the NATO defense ministers spoke of an impending NATO examination of "how the share of the United States in the civil and military budgets of NATO and in the infrastructure program might be substantially reduced."[33] An offset agreement also was

---

[30]Ibid., 6 November 1973.

[31]Irving Kristol, *Wall Street Journal,* 16 November 1973.

[32]U.S., *Statutes at Large* (1973), vol. 87, sec. 812, pp. 619–20.

[33]Final communique, defense ministers meeting, North Atlantic Council, 7 December 1973, *Atlantic Community Quarterly* 11 (Winter/1973–74): 17.

concluded with Germany involving $2.22 billion over a two-year period. This embraced military procurement, loans, and German assumption of certain real estate costs of the United States in Germany.

The spirit on both sides, however, was still sour. In fact, the German concession on offsetting U.S. dollars was accompanied by a Nixon outburst in a Chicago speech on 12 March 1974 in which he warned: "The Europeans cannot have it both ways. They cannot have the United States participation and cooperation on the security front and proceed to have confrontation and even hostility on the economic and political fronts."[34] Consequently, on the eve of its twenty-fifth anniversary the alliance looked shakier than ever. Headlines such as "Unhappy Birthday" and "NATO: End of an Era" captured the mood of leading newspapers.[35] A Gallup Poll taken at the time revealed that internationalist views in 1974 dropped 45 percent, the lowest figure since 1945. Only 48 percent of those polled approved the use of force to help Western Europe in a crisis.[36]

The Soviet press did not overlook the troubles of the alliance and took the occasion to note that the strains left from the Arab oil embargo proved that the Atlantic Alliance was obsolete. TASS observed: "Oil is only the upper layer of a compound and bitter cocktail of contradictions" between the U.S. and Europe. Europe could no longer be assigned a junior partnership. The solution was to assign NATO "to the archives."[37]

Even the official *NATO Review,* in its twenty-fifth anniversary issue, included an essay entitled "Twenty-Five Years of Ups and Downs." For the NATO Information Service to give equal weight to the "Downs" in the alliance indicates the magnitude of the distress. Yet, it could find solace in the fact that the organization always seemed to be in a state of crisis, and the editor could derive some comfort from the knowledge that NATO recovered from the shocks of the building of the Berlin Wall in 1961 and the high tensions of the Cuban missile crisis of 1962.[38] A dozen years later the alliance was able to reconcile itself to the long-term implications of the Nixon Doctrine as well as to the short-term effects of the Arab-Israeli war in the Middle East.

LIMITS OF DÉTENTE

The alliance did not collapse in the mid-1970s into the pieces antici-pated by both friends and enemies. The "Finlandization" of Europe as it

[34]Question and answer session at the Executives' Club of Chicago, 15 March 1974, *Public Papers of the Presidents* (1974), p. 276.
[35]Cyrus L. Sulzberger, *New York Times,* 4 April 1974; *Wall Street Journal,* 16 November 1973.
[36]Leslie Gelb, *New York Times,* 17 June 1974.
[37]Christopher Wren, ibid., 12 March 1974.
[38]"Twenty-Five Years of Ups and Downs," *NATO Review* 22 (April 1974): 3.

lost its NATO moorings and its faith in its own potential power did not develop from the malaise of 1974; the Soviet price for an East-West relationship remained unacceptable. A revived American isolationism never materialized, and the new but limited bilateralism between the Soviet Union and the United States underscored the limits of détente. Since the alliance did not fade out in the subsequent years, in the manner of SEATO in 1977 or CENTO in 1979 with little fanfare and no sense of loss, either the professional optimism of NATO officials was a matter of good luck or the bonds within the organization were less brittle than observers had credited.

The most pervasive answer to the question stemmed from a mutual dependence that frequently went unrecognized or when identified was given grudging respect. The growing maturity of a European Community in which the NATO powers played a predominant role assured friction between Americans and Europeans, if only because its new strength required a reevaluation of older relations. The centrality of France's presence assured as well a certain testiness in the community's outlook on the United States. The United States could do nothing to appease French suspicions since France's idea of a community was founded on its utility as an instrument to provide a distance between Europe and both super-powers, whether on diplomatic relations with the Middle East, the attack on the dollar, or projected restrictions on multinational companies. Even the rise of U.S.-Soviet détente in the 1970s distressed the French although they had been advocates of the concept a decade before. If successful, it would be seen as devaluing the position of France and Europe as a mediating force.[39]

The separate status of a new Europe would seem confirmed also by the Eurogroup, a forum of NATO defense ministers created to express a coherent European voice to the United States. It could speak from knowledge that Europeans contributed 90 percent of the ground forces of NATO, 80 percent of the navies, and 75 percent of aircraft. Most of its activities centered on furthering military cooperation among the European members, particularly in coordinating purchases of U.S. weaponry.[40]

No United Europe has yet appeared despite all the collaboration among Europeans in the direction of a single European entity. The subcommittees of the Eurogroup—Eurotraining, Europmed, or Euro-structure—helped to support a European Defense Improvement Program in the 1970s but did not conceal a continuing painful dependence on the United States. All their activities were still defined by a relationship with the Americans. Much of the debate for the past quarter of a century over

[39]Robert S. Lockwood, "NATO Gaullist Policy: NATO Withdrawal and Systemic Change" (Ph.D. diss., George Washington University, 1976).

[40]NATO Information Service, "The Eurogroup," *Atlantic Community Quarterly* 14 (Summer 1976): 76–79; communique of conference of Eurogroup defense ministers in Brussels, 8 December 1975, ibid., pp. 121–24.

"European unity" was "as much about the relationship of Europe to America," according to William Pfaff, "as about the relations of Europeans to one another."[41] Psychologically, this condition has not changed; Europe would find itself unable to cope with Soviet power without America. As the decade ended, NATO's importance to the European partners remained the major vehicle for the assurance of security.

The United States, while experiencing as many frustrations from the alliance as its allies, was no less bound to the alliance. The ambiguities of its relationship frequently obscured its importance. European unification never has been fully conceptualized in the American mind. Although sincerely desiring a "United States of Europe" that would arise as a flattering mirror image of the American model, every administration harbored fears of nurturing a Frankensteinian monster that would run amok once its creation had been completed. A Gaullist Europe was one form of apprehension; a Eurocommunist Europe susceptible to Finlandization was another. However, as with the Europeans, the bonds of a generation could not be broken without traumatic effects. On the one hand, the American industries that had invested in Western Europe—the so-called multinationals—and had bloomed with the expansion of its national economies presented a hostage of considerable significance. On the other, there was the same concern found among Europeans that U.S. disengagement could lead to Soviet pressures on the West that would be intolerable to Americans as well as Europeans. In this context the most powerful unifying force in NATO was the constraining influence imposed by the absence of alternatives.

This unwilling interdependence led NATO into a reevaluation of détente in the mid-1970s. Although originally the inspiration of European critics who deplored the unthinking bellicosity of American behavior toward the Soviet Union and its putative insensitivity to changes within the Eastern bloc in the 1950s and 1960s, it had become in the first Nixon administration part of Kissinger's apparatus for constructing complicated linkages with the Soviet. Détente as a relaxation of tension derived from a delicate balance of terror; it made SALT I possible in 1972. Since the working of détente involved Soviet-American activity outside the scope of NATO, they revived the old complaints that the United States might act in its own interests and against those of its allies. Still, if carefully undertaken with NATO participation détente between East and West could reduce troop size, inhibit development of mutually destructive weaponry, and make military costs more manageable, a divisive issue within NATO.

These considerations stimulated movement toward the Mutual and Balanced Force Reductions Program of the mid-1970s, but this was not a new conception. In 1967 the Harmel report, a broad attempt on the part of

⁴¹William Pfaff, "Unity of Europe," *New Yorker* 52 (12 April 1976): 124.

NATO ministers to redefine the goals of the alliance, first broached the idea of "mutual force reductions which should be reciprocal and balanced in scope and timing" with a "Declaration of MBFR."[42] Three years later in the meeting of the NATO council in Rome emphasis was placed on "adequate verification and controls to ensure the observance of agreements on MBFR." Specifically, the reductions were to include "stationed and indigenous forces and their weapons systems in the area concerned."[43] These precautions were understandable in the light of the Soviet intervention in Czechoslovakia in the intervening period. Negotiations were impossible until memories of that application of the Brezhnev Doctrine had dimmed.

Doubts notwithstanding, pressures for an MBFR agreement came from every quarter of NATO, propelled by the interest of Senator Mansfield and the American balance of payment problems as well as by the spirit of *Ostpolitik*. Resistance in the early 1970s then appeared on the Soviet side as NATO council approaches to Moscow were ignored. It required President Nixon's personal diplomacy during his visit to Moscow in 1972 to extract an agreement to negotiate from the Russians, and this was accomplished only as a quid pro quo for Western agreement to join a Conference on Security and Cooperation in Europe (CSCE). The proceedings finally opened in Vienna on 30 October 1973.[44]

The Soviet position was hardly based on a reluctance to capitalize on an opportunity to reduce NATO force levels; its objective in this regard had been constant. It was accompanied ever since the Rapacki Plan of the 1950s [see below pp. 40–41] with a hope that reduction of NATO forces meant removal of American forces altogether. Ideally the Russians wished to deal with "Europeans" only, not as a NATO bloc but as individual nations sharing the European continent.[45] By consenting to meet in Vienna in 1973, it temporarily gave up its intention to exclude the United States from the negotiations or to exclude NATO as a bargaining agent.

Opportunities to divide the allies were still present. Alistair Buchan, an acute British observer of NATO, remained suspicious that the MBFR would be a mask for American appeasement of Senator Mansfield. It would be a cover for dangerous reductions of American troop strength in Europe.[46] The Soviet Union helped to foster this line of thought by

---

[42]Harmel Report in *NATO Letter* 16 (March 1968): 10–13; Declaration on Mutual and Balanced Force Reductions, ibid. 16 (July/August 1968): 29.

[43]NATO ministers communique and Declaration on Mutual and Balanced Force Reductions, *Atlantic Community Quarterly* 8 (Fall 1970): 430.

[44]Joint U.S.-Soviet communique, Moscow, 29 May 1972, Department of State *Bulletin* 16 (26 June 1972): 899–901.

[45]For example, see Gromyko's speech at CSCE, directed to Western Europe, in which both the United States and NATO are omitted, trans. in *Current Digest of the Soviet Press* 25, no. 27 (1 August 1973): 1–4.

[46]Alistair Buchan, "The United States and the Security of Europe," in David Landes, *Western Europe: Trials of Partnership* (Lexington, MA: D. C. Heath, 1977), p. 300.

regularly removing "balanced" from its publicity concerning MBFR.[47]

The probable explanation for the Soviet Union's willingness to compromise over MBFR lay in the higher priority it placed on American acceptance of the CSCE. The Soviets would have preferred that a CSCE precede the MBFR discussions, since the former was a political arrangement that conceivably would provide the setting for force reduction. But its obvious interest was political legitimacy of its role in Eastern Europe, implicitly granted by the Helsinki Agreement of 1975. So anxious was the Soviet concern for the success of the CSCE that it allowed issues such as freedom of movement and freedom of information to remain on the agenda and be part of the agreement. It is worth observing that the talks at Helsinki were concurrent with the talks at Vienna, but the Helsinki negotiations culminated in a declaration of principles ratified by East and West, while the Vienna talks continued at a snail's pace throughout the 1970s.

A basic problem with the MBFR talks was the virtual impossibility of genuine parity. As with the SALT negotiations, discussions began with an assumption of Warsaw Pact superiority in conventional military capabilities in Europe. The problem of parity was complicated further by the geographical proximity of the Soviet Union to central Europe compared with the distance of the American forces from their home base. The size of force reductions must be measured against the overall capability of each side when the cut is complete. As proposed by the Soviets, the reported initial reduction of 20,000 by each side in 1974 would increase the relative superiority of the Warsaw Pact troops in the central sector. While this proposal was rejected out of hand, would the initial NATO proposal of a 30,000 troop reduction for the United States as opposed to 70,000 for the Soviet Union have achieved parity? Sheer numbers, even when substantially greater for the Warsaw countries, would be irrelevant if they could be drawn from a number of Soviet divisions without touching elite combat forces deployed near the West German boundary.[48] How to affect the Soviet capacity to initiate an attack with little or no warning was the problem disturbing NATO planners throughout the decade, and was the substance of an influential report of Senators Sam Nunn and Dewey Bartlett to the Armed Services Committee in January 1977.[49]

The ongoing MBFR negotiations have, if nothing else, increasingly sensitized Congress to the realities of Soviet military power in conventional

[47]Gerhard Mally, *Interdependence: The European-American Connection in the Global Context* (Lexington, MA: Lexington Books, 1976), p. 57.

[48]Sam Nunn, "Mutual Balanced Force Reductions: A Need to Shift Focus," *Atlantic Community Quarterly* 16 (Spring 1978): 18.

[49]U.S., Congress, Senate, Committee on Armed Services, *NATO and the New Soviet Threat: Report of Senator Sam Nunn and Senator Dewey F. Bartlett,* 95th Cong., 1st sess., 24 January 1977.

weaponry and conversely NATO's weaknesses in troops and armament. Rather than supporting the Mansfield cause they have undermined it. An earlier report of Senator Nunn in 1974 asserted: "a cut of 100,000 or more in U.S. troops would destabilize the overall military posture, but would have even more effect upon NATO's political posture. The psychological and political impact of such a cut could lead to the Finlandization of Europe and Soviet political dominance in Europe."[50] The effect then of the years of frustrating dickering over troop reduction has been to educate political leaders on the importance of "mutuality" and the difficulty in identifying it.

TOWARD MODERNIZATION

There was both a revival of faith in America's devotion to the alliance after 1975 and an upsurge in Europe's sense of its own potential. They accompanied and reinforced a common NATO perception that the Soviet Union was steadily building impressive military forces while it conducted negotiations on MBFR. Rather than demoralizing the Western allies, the growing imbalance of forces raised at least the official determination of NATO to bolster their defense systems on every front, especially in vulnerable central Europe. The Carter administration looked to more sophisticated weaponry as the Western riposte, either in tactical nuclear weapons or in technological breakthroughs in conventional arms. The United States led the way in promoting a 3-percent increase in the defense expenditures for NATO extending to 1985.[51]

The new aggressiveness in American foreign policy in the late 1970s might have been a normal concomitant of the receding of the Vietnam War from the nation's consciousness, even without new concerns about Soviet

---

[50]U.S., Congress, Senate, Committee on Foreign Relations, "Policy, Troops, and the NATO Alliance," *Report of Senator Sam Nunn,* 94th Cong., 2d sess., 2 April 1974, p. 10.

[51]"The collective deterrent strength of our alliance is effective but it can only remain so if we work to improve it. The United States is prepared to make a major effort to this end . . . in the expectation that our Allies will do the same." President Carter to the North Atlantic Council, London, 10 May 1977, *NATO Review* 25 (June 1977): 23. See President Carter's news conference, Kansas City, 9 November 1978, in *Public Papers of the Presidents, Jimmy Carter* (1978), pp. 1987–88, in which he observed that ". . . we have encouraged our Allies in particular to increase their expenditures for a joint defense of Europe and, therefore, us by 3% a year above the inflation rate. I intend to honor that commitment." See also President Carter, State of the Union Message, 21 January 1980, in which he noted that "the fiscal year 1981 budget would increase funding authority for defense to more than $158 billion, a real growth of more than 5% over my request for fiscal year 1980," in Department of State *Bulletin* 80 (February 1980): H.

military expansion to encourage it. While the effects of Vietnam and Watergate were visible in enhanced congressional authority in foreign affairs and the corresponding decline in the "imperial" presidency, American foreign policy generally observed the guidelines of the Nixon Doctrine. Fears of possible consequences of dispatching American troops abroad manifested themselves in American hesitancy over intervention in Angola, the Horn of Africa, and in Iran, not in Europe. In the late 1970s, NATO clearly enjoyed a priority that eluded the defunct CENTO or SEATO. Even the thorny political problem of Cyprus, which Turkey invaded in 1974, appeared soluble. The embargo of weapons against Turkey, forced on the Ford administration by a pro-Greek Congress, was effectively cancelled under the Carter administration in July 1978, when the fate of the southeastern hinge of NATO seemed to have been at stake.[52]

Europeans responded to the renewal of American self-confidence, but they deplored American sluggishness in dealing with oil dependence on the OPEC nations; they attempted to stand aside once more from U.S. activities in the Israeli-Egyptian negotiations of 1978 and 1979 and provided tepid responses to American cries for action over Iran and Afghanistan in 1980. In the meantime, however, China was serving to buttress NATO, and incidentally the position of the United States, not merely as an increasingly strident opponent of Soviet expansionism but also as a positive admirer of the organization. In 1970 the People's Republic spoke elliptically of the evils of all alliances, but by the middle of the decade it found new virtues in European unity and in the Atlantic Alliance. By 1977 China specifically urged Turkey not to abandon NATO despite its grievances against Greece and the United States.[53] Even though China may have acted out of a concern that a Russian-Turkish rapprochement could free Soviet troops for movement from the Turkish to the Chinese border, the public stance of a leading Communist nation had a buoyant impact on NATO spirits.

The Carter administration's decision with respect to defense spending was an expression of American wariness over the future of détente. Even before the election of 1976, President Ford had repudiated the use of the term as a symbol of a vague appeasement from which he wished to dissociate himself.[54] Less vague was his relationship with Secretary of State Kissinger who had built his structure for peace on détente and by

---

[52]*Congressional Record,* 95th Cong., 2d sess., 1978, 124:11712. The vote to lift the embargo was 57 to 42.

[53]*New York Times,* 12 June 1970, 5 December 1975, and 25 December 1977. Chinese journalists' delegation to Denmark, Great Britain, Italy, and Switzerland in November and December 1977 repeatedly endorsed Western Europe's defense against potential Soviet aggression, *Peking Review* 21 (17 February 1978): 22–26.

[54]President Ford preferred to use "peace through strength," noted in editorial in *Pittsburgh Press-Gazette,* 16 June 1976.

1976 had found himself an embarrassment to the president as Kissinger presided over linkages that did not connect, over initiatives to which the Soviets did not respond, and over American policy that left the West progressively weaker and the Eastern bloc progressively stronger. The fate of the Helsinki agreement cast a shadow on the future of the MBFR. The product of the CSCE of 1975 seemed to American critics to have been an acceptance of the inviolability of Eastern Europe's boundaries, while the promises of free exchange of information and person went unfulfilled. George Ball, former secretary of state in the Johnson administration, labeled the signing of the agreements at Helsinki "capitulation," a Kissinger submission to the logic of the Brezhnev Doctrine.[55]

The problem in the late Ford and early Carter years was how the alliance could devise a credible defense posture against an increasingly strong Warsaw Pact force in the central sector of Europe without causing excessive damage to the economies of its members. Even more difficult was the challenge of political criticism from the Left and from pacifists worried about escalating the arms race. Soviet propaganda made the most of their opportunities throughout the late 1970s, as they mobilized sentiment against the dangers of war. The blame clearly lay with NATO's aggressive designs according to their judgments.[56]

The gloom among NATO officials may have been exaggerated. How much of the Soviet activity represented a plan of ultimate aggression, and how much represented a misperception of NATO's own intention, cannot actually be resolved. However, the possibility of a mirror image exists and has relevance. At the very time Western planners were despondent over the will of the United States and NATO to stand up to Warsaw Pact powers, Soviet observers interpreted NATO's concern over its own weaknesses to be a Western rejection of détente and a return to reactionary counsels. Just as the United States observed the improvement in both conventional and nuclear arms in the East, so the Soviet commentators pointed to modernization in NATO technology. Sergei Losev, director general of TASS, made it clear that the NATO decision to build new missiles in Europe was a provocation to the Soviet Union.[57]

There were other deterrents to the excessive fear of Soviet military power, aside from the potential of a mirror image. Robert Komer, undersecretary of defense for policy, had warned even before the imbalance of

---

[55]George W. Ball, "Capitulation at Helsinki," *Newsweek* 86 (4 August 1975): 13.

[56]"The aggressive course of this military and political organization has always been based primarily on the activity of the military-industrial concerns on both sides of the Atlantic." A. Antonov and G. Ziborov, "NATO: Escalating the Arms Race," *International Affairs*, no. 8 (August 1978: 69. See *Current Digest of the Soviet Press* 31, no. 41 (9 October 1979): 5 for views of *Pravda* correspondent Vitaly Korionov over NATO plans for installing intermediate range missiles in Europe.

[57]Keith A. Dunn, "Soviet Perceptions of NATO," *Parameters* 13 (September 1978): 52–69; Sergei Losev, "Is the United States Provoking the Soviet?" from Novosti press agency, printed in *New York Times*, 24 November 1979.

forces had risen as an issue of a "self-inflicted wound" induced by a myth that a non-nuclear defense was impossible without massive military outlays. While he urged some redistribution of NATO costs, he noted the internal strains within the Warsaw Pact that limited its effectiveness. "The enemy was not 10-feet tall."[58] How reliable were the Warsaw allies in light of the Romanian model? How far beneath the surface was domestic discontent with Soviet energy practices, consumer policies, or repressed nationalism of the nation's minorities? Although the paucity of data demands caution in interpreting answers to these questions, they were factors that Komer felt should weigh in the thinking of NATO planners and that could ameliorate the apparent inferior position of NATO forces facing the imposing array of the Warsaw Pact.

A more empirically based response to the imbalance between the East and West was offered by reordering NATO's defense structure. The simplest and oldest solution to the restoration of a balance in Europe was standardization of weapons and equipment. To reduce the inevitable national rivalry that the issue has raised since the inception of NATO, the concept of "interoperability" was initiated as a superior and more manageable version of standardization. It would permit communications, or data systems, as well as weapons of a particular country to employ common elements as fuel, ammunition, and spare parts.[59] The United States greeted the idea enthusiastically in the form of the Culver-Nunn amendment on NATO standardization to a Defense Department Appropriations Act in July 1975. Deploring the wasteful duplication of efforts in NATO logistics, the amendment stated that future procurement of equipment for U.S. troops would be "standardized" or at least "interoperable with the equipment of other members of the North Atlantic Treaty Organization."[60]

Good intentions notwithstanding, present results have stimulated controversy over tanks and aircraft of the 1980s as national pressures affected the competition between the U.S. XM-1 and the German *Leopard II* tanks, between the French F-1E and the American F-16.[61] Still, there was a sense of progress abroad when the Department of the

---

[58]R. W. Komer, "Treating NATO's Self-Inflicted Wound," *Foreign Policy* (Winter 1973–74): 36–37.

[59]John B. Walsh, "Initiatives in Standardization/Interoperability," *NATO Review* 26 (October 1978): 8–10.

[60]Department of Defense Appropriation Authorization Act of 1976, U.S., *Statutes at Large*, Vol. 90, sec. 902, pp. 930–31. The Culver-Nunn amendment was constructed on evidence produced by Thomas A. Callaghan, who had been commissioned by the State Department to examine the subject. His report claimed that NATO had been wasting $10 billion a year in competitive research development and procurement of weapons. See Thomas A. Callaghan, Jr., "A Common Market for Atlantic Defense," *Atlantic Community Quarterly* 13 (Spring 1975): 161ff.; and report entitled, "US/European Economic Cooperation on Military and Civil Technologies," Center for Strategic and International Studies, Georgetown University.

[61]*New York Times*, 19 August 1976, 18 December 1975, and 9 May 1979. See Philip

Army decided on 31 January 1978 that the United States would require the German-developed 120-mm. gun for its new XM-1 battle tank. The decision consciously was intended as "an indication that the United States was sincere in its desire for a 'two-way' standardization."[62] Similarly, the principle of interoperability seemed to flourish when the first of 348 European-built F-16 aircraft was delivered to the Belgian Air Force on 26 January 1979. Four thousand suppliers and subcontractors in the United States and Europe were involved in the production of the new aircraft.[63]

A more prompt solution to coping with Soviet power in conventional arms was through employment of new antitank weapons in Europe. If sufficient funds were made available to NATO forces, the Soviet advantage in superior tank forces could be neutralized. The October War of 1973 bore witness so dramatically to the enormous potential of antitank missiles that one observer, Ian Smart, deputy director of the Royal Institute of International Affairs, was quoted as claiming that the introduction of highly mobile and simply operated antitank missiles "marks a transformation that recalls the way in which the longbow enabled the English footsoldier of the 14th century to overcome the mounted knight."[64] No matter how exaggerated the linkage of the Middle Eastern war of 1973 with the battle of Crécy in 1346 may have been, there was no doubt that the new air or ground delivered precision-guided missiles and antitank guided missiles (PGMs and ATGMs) would reduce to some degree the advantage the Warsaw powers possessed in tank superiority. It seemed to return the initiative to the West at a reasonable price. Although there were technical limitations in the use of the ATGMs, the ability of the West to employ sophisticated technology on behalf of their troops helped to mitigate the bouts of pessimism in which the NATO allies indulged periodically.

The use of the ATGM, had it been an effective panacea, would have breathed new life into MC 14/3, "Overall Strategic Concept for the Defense of the NATO Area," which had been the basis of NATO's military doctrine since its adoption by the Defense Planning Committee in March 1967. This doctrine consolidated the principle of "flexible response" and presumably would enable NATO forces to meet a conventional attack with force equal to the occasion, deliberately escalating the means of resistance when necessary. The language, as well as the style of NATO thinking, continued to be reminiscent of the Kennedy era where a premium was placed on tactical reactions with non-nuclear

J. Farley, Stephen S. Kaplan, and William S. Lewis, *Arms Across the Sea* (Washington, DC: Brookings Institution, 1978), p. 60.

[62] Scott L. Bills, "Congress and Western European Policy," in *Congress and Foreign Policy—1978*, committee print for U.S. House of Representatives (Washington, DC: Government Printing Office, 1978), p. 209.

[63] *Atlantic Community News*, February 1979.

[64] Quoted in Robert Kennedy, "Precision ATGMs and NATO Defense," *Orbis* 22 (Winter 1979):897.

arms. In this context the ATGM was an updated way of successfully deterring the Warsaw powers from initiating adventures in the central region. The superior numbers of the enemy's tanks would diminish in significance.[65]

The trouble with this vision was due partly to hyperbolic claims for the new antitank missiles. A realistic view of the Egyptian attack against Israeli forces in the Sinai would reveal that the initial Egyptian successes were produced from other sources, that the Israelis quickly countered the new weaponry with their own counterweapons, and that within two weeks of the invasion Egypt had lost control of its troops east of the Suez Canal and much territory west of the canal. Moreover, the scenario failed to take into account the technological responses that the Soviets could and did make since 1973. Tanks were not the totality of Soviet power.[66] Repeatedly, the field commanders and the supreme commanders themselves have sounded the alarm in the middle and late 1970s that the power to deter had lessened with the rapid modernization of the Warsaw forces, notably the introduction of the tactical SS-21 missile in 1979.[67]

Recognition of this problem was reflected in the attraction that the neutron bomb held for the allies in the mid-1970s. Yet, the controversy over the building of the neutron bomb was a sign that the cement that Soviet power on NATO's eastern flank provided to the alliance was riven with fissures that could destroy its unity. The neutron bomb "enhanced radiation weapon," in the language of the Pentagon, was designed to destroy attacking armor and mechanized troops while sparing nearby civilian areas, particularly buildings, from lethal damage. Its use would enable defenders to move into the blast areas quickly since the neutron weapon was basically a small hydrogen bomb that would yield about one-tenth of the heat and fallout of the older tactical nuclear weapons accompanied by a very short radioactive half-life. The space affected by the bomb could be occupied within several hours after its launching. If employed in Western Europe to halt an attack from the East, it would have none of the frightening aftereffects—fire and blast, or the destruction of civilian populations or properties—which any other tactical nuclear device would incur. By 1977 it seemed probable that all members of the alliance would endorse deployment of enhanced-radiation warheads that could be installed on the army Lance missiles, with a range of seventy-five miles. The NATO nuclear planning group gave its blessing the summer of that year.[68]

[65]Richard Hart Sinnreich, "NATO's Doctrinal Dilemma," *Orbis* 19 (Summer 1975): 461ff.

[66]Ori Even-Tov, "The NATO Conventional Defense: Back to Reality," *Orbis* 23 (Spring 1979): 35ff.

[67]For example, see Andrew Goodpaster, "NATO Strategy and Requirements, 1975–1985," *Atlantic Community Quarterly* 13 (Winter 1975–76): 461ff; and Alexander M. Haig, "NATO: An Agenda for the Future," *NATO Review* 27 (June 1979): 3–5.

[68]*New York Times,* 8 July 1977.

A political blast deferred production of the neutron bomb despite the blessings of NATO officials. Its failure forced the allies to face the consequence of failing to develop a clear doctrine on use of tactical nuclear weapons.[69] The issue had lurked in the background for twenty years, from the time when Henry Kissinger's *Nuclear Weapons and Foreign Policy* thrust it into NATO's consciousness in 1957 as an alternative to "massive retaliation."[70] But it never amounted to more than a vague deterrent as opposed to a developed tactic of containment. The older tactical "dirty" bombs were so destructive to friend and enemy alike that their utility in a crisis was doubtful. It was the very practicality of the neutron bomb that distressed congressional critics like Mark Hatfield who called the effort to put the bomb into production "unconscionable."[71] A threatened Senate filibuster in 1977 did not prevent the Carter administration from continuing to seek funds for the neutron bomb, but the fallout in the Senate and abroad prevented it from being part of the NATO arsenal during the 1970s.

The neutron issue sparked a major debate among the allies because of its association at the time with another weapon that was of major concern to Europeans: the cruise missile, a low-flying, pilotless aircraft that could elude Soviet radar and deliver either nuclear or conventional warheads with great accuracy inside the territory of the Warsaw Pact powers. Both became entangled in European apprehension over the potential impact of the Soviet-American SALT II negotiations upon their security of the allies. When the United States agreed in 1977 to a three-year delay in extending the cruise missiles to the Western allies as a ploy in the SALT talks, this concession was seen as an example of American waffling in the face of Soviet pressure. Failure to develop the neutron bomb would be another American weakness.[72]

General H. F. Zeiner-Gundersen of Norway, chairman of the NATO Military Committee, helped dim this image and urged the introduction of the neutron weapon at a meeting of defense ministers in December 1977; and in the United States the influential voice of the *New York Times* praised the deterrent value of the bomb. Its expected effectiveness against massed tank formations made it a formidable bargaining chip in MBFR negotiations.[73] Soviet concern would be understandable. Twenty thousand tanks, sealed against conventional radiation

---

[69]R. G. Shreffler, "The Neutron Bomb for NATO Defense: An Alternative," *Orbis* 21 (Winter 1978): 959ff.

[70]Henry A. Kissinger, *Nuclear Weapons and Foreign Policy* (New York: Harper and Row, 1957).

[71]*New York Times,* 8 July 1977.

[72]Ibid., 9 December 1977; Defense Planning Committee, final communique, *NATO Review* 26 (February 1978): 28.

[73]*New York Times,* 7 December 1977, 30 March 1978.

fallout, would be rendered virtually obsolete if the new weapon were deployed.[74]

However, subterranean uneasiness on both sides of the Atlantic stayed the president's hand. For all their generalized support the European allies sent out confusing signals. While demanding that the United States begin production of the bomb, they refused to take any initiative in offering their territories as sites for its deployment. Conceivably, the neutron weapon could be held in abeyance or suspended for eighteen months or two years until the Soviet Union had been tested. A withdrawal of the SS-20 might be a worthwhile quid for a neutron quo. Germany was formally on record favoring production of the bomb, but this was not the impression Chancellor Helmut Schmidt left with Carter in the spring of 1978. Despite his private wishes, Schmidt faced strong opposition within his party that stilled his voice at the critical moment of decision. Germans looked for and could not find other continental nations to join them.[75]

The president's indecisive deferral in April 1978 on the decision to produce the neutron bomb reasonably may be regarded as a rebuke to the timidity of the allies. It also could be a product of the Soviet Union's own shrewd and massive European campaign of intimidation and cajolery, even when its coarse ideological language threatened to blunt its impact. Labeling the neutron bomb "the ultimate capitalist weapon," its propaganda worked to exploit the discomfort of those who believed that the weapon was inhumane or would increase the likelihood of future war.[76] Additionally, it was obvious that the president harbored a deep-seated reluctance to take responsibility for lowering the threshold of nuclear war.

Today the neutron bomb is still an issue, not because all the foregoing fears have been exorcised but primarily because Soviet improvements in their first-strike capabilities have limited alternatives to both the cruise missile and the neutron bomb in the opinion of Europeans. The Warsaw power's new intermediate-range missile, the SS-20, which could hit any part of Europe, and its short-range missile, the SS-21, based in East Germany, help to explain why the Nuclear Planning Group of NATO would raise again the issue of the neutron option less than two weeks after the president had dismissed it.[77] In January 1979 at a meeting of the leaders of the major NATO powers in Guadeloupe, Chancellor

---

[74]Soviet opposition was customarily expressed in more humanistic terms. See, for example, A. Stoleshnikov, "The Neutron Weapon: A Threat to Peace," *International Affairs* (May 1978): 66–69. The author emphasizes international opposition: Swedish foreign minister, World Peace Council, World Federation of Scientific Workers, and U.S. Senators Mark Hatfield and John Heinz.

[75]Note the even-handed criticism of Lothar Ruehl, "Die Nichtentscheidung über die 'Neutronenwaffe': Ein Beispiel Verfehlter Bundespolitik," *Europa Archiv* 34 (March 1979): 137–50.

[76]*New York Times,* 29 April 1978.

[77]Ibid., 20 April 1978.

Schmidt brought with him a continuing, but now more public, conviction that the neutron bomb was the only weapon that could balance Soviet superiority in tank numbers in the central sector of Europe.[78] The decision of the NATO council in December 1979, in the face of strong Dutch and Belgian political opposition, to develop and deploy 572 U.S.-made *Pershing II* and cruise missiles on the European continent was made vital by the perceived need to counter the rising Soviet power in Europe as well as to demonstrate American recovery from the indecisiveness over the neutron issue. At the same time the council announced its willingness to enter into arms negotiations with the Soviet Union in order to reduce numbers of all medium-range missiles in Europe. It was this hope that permitted wavering Belgium and Holland to give at least tentative and reserved approval of the counterforce plan. In this context SALT II seemed to be an urgent priority for NATO, preceded by decision for installation of new missiles in Western Europe, but to be followed by new negotiations in a forthcoming SALT III for the reduction of both NATO and Warsaw Pact weapon systems.[79]

CONCLUDING OBSERVATIONS: CHANGE IN CONTINUITY

Where then did NATO stand as it entered its fourth decade? The most conspicuous position still is a state of disarray. Whether or not the components of its disarray—problems of standardization, increasing Soviet military strength, shortcomings in European functional cooperation, or fragile relations with the Balkan members—are more serious challenges than they had been in the past are debatable. A case may be made that the Korean War of 1950, or the Suez invasion of 1956, or the French withdrawal from the organization in 1966, or even the specter of Eurocommunism in France and Italy in the mid-1970s were more severe challenges than any of the centrifugal forces presently at work in the alliance. Its record suggests that NATO always will be in turmoil and that it will have a continuing capacity to cope with it. As one NATO official expressed it, "... don't exaggerate the difficulties. The shape of the alliance can be described with the words Mark Twain used about Wagner's music—it isn't as bad as it sounds."[80]

The future may witness major changes in the alliance. Global cooperation between NATO and China and Japan might require a new

---

[78]Drew Middleton, ibid., 5 January 1979.
[79]Communique, special meeting of foreign and defense ministers, 12 December 1979, *NATO Review* 28 (February 1980): 25.
[80]Flora Lewis, *New York Times,* 1 April 1978.

framework for the alliance in the 1980s. The lengthy birth pangs of a united Europe capable of concerted action independent of the United States may be announcing the onset of its final trimester. The coordination of NATO's activities outside the boundaries of the treaty, as in the Middle Eastern crisis of 1973 and the Iranian crisis of 1979, should be addressed immediately.[81] Subsequently, all of these prospects are still subsumed under a precarious balance that has kept Europe reasonably stable in the 1970s.

What is missing, however, from many of the evaluations of the present and future of NATO is a recognition that the original purposes of the treaty are still valid, and that they override every other consideration of its functions. For all the changes in the balance of power within the alliance and between the Western and Eastern blocs, the perceived need for security in a continent dominated by fears of Soviet power still requires an American connection. Neither *Ostpolitik,* nor détente, nor the split in the Communist world sufficed to replace it. As Walter Laqueur commented at the end of the decade: "An interim balance sheet of détente in Europe shows that the dramatic transformation of the world and European scene that had been predicted in 1971 certainly had not materialized."[82] The imbalance of power, at least psychologically, between East and West may be no less in 1980 than it was in 1950.

The shared perception of threat from the East may not of itself continue to serve as a centripetal force for NATO. The continuing crisis of confidence in American leadership, unfolding with undiminished force in 1980, could fragment the alliance in the 1980s. American failures to check the Soviet Union in Afghanistan and to provide a ready solution to relations with Iran could erode the alliance as European sense of dependence on American power is overcome by a sense of American impotence in the Middle East and elsewhere. The future then could result in accelerating the pace toward a united Europe; more likely it would be a case of *sauve qui peut* as European nations move toward an accommodation with the Soviet vision of the world.

---

[81]As early as 1956, NATO heads of government had agreed to consultation on problems outside the North Atlantic Treaty area but in successive announcements had reached the point where they could accept that the common interests of the Alliance "can be affected by events in other areas of the world." See "Declaration on Atlantic Relations," 26 June 1974, in Department of State *Bulletin* 71 (1974): 42–44. The absence of obligatory action was noted by Frederic L. Kirgis, "NATO Consultations as a Component of National Decisionmaking," *American Journal of International Law* 73 (July 1979): 376–78.

[82]Walter Laqueur, *A Continent Astray: Europe, 1970–1980* (New York: Oxford University Press, 1979), p. 220.

The foregoing is a picture of the alliance at the brink of destruction.[83] It is not, however, a new image. NATO's history is replete with predictions of fatal crises. Hitherto the alliance has coped with the centrifugal elements that always have been present in its structure. It can cope again but only if NATO achieves a unity within which both authority and responsibility are more widely distributed than in the past. The call to "unite their efforts for collective defense and for preservation of peace and security" was made in the preamble of the Treaty of Washington in 1949. Its message is as valid for the second generation as it had been for the first.

---

[83] See, for example, James O. Goldsborough, "Europe Cashes in on Carter's Cold War," *New York Times Magazine*, 27 April 1980, pp. 42ff.; Hans Scheuer, "Veränderte Rolle der USA in der Weltpolitik," *Aussenpolitik* 31 (January 1980): 84–91; and André Fontaine, "Comment parler fort avec un petit bâton?" *Le Monde*, 23 April 1980.

The United States and NATO, 1953–69

NORMAN A. GRAEBNER

WEST GERMANY AND THE COMPLETION OF NATO

Dwight D. Eisenhower, defying the Asia-first orientation of his party, assured the country as president that he regarded Europe's continuing improvement the primary goal of his administration. For high Republican officials, NATO was indeed their party's central inheritance from the Truman years. "Nothing that has happened," declared Secretary of State John Foster Dulles in April 1953, "has induced in us a mood of relaxation or any desire to weaken NATO."[1] The alliance satisfied two essential and intertwined requirements of American policy—defense of a specific area of major historical concern and loyalty to the principle of international cooperation. NATO symbolized the country's rejection of the isolationism that had governed its relations with Europe before 1939. It offered security to the Atlantic world even while it permitted each participating country the freedom to pursue its traditional interests in Europe and elsewhere. That the international commitments of the United States after 1953 became increasingly unilateral and global in no way undermined Western Europe's significance. Rather it was the soundness of the trans-Atlantic partnership that enabled Washington to pursue its far more extravagant and controversial policies in Asia, Latin America, and the Middle East.

For security-minded Washington, NATO's major unfinished business in 1953 was the incorporation of West Germany into its military structure. France had opposed it, convinced that a revived Germany, militarily strong and free to pursue its historic ambitions, would unleash unwanted tensions across Europe. To assure its future security against an armed Germany, France proposed the creation of a European Defense Community (EDC), a supranational body within NATO that would limit and control Germany's contribution to Europe's defense. The EDC proposal, as finally adopted by the NATO governments in May 1952, ended the allied occupation of Germany and provided for a German contribution of twelve divisions to Europe's defense, with all military units

---

[1] John Foster Dulles, "The First 90 Days," Department of State *Bulletin* 28 (27 April 1953): 604–5.

above division level under multinational control. NATO's Supreme Allied Commander would direct the entire European army. Equally important for French security, EDC would deny Germany the right to manufacture aircraft, heavy ships, or atomic, chemical, and biological weapons unless the NATO Council approved such production unanimously. Germany ratified EDC despite the widespread fear among Germans that NATO membership would challenge Soviet interest and thus guarantee the permanent division of their country.[2] In Paris the French Assembly balked at its own government's proposal.

In February 1953, Secretary Dulles visited six EDC countries and Great Britain to warn them that a policy of continuing drift on matters of defense would dry up the sources of U.S. military and economic aid. He urged the countries of Europe to perfect the organization of EDC. Having revived the project, Dulles predicted on his return to Washington that the Europeans would shortly push it to completion. It had become, he informed the nation, "the liveliest single topic before the six parliaments of continental Europe."[3] Unless the French approved EDC quickly, he warned, the United States would undertake an "agonizing reappraisal" of its commitment to Europe's defense. Europe recognized in Dulles's statement a veiled threat that the United States would either limit its defense effort to the Western Hemisphere or rearm West Germany without French approval. To European observers both alternatives appeared unreasonably severe; French radicals and nationalists who opposed EDC were not impressed. Radical Socialist Premier Pierre Mendès-France revealed little enthusiasm for EDC but affirmed France's devotion to an alliance of equal partners "discussing together their common interests while each member remains judge of its own vital and essential national interests."[4]

Through 1953 and the early months of 1954 Dulles continued to apply the "shock treatment" to France in an effort to force the issue of EDC ratification on both the French Assembly and the French people.[5] Anticipating a French rejection of EDC, the United States Senate, by a vote of 88 to 0, argued for a unilateral American approach to German rearmament. The Senate Armed Services Committee made clear its determination to cut future aid to France unless that country ratified EDC. In August 1954 the French Assembly delivered its predictable coup de grâce to EDC—a resounding defeat for American policy.

---

[2]For a brief survey of U.S. efforts to bring West Germany into NATO, see Lawrence S. Kaplan, "The United States and the Atlantic Alliance: The First Generation," in John Braeman, Robert H. Bremner, and David Brody, eds., *Twentieth-Century American Foreign Policy* (Columbus, OH: Ohio State University Press, 1971), pp. 317–21.

[3]Dulles, "The First 90 Days," p. 604.

[4]Edmond Taylor, "This Long NATO Crisis," *The Reporter* 24 (21 April 1966): 17.

[5]C. L. Sulzberger, *New York Times*, 20 December 1953.

Dulles swallowed France's rejection with scarcely a murmur; American interests in Europe would not permit an "agonizing reappraisal." But the French decision left the West scrambling for the means to tie West Germany into an integrated West European alliance. Into this vacuum moved the British, deserting their traditional isolation from the continent. The London government feared that any U.S. effort to rearm West Germany without French concurrence would excite French feelings of insecurity and aggravate that country's internal dissension. Britain, moreover, shared France's distrust of German power and opposed a combination of uncontrolled German and American forces in Western Europe that might increase pressure on the Soviet Union and thereby endanger a totally acceptable status quo.

Britain's Anthony Eden resolved the crisis by committing four British divisions to the continent "as long as a majority of the Brussels partners want them there." The channel had ceased to be a special guarantee of British security.[6] Eden saved NATO by placing curbs on Germany satisfactory to the French. Suddenly the Western Europeans shared a renewed spirit of unity. President Eisenhower lauded the prospective accord as perhaps "one of the greatest diplomatic achievements of our time." At the London nine-power conference in September 1954, American policy revealed a more compromising tone.[7] Dulles listened calmly to French demands for arms control. During October the foreign ministers met in Paris to approve the new agreements with Germany. Chancellor Konrad Adenauer of West Germany accepted the necessary concessions to France. France received guarantees of British and American protection. The Supreme Allied Commander in Europe maintained direct control of Germany's military forces. In addition, the new arrangements retained the provisions of the rejected EDC that barred Germany from the production of biological, chemical, and atomic war materials. Germany received membership in the Atlantic and European communities as an equal partner and the promise of national reunification. The United States received what it had long desired: the full integration of German power into the Western alliance. In May 1955 West Germany became the fifteenth member of NATO. Supported by United States military assistance, that country soon embarked on an ambitious program of rearmament.[8] The Soviet Union responded to the new challenge by

---

[6]For an excellent evaluation of British Policy, see Woodrow Wyatt, "Geography Closes in on the British," *New York Times Magazine* 12 (17 October 1954): 68–71.

[7]Drew Middleton noted John Foster Dulles's efforts to find the necessary compromises, *New York Times,* 3 October 1954.

[8]For the United States-West German mutal defense agreement, 30 June 1955, see Department of State *Bulletin* 33 (25 July 1955): 142–44; James B. Conant, ambassador to the Federal Republic, discusses United States-West German relations, 23 March 1956, Department of State *Bulletin* 34 (9 April 1956): 585–87.

organizing its Warsaw Pact across Eastern Europe. Containment thereafter would reinforce the division of Europe and Germany; it would not do
more.

ENDS WITHOUT MEANS

After mid-century Washington had rationalized its burgeoning
defense effort as a prerequisite for successful negotiations with the USSR.
By 1953 it seemed clear that the Marshall Plan and NATO, backed by the
economic power and atomic supremacy of the United States, had halted
the threatened landslide into disaster. Convinced that Western power vis-
à-vis the Soviet Union would never be greater than it was at that moment,
Europeans and Americans alike argued that the time had arrived to begin
the arduous task of negotiating a general European settlement. Even many
who distrusted Soviet diplomacy believed that the West had no choice but
to use whatever advantages its atomic lead afforded in an immediate
search for an acceptable economic and political division of the continent.
Those who commanded Western policy, however, concluded that Western
gains after mid-century warranted further delay to enable Western
diplomats to approach the Kremlin with total military superiority. Some
warned indeed that Winston Churchill's widely publicized demand for a
Big Four meeting merely injured Western unity and encouraged a
dangerous euphoria in the democracies.[9] What would determine the
success of any peacetime negotiations would be the compatibility of the
opposing national objectives. Unfortunately, Washington's minimum
requirements demanded no less than a Soviet diplomatic capitulation. It
was not strange that Eisenhower and Dulles anticipated little progress in
East-West diplomacy.
    For Dulles the goal of liberating Eastern Europe, proclaimed
without restraint during the presidential campaign, became a logical and
necessary extension of the policy of containment. In his appearance before
the Senate Foreign Relations Committee on 15 January 1953, Dulles
complained of the limited objectives of past containment policy. He
warned the committee:

> [W]e shall never have a secure peace or a happy world so long as
> Soviet Communism dominates one-third of all of the peoples that
> there are. . . . These people who are enslaved are people who deserve
> to be free . . . and ought to be free because if they are the servile

---

[9]For the debate on the proper timing of negotiations, see C. L. Sulzberger, *New York
Times,* 1 November 1953. Anthony Eden favored early talks. See the *Des Moines Register*,
1 December 1953.

instruments of aggressive despotism, they will eventually be welded into a force which will be highly dangerous to ourselves and to all of the free world. Therefore, we must always have in mind the liberation of these captive peoples. . . .Liberation can be accomplished by processes short of war.[10]

Dulles reaffirmed the need of liberation when he addressed the American Society of Newspapers Editors on 18 April 1953: "It is of utmost importance that we should make clear to the captive peoples that we do not accept their captivity as a permanent fact of history. If they thought otherwise and became hopeless, we would unwittingly have become partners to the forging of a hostile power so vast that it could encompass our destruction."[11] Unless the United States reduced the Soviet presence in Eastern Europe, Dulles warned repeatedly, not even the established lines of demarcation would hold. Containment would triumph when it achieved liberation.

President Eisenhower, in his first State of the Union Message on 2 February 1953, condemned the wartime agreements which, Republicans insisted, had brought Soviet dominance to millions of Europeans. He would ask Congress to pass a resolution declaring that the government of the United States recognized no past accords that condoned such enslavement. Dulles explained the resolution before the House Foreign Affairs Committee on 26 February. "The aim," he said, "is to make totally clear the integrity of this Nation's purpose in relation to the millions of enslaved peoples in Europe and Asia."[12] The proposed resolution condemned Soviet behavior rather than Franklin D. Roosevelt's alleged sellout at Yalta; Senate Republicans rejected it. Senator Arthur Watkins of Utah reminded his Republican colleagues of the campaign pledge. Thereafter, Republican leaders in Congress demanded that the administration fulfill its promise to free the Slavic peoples of Europe. The failure of the wartime conferences argued against any further negotiations until the Kremlin made the necessary guarantees of liberation in advance. Former President Herbert Hoover charged that American acquiescence had enabled the Soviet Union to extinguish "the liberties of tens of millions of people" in Eastern Europe; no Republican administration should recognize the consequences of such behavior. Senator Robert A. Taft of Ohio rebuked the British and French in May 1953 for their

[10]U.S., Congress, Senate, Committee on Foreign Relations, *Hearings before the Senate Committee on Foreign Relations on the Nomination of John Foster Dulles, Secretary of State Designate, January 15, 1953,* 83d Cong., 1st sess., 1953, pp. 5–6.

[11]Dulles, "The First 90 Days," p. 606.

[12]Resolution appears in U.S., Department of State, *American Foreign Policy, 1950–1955: Basic Documents II,* General Foreign Policy Series 117, Publications 6446 (1957); and J. F. Dulles's PP1958–1959 statement, 26 February 1953, U.S., Department of State, *American Foreign Policy, 1950–1955, II,* General Foreign Policy Series 117, Publication 6446 (1957), p. 1959.

apparent willingness to abandon the Poles, Czechs, Hungarians, and Romanians to the mercies of the Soviets; and Senator Joseph McCarthy of Wisconsin warned the administration late that year against adopting the Truman-Acheson policy of "whining, whimpering appeasement."[13]

Dulles assumed that he could weaken the Soviet Union by denying it the moral respectability and needed resources of the Western World. Following Stalin's death in March 1953, his successor, Georgi Malenkov, argued for peaceful coexistence and new measures to guarantee the peace. When Eisenhower advocated a hopeful and positive response to the Soviet overtures, Dulles made clear his displeasure: ". . . I think there's some real danger of our just seeming to fall in with these Soviet overtures," he cautioned. "It's obvious that what they are doing is because of outside pressures, and I don't know anything better we can do than to keep up these pressures right now."[14] The East German riots of June 1953, followed in July by the execution of Lavrenti Beria, notorious head of the Soviet secret police, convinced Dulles that the Soviet empire was seething with discontent and that greater Western pressure could break Soviet control of Eastern Europe completely. "This is the kind of time when we ought to be *doubling* our bets, not reducing them—as all the Western parliaments want to do," he informed the cabinet on 10 July. "This is the time to *crowd* the enemy—and maybe *finish* him, once and for all." At the same time Dulles assured the nation: "[T]he Communist structure is over-extended, over-rigid and ill-founded." As oppressed populations demonstrated their spirit of independence, the secretary continued, the Kremlin "would come to recognize the futility of trying to hold captive so many peoples who, by their faith and their patriotism, can never really be consolidated into a Soviet Communist world."[15]

Disturbed by West European complacency toward Soviet repression, Dulles opposed the president's attendance at the Bermuda conference of the three Western heads of state in December 1953. Shortly before the meeting the secretary assured a House committee that the United States would welcome the opportunity to settle specific disputes with the Soviet Union, but he added: "We do not look on the conference table as a place where we surrender our principles, but rather as a place for making principles prevail."[16] If Churchill and French Premier Joseph

---

[13]Republicans continued to exert pressure on the Eisenhower administration. For example, California Senator William F. Knowland warned the administration in December 1954 to avoid any conference in which the Western allies might recognize the Iron Curtain. "I think," he said "that is a direct contradiction of the Party platform of 1952 under which the Republicans came to power," *New York Times Magazine* (5 December 1954).

[14]Quoted in Emmet John Hughes, *The Ordeal of Power: A Political Memoir of the Eisenhower Years* (New York: Dell Publishing, 1964), pp. 95–96.

[15]Ibid., pp. 95, 96, 120. See also U.S., Department of State, *American Foreign Policy, 1950–1955, II,* General Foreign Policy Series 117, Publication 6446 (1957), p. 1746.

[16]Quoted by Richard Wilson in *Des Moines Register,* 1 December 1953.

Laniel hoped to extract a more realistic policy toward the Soviet Union from the United States, they were disappointed. The Bermuda declaration embodied America's rollback policy toward the Soviet Union; it reassured the people behind the Iron Curtain: "We cannot accept as justified or permanent the present division of Europe. Our hope is that in due course peaceful means will be found to enable the countries of Eastern Europe again to play their part as free nations in a free Europe."[17] Unfortunately, liberation required the withdrawal of Soviet military power and political influence from Eastern Europe. What peaceful means could achieve such purpose was not clear. As the London *Economist* observed on 30 August 1952: "Unhappily 'liberation' applied to Eastern Europe . . . means either the risk of war or it means nothing. . . . 'Liberation' entails no risk of war only when it means nothing."

Eventually American revisionism focused on the issue of German reunification; anything less would upset West Germany's internal stability. For political reasons the Bonn government would not accept as permanent the Soviet subjugation of 17 million East Germans. If the West could not satisfy this German interest, some Americans feared, Bonn eventually might negotiate with the Kremlin on its own. Few American leaders entertained much hope of immediate reunification, but they were determined to prevent the Western alliance from using the East Germans as pawns in allied diplomacy. As early as July 1953, Eisenhower declared that an honorable European peace would require the reemergence of a united German republic, dedicated to the welfare of its own people and to the peace of Europe. "The continued partition of Germany," Dulles declared more forcefully in September, "is a scandal. It is more than that. It is a crime. . . .[I]t is not only wrong to the Germans; it is a menace to the peace."[18] Certainly the incorporation of West Germany into NATO was a net gain. But Dulles never explained how a rearmed West German state, tightly integrated into the Western alliance, could achieve reunification without a Soviet capitulation. Soviet power and determination rendered the goal of German reunification unachievable, but it kept allied purposes simple and sustained objectives on which the partners could agree.[19]

In February 1954, Dulles, with allied approval, made German reunification the central issue at the Berlin conference. "I am firmly convinced," he said, "that a free and united Germany is essential to stable peace in Europe. . . .It is the disagreement of our four nations which perpetuated the present division of Germany, and it is only we who can end this division of Germany." Dulles condemned the Soviet effort to defend its interests in a regime placed in power and held in power by the presence of Soviet divisions. In his central argument Dulles denied that

---

[17]*American Foreign Policy, 1950–1955, II,* pp. 1747–48, 1843–44.
[18]See Edmund Stillman, " 'Containment' has won, but . . . ," *New York Times Magazine* (28 May 1967): 27.
[19]*American Foreign Policy, 1950–1955, II,* pp. 1850–52, 1854–55.

such a regime had the right to negotiate with the West German government on equal terms. Dulles appeared to succeed in his quest for a free,
united Germany when the Big Four Geneva conference of July 1955
adopted a resolution that declared: "The Heads of Government, recognizing their common responsibility for the settlement of the German
questions and the reunification of Germany, have agreed that the settlement of the German question and the reunification of Germany by means
of free elections shall be carried out in conformity with the national
interests of the German people and the interests of European security."[20]
Eisenhower at Geneva insisted that European security and German reunification were inseparable issues. The foreign minister, returning to
Geneva in October, would make the final arrangements for free German
elections.

   At the October meeting Dulles faced only frustration and failure.
The Soviets based their formula for German unification on the negotiation
of an all-European security treaty. Dulles declared that the three Western
powers would agree only to a security treaty that provided for a free,
united German republic. Anthony Eden's countering plan insisted, furthermore, that an all-German government should have the right to accept
or reject membership in NATO as it preferred. At Geneva Dulles
repeatedly demanded a reunited Germany under free elections. "We urge
upon the Soviet Government," he declared on 9 November, "that it
should not perpetuate the injustice of a divided Germany with the menace
which it carries to European security. Can we not learn from the lesson of
Versailles? We make the plea, and we shall go on making it, in the hope,
and, indeed, in the expectation that before it is too late wisdom will
prevail."[21] Western demands exceeded the limits of diplomatic possibility;
still allied unity required the rejection of compromise.

NUCLEAR STRATEGY: THE GREAT DEBATE

   For official Washington the concept of peaceful liberation was not a
contradiction in terms. Dulles shared Dean Acheson's conviction that
time favored the West; ultimately Western supremacy would force a
Soviet retreat and gain the fulfillment of Western revisionist goals.
Western military policy need only hold the lines of demarcation and await
the disintegration of the Soviet structure. Eisenhower accepted the
Truman consensus on the need for an adequate national defense, one
that included the European theater. He was determined as well to fulfill

---

[20]Ibid., p. 2015.
[21]Ibid., pp. 1910, 1924.

his campaign pledge of budget reduction. In February 1953 the new president declared: "Our problem is to achieve military strength within the limits of durable strain upon our economy." During May he spoke of a budget cut of $8 billion to achieve his goal "of creating a situation of maximum strength within economic capabilities." In January 1954, Eisenhower unveiled his "New Look" in military policy; the country's defense would emphasize air-atomic power, permitting it to wield maximum destructive force at minimum cost.[22] Secretary Dulles soon elevated the military New Look into a broad strategic concept that assured superior national performance at reduced costs and risks of war.

Dulles defined his new strategy on 12 January 1954, when he informed the New York Council on Foreign Relations that the United States in the future would rely less on conventional forces than on its "great capacity to retaliate, instantly, by means and places of our own choosing." The new strategy would eliminate future losses to enemy attack by assuring aggressors that their urban centers might be reduced to rubble. But Dulles promised more, binding the promise of liberation to American defense policy in Europe. The achievement of world stability through the threat of massive disaster, he assured the nation, would permit time and the human desire for freedom to work their destruction on the Communist enemy. "If we persist in the course I outline," he said, "we shall confront dictatorship with a task that is, in the long run, beyond its strength. . . .If the dictators persist in their present course, then it is they who will be limited to superficial successes, while their foundations crumble under the treads of their iron boots. . . ."[23] Critics noted that the doctrine of massive retaliation limited Soviet options, in the event of war, to capitulation or annihilation.[24] Dulles's successive modifications of the doctrine admitted the need for additional choices, but the continuing American commitment to European security comprised, fundamentally, the nuclear deterrent as the surest guarantee against war. Massive retaliation might punish the Soviet Union in war; it would not save Europe. NATO's strategy, based on massive retaliation, could serve allied interests only as long as the Soviets did not put the alliance to the test.

Some analysts charged that NATO's diplomatic inflexibility, backed by a huge nuclear arsenal, assumed dangers that did not exist and

---

[22]Donald W. Mitchell criticizes Eisenhower's "New Look" in military policy, in "The New Look," *Current History* 27 (October 1954): 214–19.

[23]U.S., Department of State, Department of State *Bulletin* 30 (25 January 1954): 107–10. Dulles explained his strategy more fully in "Policy for Security and Peace," *Foreign Affairs* 32 (April 1954): 353–64.

[24]For a standard critique of Dulles's strategy of massive retaliation, see Hans J. Morgenthau, "Instant Retaliation: Will it Deter Aggression," *The New Republic* 130 (29 March 1954): 11–14.

perpetuated goals that ruled out negotiations and reinforced the continent's divisions. NATO seemed less a source of strength for effective diplomacy than an agency for eliminating diplomacy altogether. Dulles's critics also accused him of conducting an ideological crusade against the USSR. Under American guidance, by late 1957 NATO had redefined the danger that it faced from Soviet power to the more insidious and ideological "international communism" backed by Soviet power.[25] The purpose of the alliance, some complained, was not to war against communism but to protect Western Europe from the physical power of the Soviet state. Had the United States accepted the goal of containing the Soviet Union within the limits that it had reached in 1945, the alliance might have created some balance between its power and its avowed intentions. But when the Eisenhower administration insisted that it could go beyond the negative, static policy of containment combined with nonrecognition and attempted to give a positive implementation to the goal of liberation, it tied the alliance to objectives that had no relevance to either the West's minimal interests in eastern Europe or its major interest in peace.

What troubled George Kennan in NATO's military posture was the uncompromising nuclear confrontation that it sustained in the heart of Europe. The West's decision to rebuild West German power inside NATO merely accentuated the confrontation. Kennan challenged Western policy directly in his widely publicized Reith Lectures over BBC in the autumn of 1957. He proposed a disengagement of forces that would free Germany of foreign troops and thereby reduce the level of tension across Europe. By reducing both American and Soviet influence in continental affairs, Europe might still escape its reliance on atomic weapons. "[I]f there could be a general withdrawal of American, British, and Russian armed power from the heart of the Continent," Kennan wrote, "there would be at least a chance that Europe's fortunes might be worked out, and the competition between two political philosophies carried forward, in a manner disastrous neither to the respective peoples themselves nor to the cause of world peace. I would not know where else this chance is to be looked for."[26] What lay behind Kennan's proposal was his conviction that Germany could not have both unification and military power. Only a neutralized Germany, he feared, would ever achieve reunification. To Kennan the purpose of containment was precisely that of negotiating such compromises, not dictating terms of peace to the Kremlin.

In February 1959 Poland's foreign minister, Adam Rapacki, presented a plan for a nuclear free zone in Central Europe, including both

[25]Cyrus L. Sulzberger, *What's Wrong with U.S. Foreign Policy* (New York: Harcourt, Brace, 1959), pp. 135–36; Aneurin Bevan, "Some Sharp Words from a Tough Welshman," *Look* 22 (18 March 1958): 128.
[26]George F. Kennan, *Russia, the Atom and the West* (New York: Harper and Row, 1957), p. 61; Robert Endicott Osgood, *NATO the Entangling Alliance* (Chicago: University of Chicago, 1962), pp. 331–32.

Germanies, as a further guarantee of peace and the eventual reunification of Germany. Washington rejected both the Rapacki Plan and the Kennan proposal. Acheson answered Kennan in the April 1958 issue of *Foreign Affairs*. For him Europe's defenses required a maximum of power and determination, not a withdrawal that would create a power vacuum and risk the loss of Central Europe to the Kremlin.[27] Dulles denounced disengagement as a sellout of West Germany. "If I had to choose between a neutralized Germany and Germany in the Soviet bloc," he wrote, "it might be almost better to have it in the bloc. That clearly is not acceptable but disengagement is absolutely not acceptable either."[28] Dulles assured Adenauer that the United States had no intention of weakening West Germany through any program of disengagement or neutralization.

CHALLENGES TO WESTERN UNITY

Historically alliances have demonstrated little success in dealing with long-term challenges; changing circumstances tend to weaken if not dissolve them. The fact that the North Atlantic Alliance, as it approached its tenth anniversary in 1959, had never encountered the problems that led to its formation caused some observers to wonder whether those problems existed at all. Amid actual conditions of peace in Europe the perennial warnings of danger lost their seriousness. The renewal of confidence encouraged the allies to reassert their sovereignty and to pursue independent and self-interested foreign policies. If NATO remained a viable defense organization, ten years without war had weakened the connection between the alliance and western European progress.[29]

Three factors sustained the Atlantic Alliance during its initial years: the atomic monopoly of the United States, the economic collapse of the West European countries, and the intransigence of Stalinist policies. After the mid-1950s Europe's postwar transformation effectively undermined them all. First, American nuclear weapons no longer appeared to guarantee western European security against Soviet attack. If their putative advances in weaponry had substance, they created a stalemate in nuclear power. By 1955 it seemed apparent to much of the world that the United States and the Soviet Union had reached a "parity of horror" that threatened destruction not only to themselves but also to all Western

---

[27]Dean G. Acheson, "The Illusion of Disengagement," *Foreign Affairs* 36 (April 1958): 373–81.
[28]Quoted in Walter LaFeber, *America, Russia and the Cold War* (New York: Wiley, 1976), p. 207.
[29]Thomas N. Etzold, "The Trouble with Alliances....," *U.S. Naval Institute Proceedings* 103 (March 1977): 47–49.

Europe. This dread of a nuclear confrontation led to the famed Geneva Summit Conference of July 1955. Second, the economic recovery of the western European countries greatly diminished their dependence upon the United States. So successful were the Marshall Plan and NATO in underwriting Europe's recovery that it was no longer certain in the late 1950s whether the region's confidence emanated from the alliance or from the sheer energy and productivity of Western Europe itself. If these countries still desired American aid, it was no longer a matter of life and death. The development of the Coal and Steel Community, Euratom, the Common Market, and the burgeoning trade with the Soviet bloc tended to decrease allied economic dependence on the United States even further.[30]

Third, the Soviet Union weakened Western unity with its "New Look" foreign policies. Having earlier created the image of a ruthless nation, guided only by considerations of military power, the Soviets struck a new pose after 1953 designed to relieve a world living in dread of war. Because of massive U.S. superiority the Soviets recognized that nothing could be settled by nuclear war. The Kremlin leaders after 1955 began to reveal amazing vigor, agility, and pragmatism in their use of diplomacy. They moved into South Asia and the Middle East with offers of trade and economic assistance. This shift in Soviet methods and the arena of activity turned countries from North Africa to Indonesia from passive objects to arbiters in the East-West struggle. In its global contest with the Kremlin, American policy outside Europe became increasingly divorced from that of its NATO allies; this aggravated the tensions within the alliance.[31] In Europe, Soviet proposals stressed peaceful coexistence, attributing the failure of diplomatic progress to the dogmatism and rigidity of Western policy. Western revisionism gave the Soviets a tactical advantage. Henry A. Kissinger noted in *Foreign Affairs:* "One of the difficulties the free world has had in dealing with the Soviet bloc is that we have been clearer about the things we oppose than those we stand for. This has given much of our negotiations with the Soviet Union the quality of a stubborn rearguard action designed primarily to thwart Soviet overtures." The rapid recovery of West Germany, with all the fears that German political, economic, and military eminence created throughout Europe, contributed to the opportunities confronting Soviet policy. Lester B. Pearson, Canada's noted diplomat, responded to the changing times when he wrote in 1958: "We must take full advantage of every opportunity, even more, create opportunities through a dynamic diplomacy, to negotiate differences with those whom we now fear."[32]

---

[30]Hans J. Morgenthau, "Alliances," *Confluence* 6 (Winter 1958): 317–20; Norman A. Graebner, "Alliances and Free World Security," *Current History* 38 (April 1960): 215.

[31]Dean Acheson, "To Meet the Shifting Soviet Offensive," *New York Times Magazine* (15 April 1956); Claude Delmas, "How the Third World Splits NATO," *Western World* 1, no. 20 (December 1958): 43–47.

[32]Henry A. Kissinger, "Nuclear Testing and the Problem of Peace," *Foreign Affairs* 31 (October 1958): 15; Lester B. Pearson, *Diplomacy in the Nuclear Age* (Cambridge, MA: Harvard University Press, 1959), p. 88.

These subtle changes in the relationship between American power and the security of Western Europe did not destroy the common interest of the Atlantic nations in a system of collective defense. But NATO's acceptability rested less on the hope that the organization would bring victory in war than on the need to prevent war. NATO would fail at the moment that a nuclear war came to Europe. At the core of NATO's strength, unity, and effectiveness was the American commitment to Western defense. Without the steady conviction that the United States would fulfill its obligation to the NATO members, the alliance would cease to exist. This essential guarantee Washington sought to sustain. Secretary Dulles observed at a news conference in November 1957: "I think that the commitment, as far as the treaty is concerned, is as strong as it could be made. It is hard to get much further in an agreement than 'an attack upon one is an attack upon all.' That is, in turn, reinforced by the presence at the forward positions of American forces which would presumably be themselves attacked." President Eisenhower repeated that assurance at Paris a month later: "Speaking for my own country, I assure you in the most solemn terms that the United States would come, at once and with all appropriate force, to the assistance of any NATO nation subjected to armed attack. This is the resolve of the United States—of all parts and of all parties."[33]

America's capacity to protect Western Europe against war lay in nuclear weapons and the means of conveying them to targets in Eastern Europe and the Soviet Union. Since few assumed that a European war could be localized, the region's survival was synonymous with peace. This compelled NATO to cling to the threat of thermonuclear reprisal as the only available means of keeping aggression away from its door. But anchoring strategy to mass destruction exposed NATO to the pressures of technological change. When Dulles in 1954 announced the American reliance on massive retaliation, the defense of the United States was not at issue. Nuclear strategy would insure the peace of Europe with reduced military forces. As long as the airplane was the only vehicle available for delivering nuclear weapons in a European confrontation, the United States required its forward NATO bases. This created a convergence of interests, for without American weapons Europe had no deterrent and without Europe the United States had no means of reaching its prospective targets. But many Europeans doubted that this mutual interest would survive the replacement of aircraft with long-range guided missiles as the chief means of delivering nuclear weapons. Western Europe would no longer be essential for American strategy.

What brought the technological revolution into focus was the development of Soviet intercontinental ballistic missiles (ICBMs) that

---

[33]"NATO Talks on Disarmament," *Manchester Guardian* 77 (19 December 1957): 3. See also Department of State *Bulletin* 38 (6 January 1958): 7. *Guardian* writer Max Freedman regarded these verbal assurances more important than missiles for Europe's defense.

could reach American targets. Now that the United States itself would be vulnerable to attack, would that nation under all circumstances come to the rescue of Western Europe with nuclear weapons? Somehow the United States seemed more reliable when it was less vulnerable. For some Europeans the answer to this new challenge lay in the development of purely European nuclear deterrents. British Minister of Defense Duncan Sandys justified the new British emphasis on nuclear armaments in 1957 by citing the possible unreliability of some future Washington administration. On 9 February 1959 in the London *Daily Mail,* T. F. Thompson stated the British rationale for developing its own deterrents.

> Soon the United States will have its inter-continental missile bases established on its home territory. Relationships then will change. Not only between the U.S. and Russia, but the U.S. and Europe. For the first time in the history of modern war, America will be in a position to guarantee its own territory without having to bother with advance bases in Europe. . . .The position will then be that the United States would not dare attack Russia nor the Soviet Union the American homeland. . . .It is at this point that the British deterrent becomes important. We are in Europe. We are of Europe. . . .Britain would have to retaliate with nuclear weapons at the outset of a major attack in Europe with conventional forces. The alternatives would be the end of our way of life.

The assumption that nuclear weapons assured peace rendered conventional forces almost irrelevant. British writer Alexander Bregman argued in *Western World* (October 1959) that even the strongest nation would not attack a weak country as long as it faced the danger of nuclear retaliation. The British deterrent, declared one government spokesman, "removes any danger that the Soviet Union may be tempted to invade Western Europe in the misguided belief that the United States of America, faced with the possibility of bombardment by intercontinental missiles, would shrink from saving countries which are distant from her."[34]

By 1960 the international division of military labor was taking its toll of allied unity. The heart of the problem was the question of nuclear control. An effective coalition requires some limitations on national sovereignty, but Europe's total reliance on American-controlled nuclear weapons for its peace and survival placed that continent's destiny in the hands of a non-European power whose global commitments often defied European interests. The greater the disproportion of military power between the United States and its NATO allies, the more obvious the centripetal force of Washington's decisions. That alignment of power and fear that underwrote Europe's defense compelled the allied governments,

---

[34]Alistair Buchan, "Britain and the Bomb," *The Reporter* 20 (19 March 1959): 23; Alexander Bregman, "The Nuclear Club Should be Expanded," *Western World* 2 (October 1959): 12–15.

in any crisis, to accept Washington's conceptualization of its own and Europe's interests. "The alliance is out of balance," observed James Reston, "mainly because Europe is not doing what it could do, and it is not doing what it could do, partly because it has abdicated and partly because the United States has been willing to carry the load long after Europe was able to do much more in self-defense."[35] Europe's survival in a crisis depended on America's strategy for initiating the use of nuclear weapons. That strategy created the most doubtful, yet the most essential, aspect of NATO's nuclear credibility. Europe remained hostage to American foreign and military policy long after many Europeans questioned Washington's reliability. It was not strange that France's Charles de Gaulle sought an escape.

De Gaulle inaugurated his assault on America's virtual monopoly of allied leadership in 1958 when he proposed a global directorate to control NATO's decisions that would include the United States, Britain, and France. Washington rejected the plan with the argument that the United States could not designate one or two European powers to speak for the others.[36] Dulles recognized the need for more liberal American atomic secrecy laws to facilitate allied collaboration in the development of NATO's nuclear strategy. In 1958 a modification of the Atomic Energy Act permitted the United States to provide nuclear materials and information to any ally that had "made substantial progress in the development of atomic weapons." Obviously Britain was the only country that could qualify. America's rebuff of de Gaulle's tripartite proposal and refusal to share atomic secrets with France reinforced the French leader's determination to build a French nuclear deterrent without American help, both to strengthen France's voice in European affairs and to increase the confidence of the French army following France's politically imposed defeat in Indo-China. As de Gaulle explained in 1958, France would attempt to "bring together the states along the Rhine, the Alps, and the Pyrenees into a political, economic, and strategic group—to make of this organization one of the three world powers and if necessary one day the arbiter between the Soviet and Anglo-Saxon camps." On 5 September 1960, de Gaulle issued an edict forbidding nuclear weapons on French soil unless France shared in their control. The United States shifted its nuclear bomb-carrying aircraft from French to British and German bases.[37]

---

[35]James Reston, *New York Times,* 28 May 1961.

[36]Henry A. Kissinger, "The Invisionist: Why We Misread de Gaulle," *Harper's* 230 (March 1965): 74; Drew Middleton, *New York Times,* 14 August 1966; editorial, *New York Times,* 28 August 1966.

[37]Sulzberger, *New York Times,* 28 July 1966; Hanson W. Baldwin, "NATO's Uneven Steps toward Integration," *The Reporter* 3 (11 March 1965): 34; Malcolm W. Hoag analyzed the problem of European deterrents in "What Interdependence for NATO," *World Politics* 12 (April 1960): 389–90. Raymond Aron argued that de Gaulle would never

THE RISE AND FALL OF KENNEDY'S GRAND DESIGN

After January 1961, President John F. Kennedy scarcely could ignore de Gaulle's direct challenge to American leadership in Europe. To counter the divisive tendencies within the Atlantic Alliance, the Kennedy administration, through its Grand Design for Europe, determined to make the West's political and economic institutions and attitudes conform to the outsized requirements of NATO. At Philadelphia on Independence Day of 1962, Kennedy declared that the United States contemplated the European movement toward union, as embodied especially in the Common Market, with hope and admiration. "We do not," he said, "regard a strong and united Europe as a rival, but a partner." Then he continued: "I will say here and now on this Day of Independence that the United States will be ready for a declaration of interdependence, that we will be prepared to discuss with a United Europe the ways and means of forming a concrete Atlantic partnership. . . ."[38] At his news conference that followed, the president refused to define what kind of partnership he had in mind, observing that it would be premature to do so before the European nations themselves had made greater progress toward unity. Although the design was idealistic, it was rooted in the conviction that the major economic and financial concerns of the world had passed beyond the control of individual national governments.

Kennedy doubted the adequacy of Western defense. To broaden the options required to make limited war more feasible and the nuclear deterrent more credible, he stressed the need for a "wider choice than humiliation or all-out nuclear action."[39] The new American strategy called for the creation at last of non-nuclear capabilities sufficient to

permit Britain to have a privileged nuclear position. "De Gaulle and Kennedy—the Nuclear Debate," *The Atlantic* 210 (August 1962): 36. Many other writers explained de Gaulle's determination to achieve French independence from Great Britain and the United States. Among them were Edward Ashcroft, "Behind de Gaulle's Quarrels with His Allies," *New York Times Magazine* (September 1962): 62, 74–82; Andre Fontaine, "De Gaulle's View of Europe and the Nuclear Debate," *The Reporter* 27 (19 July 1962): 33–34; Edmond Taylor, "De Gaulle's Design for Europe," *The Reporter* 26 (7 June 1962): 15–16; and Bernard B. Fall, "Why the French Mistrust Us," *New York Times Magazine* (6 September 1964): 6, 33–37.

[38]For a detailed discussion of J. F. Kennedy's Grand Design, see Sidney Hyman, "In Search of the Atlantic Community," *New York Times Magazine* (6 May 1962): 17, 111–14; *New York Times,* 26 May 1963; and Kennedy's Philadelphia speech quoted in *New York Times,* 8 July 1962. Louis J. Halle criticized Kennedy's speech in "Appraisal of Kennedy as World Leader," *New York Times Magazine* (16 June 1963): 42. Philip H. Irezise analyzed at length the rationale for Kennedy's idea of trans-Atlantic partnership, Department of State *Bulletin* 48 (24 July 1963): 971–76.

[39]U.S., Congress, Senate, *Problems and Trends in Atlantic Partnership II: Staff Study Prepared for the Use of the Committee on Foreign Relations, June 17, 1963,* 88th Cong., 1st sess., doc. 21 (1963), pp. 11–12.

contain limited aggressions. The purpose was not necessarily to concentrate power in conventional forces but rather to permit a "pause" in any future fighting long enough to enable the two contestants to negotiate a cease-fire or give the aggressor time to contemplate the consequences of further escalation. To achieve the anticipated conventional force levels, Washington required a larger allied commitment to Europe's defense. The maintenance of 300,000 U.S. military personnel in the European theater gradually had destroyed the American balance of payments structure whereas Europe, enjoying unprecedented prosperity, refused to contribute its share to either the European defense force or the economic development of the Afro-Asian world. Western Europe by 1962 had not only closed the dollar gap but also held gold and dollar reserves that exceeded the combined holdings of the United States and Britain. This shifting economic balance motivated President Kennedy's urgent request for the Trade Expansion Act of 1962 as well as Congress's overwhelming approval of the legislation. Some Europeans admitted that Western Europe had become the special beneficiary of American insecurity. As Italian leader Altiero Spinelli observed in July 1962: "Western Europe, thanks to American protection, has become a paradise of political, military and social irresponsibility."[40]

To maximize Europe's contribution to conventional defense, the Kennedy administration opposed expenditures for independent nuclear deterrents, especially those of France. At Ann Arbor, Michigan, on 6 June 1962, Defense Secretary Robert McNamara declared: "Limited nuclear capabilities, operating independently, are dangerous, expensive, prone to obsolescence, and lacking in credibility as a deterrent." He asked Europe to avoid conflicting and competing strategies to meet the contingency of nuclear war. "We are convinced," he continued, "that a general nuclear war target system is indivisible, and if, despite all our efforts, nuclear war should occur, our best hope lies in conducting a centrally controlled campaign against all of the enemy's vital nuclear capabilities, while retaining reserve forces, all centrally controlled."[41] McNamara asked that the NATO partners leave full responsibility for nuclear warfare to Washington. In Copenhagen on 27 September, White House adviser McGeorge Bundy reminded Europeans of the American commitment to Europe's defense. Writing in the October 1962 issue of *Foreign Affairs,* Bundy explained why the United States could not escape a European war:

---

[40]Washington's criticism of European defense policy was continuous in 1962. What disturbed Kennedy especially was the refusal of the allies to support the United States during the Berlin crisis of 1961. See James Reston, *New York Times,* 18 May 1962; Sulzberger, *New York Times,* 19 November 1962; and Middleton, *New York Times,* 21 April 1962.

[41]Robert McNamara's address appeared in *New York Times,* 17 June 1962. For commentary on Kennedy's nuclear policy, see Middleton, *New York Times,* 25 May, 1 July 1962.

The general nuclear war the world fears would be a disaster to the whole race, but it is the stronger members of the two great opposed alliances who would be most certainly caught in its horror. The present danger does not spare either shore of the Atlantic—or set Hamburg apart from San Francisco. . . .[W]hile our experience of the cost and burdens of genuine membership in the nuclear club makes us believe that countries which do not apply are wise, we fully recognize that this sovereign decision is not ours to make for others. But we may reasonably ask for understanding of the fact that our own place at the center of the nuclear confrontation is inescapable.[42]

The administration's preference for a more flexible strategy did not anticipate any curtailing of the quest for nuclear weapons systems of the highest efficiency and accuracy.

Convinced that de Gaulle would not conform to American wishes, Washington sought a compromise in which a European nuclear force, closely linked with that of the United States, would encompass the French deterrent as well. But this objective seemed to require the creation of an effective political and economic union in Europe that included Britain. To that end the administration placed the full force of American influence and prestige behind the British bid for membership in the Common Market.

Europe's response to American demands for a more equitable distribution of the Western defense burden was hardly enthusiastic. Whatever its lack of military flexibility, the Western deterrent had granted Europe a decade of peace without recurrent crises or prosperity-curtailing defense expenditures. Many concluded that it was precisely Europe's inability to fight a conventional war that had made the deterrent effective; apparently the Kremlin understood that any Western decision to resist even a minor Soviet attack could quickly degenerate into a nuclear war. Kennedy's new emphasis on conventional weapons seemed to endanger the credibility of the nuclear deterrent and undermined further Europe's confidence in the American commitment to its defense. Some Europeans feared that the United States, in an effort to avoid the extremity of a nuclear exchange, might refuse to act until much of Europe again lay in ruins.[43] Not even Kennedy's success in the Cuban missile crisis of October 1962 could counter the burgeoning distrust of America's nuclear commitment. The United States and the USSR had demonstrated more vigorously than ever before their fear of nuclear war and their readiness, in a moment of peril, to reach a settlement with scarcely a nod at their respective allies. Europe emerged from the crisis thankful but was

---

[42]McGeorge Bundy, "Friends and Allies," *Foreign Affairs* 41 (October 1962): 21.

[43]U.S., Congress, Senate, Committee on Foreign Relations, *Problems and Trends in Atlantic Partnership I: Some Comments on the European Economic Community and NATO, Sept. 14, 1962*, 87th Cong., 2d sess., doc. 132 (1962), p. 33; Bernard Brodie, "What Price Conventional Capabilities in Europe," *The Reporter* 27 (23 May 1963): 25–33.

reminded dramatically of its helplessness in the face of Soviet and American decision making.

Nowhere in his Grand Design did Kennedy resolve the question of nuclear control. The alliance could go forward or backward; those who favored stronger ties agreed that Atlantic unity required a sharing of responsibility for nuclear decision making. Paris's *Le Monde* answered Kennedy's Fourth of July speech of 1962: "The idea of interdependence could become exalting . . . only if Europeans and Americans really agreed to transform into an *equal* partnership relations that are now those of clients to protectors." Writing in the January 1963 issue of *Foreign Affairs*, Malcolm W. Hoag observed: "We cannot simultaneously preach Atlantic community and practice unimpaired sovereignty on life-and-death matters. To try to satisfy proud and militarily vulnerable allies with vague and secretive reassurances will increase anxiety and resentment rather than produce cooperation. We must somehow reconcile the operational need for unitary nuclear control with allied political participation and partnership."[44] Not even in his noted Nassau agreement on a multilateral defense force did Kennedy accept the challenge. When his administration informed the British government in November 1962 that it would cancel the Skybolt air-to-ground ballistic missile program, it turned to the frequently discussed concept of a mixed-manned naval nuclear defense force, equipped with Polaris missiles. Still the British-American agreement on a sea-based, mixed-manned nuclear force, announced at Nassau by the president and Prime Minister Harold Macmillan in December 1962, scarcely satisfied the NATO allies.[45] The proposal contained no arrangement for an integrated strategy; the United States gave up none of its control of the nuclear deterrent. The multilateral force (MLF) remained totally separate from American nuclear strategy.

De Gaulle, in a dramatic press conference on 14 January 1963, challenged every facet of the American Grand Design. In rejecting the British application for Common Market membership, the French leader charged that Britain was not sufficiently European-minded to break its ties with the United States and the Commonwealth. He was, he said, simply furthering the emancipation of Europe. British membership in the Common Market would lead to the formation of "a colossal Atlantic Community under American dependence and leadership." France could

---

[44] Malcolm W. Hoag, "Nuclear Policy and French Intransigence," *Foreign Affairs* 41 (January 1963): 294. Also on the problem of nuclear sharing is Sir John Slessor, "Atlantic Nuclear Policy," *International Journal* 20 (Spring 1965): 143–57. American officials argued that the problem of allied partnership on matters of nuclear sharing lay in the unequal distribution of power in the alliance. See Undersecretary George Ball, 6 February 1962, Department of State *Bulletin* 46 (5 March 1962): 366; Counselor W. W. Rostow, 9 May 1963, Department of State *Bulletin* 48 (3 June 1963): 858.

[45] On the "Sky Bolt" affair and the Nassau agreement, see Henry A. Kissinger, "The Sky Bolt Affair," *The Reporter* 28 (17 January 1963): 15–18; and Ward S. Just, "The Scrapping of Sky Bolt," Ibid., (11 April 1963): 19–21.

accomplish little without sacrifice, he informed a French audience in April, "but we do not wish to be protégés or satellites; we are allies among allies, defenders among the defenders."[46] De Gaulle rejected the principle of the multilateral defense force with equal determination. "France has taken note of the Anglo-American Nassau agreement," he declared at the press conference. "As it was conceived, undoubtedly no one will be surprised that we cannot subscribe to it." De Gaulle dismissed completely the question of the integration of nuclear forces. France, he warned, would provide its own nuclear deterrent. The reason France required a nuclear strike force was made clear by French Minister of Armed Forces Pierre Messmer in the April 1963 issue of *Revue de Défense Nationale:*

> For Europe to exist it must take charge of and responsibility for its own defense, and for that it must possess nuclear arms. When we reach that point it will be seen that French possession of national nuclear arms will be a key piece in the construction of Europe. . . . The decision taken by General de Gaulle to provide France with nuclear armaments is the dominant factor of our military policy. This decision is of such importance that it will orientate the destiny of our country for a long time.[47]

By no means did the French deterrent exclude the possibility of future cooperation between that force and the similar deterrents of the allies. The French leader admitted that the defense strategy of the United States covered all European targets; what he questioned, he said, was the American willingness to engage in a nuclear exchange over issues which Washington might regard as secondary. "[N]o one in the world, particularly no one in America," he charged, "can say if, where, when, how and to what extent the American nuclear weapons would be employed to defend Europe."[48] The United States, involved globally as it was, might permit the USSR to blackmail Western Europe. In a further assault on American influence in Europe, de Gaulle, one week after his January press conference, announced the signing of a Franco-German treaty whereby the two governments agreed to "consult before any decision on all important questions of foreign policy . . . with a view to reaching as far as possible parallel positions."[49] At the very least de Gaulle had placed the movement for trans-Atlantic partnership in temporary eclipse. His action terminated abruptly the expansion of the European Economic Community and administered a decisive blow to Europe's community spirit.

---

[46]April statement in *New York Times,* 28 April 1963. For a full analysis of de Gaulle's reaction to Kennedy's Grand Design, see *Problems and Trends in Atlantic Partnership, II, June 17, 1963,* pp. 1–8. De Gaulle's press conference of 14 January 1963 appears in ibid., pp. 57–65.

[47]Ibid., p. 14.

[48]Ibid., p. 61.

[49]For a full text of the treaty see ibid., pp. 50–53.

De Gaulle's news conference evoked expressions of muffled rage in Washington and professions of disappointment in Britain. At his own news conference on 8 February, President Kennedy voiced regret that France had denied Britain membership in the Common Market. He challenged de Gaulle's assertion that the United States did not deal with Europe as an equal partner. "We supported strongly," he said, "the Common Market, Euratom, and the other efforts to provide for a more unified Europe, which provides for a stronger Europe, which permits Europe to speak with a stronger voice, to accept greater responsibilities and greater burdens, as well as to take advantage of greater opportunities."[50] The United States, he added, was prepared to work with Europe to strengthen its voice and authority. Kennedy selected Ambassador Livingston T. Merchant to initiate official talks with NATO governments on the question of participation in the multilateral defense force. Only West Germany indicated a willingness to join and defray its share of the cost. Critics noted immediately that the multinational force satisfied no outstanding strategic requirement and offered Europe no significant political or diplomatic responsibility for nuclear deterrence. In addition, Europeans objected to the use of highly vulnerable surface vessels rather than submarines. To many international observers the new defense establishment was nothing more than a small effort to involve West Germany in a system of nuclear defense without upsetting the delicate cold war balance in Europe. Some charged that the United States was more concerned with outbidding de Gaulle for German support than with creating an effective system of nuclear sharing.[51]

To demonstrate his administration's desire to bridge the Atlantic gap with new forms of allied cooperation, Kennedy, in late June 1963, visited West Germany, Ireland, Britain, and Italy. The trip quickly assumed the form of a ceremonial spectacle. In West Germany the president stressed the concept of partnership. At historic Paulskirche in Frankfort he designated the United States and West Germany as "partners for peace." The greatest necessity confronting the alliance, he stressed, was "progress toward unity of political purpose." In a clear thrust at de Gaulle Kennedy declared: "Those who would separate Europe from America or split one

---

[50]Max Frankel discusses American and British reaction to de Gaulle's press conference, *New York Times,* 7 April 1963. Kennedy's 8 February statement appears in U.S., Department of State, *Foreign Policy Briefs* 12 (18 February 1963): 1. Secretary of State Dean Rusk made a similar appeal for European unity, 12 July 1963, Department of State *Bulletin* 49 (5 August 1963): 192.

[51]Writers condemned MLF as both a political and a military venture. Among the criticisms are: *New York Times,* 23 June 1963, (editorial); a major discussion in *New York Times,* 30 June 1963; Hanson W. Baldwin, *New York Times,* 15 December 1963; Henry A. Kissinger, "The Unsolved Problems of European Defense," *Foreign Affairs* 40 (July 1962): 535; "Multilateral Force or Farce," *New York Times Magazine* (13 December 1964): 25, 100–7; and Ronald Steel, "The Place of NATO," *The New Republic* 151 (14 November 1964): 19–22.

ally from another—could only give aid and comfort to the men who make themselves our adversaries and welcome any Western disarray. The United States cannot withdraw from Europe, unless and until Europe should wish us gone. We cannot distinguish its defenses from our own. We cannot diminish our contributions to Western security or abdicate the responsibility of power." At Bonn the president issued the same assurance: "Your safety is our safety, your liberty is our liberty, and an attack on your soil is attack on our own."[52]

Kennedy effectively challenged de Gaulle's assumptions of America's unreliability, but he had no measurable effect on French policy. De Gaulle's effort to defend French economic interests still determined the course of Common Market discussions. When the United States during the autumn of 1963 pressed its allies for greater defense contributions, de Gaulle replied that the American concept of a "pause" would not prevent nuclear war as effectively as reliance on instant nuclear retaliation. Nothing in the entire spectrum of Soviet behavior disproved his contention. Late in January 1964 in another dramatic press conference, the French leader defied U.S. Far Eastern policies by announcing the French recognition of mainland China and stressing again the need for the neutralization of Southeast Asia.[53] Never before had French policies clashed so directly and universally with those of the United States. During the summer of 1965, de Gaulle announced that France would no longer tolerate its subordinate position in the Atlantic Alliance. Then in April 1966 he informed NATO that he would withdraw all French officers and troops from its integrated military system and would remove all military installations not under exclusive French control. He stated that French independence would permit nothing less.[54] Premier Georges Pompidou explained the French decision to the French Assembly:

> What we criticise about that doctrine [of flexible response] is its being specifically conceived on the basis of America's geographic location, . . . limiting the atomic battlefield by sparing the territory of the Soviet Union, and therefore the territory of the United States, and thereby creating a psychological risk, that of making it believed that the war could remain localized between the Atlantic and the Polish frontier in the East, that is to say, in Europe, but a Europe doomed to destruction.

---

[52]Kennedy's Frankfurt speech appears in U.S., Department of State, *Foreign Policy Briefs* 12 (8 July 1963): 1; Middleton, *New York Times,* 30 June 1963; and Arthur J. Olsen, *New York Times,* 7 July 1963.

[53]On U.S. pressure for larger European defense contributions, see Arthur J. Olsen, *New York Times,* 27 October 1963; and Middleton, *New York Times,* 3 November 1963. De Gaulle's January 1964 press conference is analyzed in *New York Times,* 26 January 1964.

[54]Henry Tanner, *New York Times,* 24 April 1966.

Only nuclear deterrence could guarantee the peace. "You tell us: NATO has guaranteed peace in Europe for 15 years," Pompidou concluded. "What an error if you are referring to the integrated organization! What has guaranteed peace is the alliance, insofar as it brought to bear the threat of the American Strategic Air Command. . . . "[55] In compliance with French policy, NATO moved its military headquarters from Paris to Brussels.

American reaction to de Gaulle's repeated assertions of French independence was not unanimous. Washington denounced the French leader as rude and malicious. For American officials there was still too much unfinished business before the alliance to permit such contention with an obstreperous ally. Wherever the United States was in trouble, they complained, de Gaulle was sure to appear, establishing himself as an arbiter, investing little but words to reap the benefits of confusion, national rivalry, and big power humiliation. For those who placed their faith in Western power and unity, de Gaulle's policies were both dishonest and disastrous. Declared the *Detroit News* early in March 1964: "Whether it is his intent or not, Charles de Gaulle is doing a pretty effective job of wrecking the Atlantic Alliance, the most effective instrument devised so far for containing Communist expansion. . . . All de Gaulle's dreams, all this scheming, all this pontificating is possible only because of one factor—the nuclear might of the United States—which stalls the Communist drive. . . . Under that umbrella he berates the real custodian of France's security."[56] Dean Acheson, a key architect of the NATO alliance, termed de Gaulle's policies as "an erosion on one side of the Grand Alliance." French policy, he added, "increases the difficulty of action within the alliance by opposition to joint and integrated measures to advance common interests and solve common problems."[57]

To other American analysts, conscious of the changes that fifteen years had wrought in Europe's economic and military progress, de Gaulle's challenge to American policies was both rational and predictable.[58] In an alliance among nations of unequal power, the dependence of the weaker is tolerable only as long as there exists a complete identity of interest between the weaker and the stronger. After fifteen years the Atlantic Alliance remained what President Truman once described as a

---

[55]Georges Pompidou quoted in *New York Times,* 24 April 1964.

[56]Max Frankel, *New York Times Magazine* (5 December 1965): 54–55, 173–88; Frankel, *New York Times,* 8 March 1964; *Detroit News* quoted in *New York Times,* 8 March 1964.

[57]Dean Acheson, "Withdrawal from Europe? An Illusion," *New York Times Magazine* (15 December 1963): 67.

[58]For a defense of de Gaulle, see John Grigg, "In Defense of Charles de Gaulle," *New York Times Magazine* (23 February 1964): 66–68; Stephen R. Graubard, "After Five Years, de Gaulle Still Towers," *New York Times Magazine* (15 December 1963): 21, 54–60.

"shield against aggression." But even this common and continuing interest in mutual defense did not in itself create a body of policy. Indeed, after fifteen years of NATO the common policies required to implement the alliance remained elusive. There was not one major European issue, political or military, on which all allies agreed. On questions outside Europe the United States stood almost alone. Ultimately, the challenge to allied unity rested in the sheer quality of U.S. foreign policy. The central issue was inescapable. Could the United States establish and maintain a clear relationship between its considerable power and the objectives that it pursued? If it was true, as the Sacramento *Morning News* insisted, that de Gaulle was making "a confused tangle of American diplomacy," one could ask in good conscience why the policies were so easily tangled.

THE LIMITS OF REVISIONISM

In limiting NATO to twenty years Western leaders assumed that the original agreement, if anchored to a unified and reasonable body of objectives, would, in negotiation with the Kremlin, achieve some resolution of Europe's divisive issues. Washington accepted no less a goal for containment than the opportunity to negotiate from strength. President Kennedy declared characteristically in 1960: "It is only when we have military force strong enough to convince the Russians that they will never be able to gain any advantage through military strength that we can hope for fruitful negotiations." Similarly, Secretary of State Dean Rusk assured the country a year later: "We are not dealing in the world these days from a position of weakness. . . . I have no doubt the Soviet government knows a good deal about our strength and has an accurate assessment of it." In defending the nation's decision to construct the antiballistic missile system (ABM), Defense Secretary Clark Clifford asserted: "You deal much better with the Soviet Union when you deal from strength." That the United States had long possessed sufficient strength for successful negotiation seemed clear enough. Indeed, after mid-century U.S. diplomats enjoyed the support of a universally recognized national capacity to reduce much of the earth's surface to rubble in a period of hours. Still there were no fruitful negotiations.

Fortunately for Europe the failure of East-West negotiations was a matter of limited consequence. The Soviets gained control of Eastern Europe as early as 1945. Thereafter the actual policies of the United States and the USSR, whatever the rhetoric both countries employed, were designed primarily to stabilize a Europe already divided. This simple goal rendered power the essence of policy. But if negotiation was the declared end of containment, why was there no settlement? No negotiation from strength? In part the answer lay in the fallacy of the concept itself. Coral Bell, in *Negotiation from Strength* (1962), suggested two reasons why governments avoided negotiation: If a nation is weak it cannot afford to negotiate; if it is strong it does not need to. It is never clear, moreover, when a country has achieved the optimum conditions for successful negotiation.[59] As Kennan once wrote, the search for the ideal military posture is the enemy of negotiation.

Actually the failure of diplomacy resulted less from the elusiveness of power than from the objectives pursued. Whereas the United States and the Soviet Union in their day-to-day decisions accepted the status quo as a necessity, their official purposes eliminated, as politically and ideologically unacceptable, the only world available to them. What the United States sought was not hegemony but instead a compatible world in which all countries would accept the liberal principles of self-determination, peaceful cooperation, and the rule of law. Secretary of State Rusk reminded a national television audience on 24 September 1962 that the United States desired "a peaceful world community of free and independent states, free to choose their own future and their own system so long as it does not threaten the freedom of others." Rusk explained why the United States would continue to avoid negotiation with the Soviet Union. "Our goal, the goal of all free men," he said, "is incompatible with the communist goal. This contest between two incompatible systems and concepts will continue until freedom triumphs. Our objective is a worldwide victory not of one people or one nation over another, but a worldwide victory for all mankind, for freedom and a decent world order."[60] Such goals exceeded the possibilities of negotiation, even of war.

Keeping West Germany a satisfied member of the Atlantic Alliance took a heavy toll on Western diplomacy. The West remained committed to German reunification and the revision of the Oder-Neisse line. Rusk insisted in October 1963 that the West could never come to terms with the Soviet Union until the German people received the right of self-determination. Kennan questioned NATO's uncompromising mood in a *Look* magazine interview, published on 19 November 1963:

> This coalition is incapable of agreeing on any negotiated solutions except unconditional capitulation and the satisfaction of the maximum demands of each of our allies. It is easier for a coalition to agree to ask for everything but the kitchen sink, rather than take a real negotiating position. This worries me [said Kennan] because there is not going to be any capitulation. Our adversaries are not weak. If we

---

[59]Coral Bell, *Negotiation from Strength: A Study in the Politics of Power* (New York: Alfred A. Knopf, 1963), pp. 210–11, 240–41. The concept, writes the author, had the effect of maintaining a "hopeful vagueness" in allied purposes, ibid., p. 212.
[60]Dean Rusk, Department of State *Bulletin* 47 (15 October 1962): 547.

cannot find any negotiating position, the Cold War will continue, and the dangers will not decrease.[61]

How the Western allies intended to achieve self-determination within the Soviet sphere was still not apparent. Russian interests alone governed the major political trends of Eastern Europe. The Kremlin demonstrated that in 1968 when it overthrew Czechoslovakia's liberal Alexander Dubček in order to reinforce its control over the internal evolution of the Soviet bloc countries. After twenty years NATO remained a body of means, concerned with stability rather than change.[62]

As a stabilizing force NATO's contribution to postwar Europe was profound. Western policies of containment underwrote the continent's astonishing political and economic achievements; they failed to eliminate the unforeseen and unwanted consequences of the allied victory over Germany. They did not unify Germany or erase the Soviet hegemony in Eastern Europe. In the absence of major cold war victories or defeats for either side, time merely confirmed Europe's de facto postwar boundaries. For most western Europeans this mattered little; Soviet policy did not infringe on their prosperity or welfare. No sense of urgency encouraged NATO leaders to test their unity by proposing major changes in East-West relationships. Still the persistence of cold war issues, never threatening but never resolved, troubled some thoughtful observers, as Idaho's Senator Frank Church noted in his May 1966 report on Europe:

> Although reasonably satisfied with the present and sanguine about the future, there is still a feeling of uneasiness when our allies in Europe look either to the East or to the West. In the East, Western Europeans see a less militant Soviet Union and her neighbor Communist countries evolving, some more rapidly than others, in the direction of a more independent relationship with Russia. At the same time, Western Europeans see no evidence of any present disposition on the part of the Soviets to release their hold on East Germany to permit a reunification that would end the uneasy, potentially explosive, military confrontation in the heart of the continent. . . . Looking westward, many Europeans suspect that the United States is

---

[61]Rusk, Department of State *Bulletin* 49 (28 October 1963): 656–57; George C. McGhee, 16 July 1964, Department of State *Bulletin* 51 (3 August 1964): 142. For an evaluation of allied policy toward German reunification, see Torence Prittie, "Again the Issue of Two Germanys," *New York Times Magazine* (16 August 1964): 10, 58–60; and Norman A. Graebner, "Germany Between East and West," *Current History* 62 (May 1972): 225–28. Henry A. Kissinger outlined a program for reunification, beginning with self-determination for East Germany, in *The Troubled Partnership: A Re-Appraisal of the Atlantic Alliance* (New York: McGraw-Hill, 1965), pp. 216–23. Kennan's statement in J. Robert Moskin, "Our Foreign Policy is Paralyzed," *Look* 27 (19 November 1963): 26.

[62]Norman A. Graebner studied NATO's general complacency toward a stable Europe in the late 1960s. See "NATO: An Uneasy Alliance," *Current History* 58 (May 1970): 86–92.

unattuned to the changing sentiment in Europe—that we are not moving with the times but remain wedded to concepts which reflect the old status quo. In particular, Europeans would welcome our placing less emphasis upon NATO's role as a fort and more upon its use as a forum for reaching agreement on Western initiatives directed toward the normalization of relations with Eastern Europe and the Soviet Union.[63]

What NATO lacked from its initial formulation was a set of clearly defined goals achievable within the constraints placed on power by the irrationality of war. Nothing would demonstrate so effectively the limited choices confronting the West as the outbreak of a conventional war involving the forces of both the United States and the Soviet Union. For military conflicts in the 1960s could be limited only by an unequivocal acceptance of the status quo as the object of policy. If a nation at war fighting under the immediate threat of nuclear escalation faced the simple alternative of announcing the limits of its intentions or inviting a thermonuclear attack, then it was unreasonable to suggest that it regard negotiable in time of peace what it would of necessity regard negotiable in time of war. Containment achieved its initial purpose when it brought the full power of the United States to bear on world politics as an essential element in Europe's postwar success. How that great power could best serve the needs of a divided Europe remained the unanswered, yet inescapable, challenge still confronting the people and government of the United States.

---

[63]U.S., Congress, Senate, *Europe Today: A Report to the Committee on Foreign Relations,* by *Senator Frank Church, May 1966,* 89th Cong., 2d sess. (1966), p. 1.

NATO and the Larger European States

COLIN GORDON

As the Atlantic Alliance enters its fourth decade, its membership unchanged since the adherence of the German Federal Republic in 1955, it is piquant to recall that the very first postwar European security arrangement was the Dunkirk Treaty of March 1947 struck between Britain and France and expressly designed to circumvent any possible aggression by a resurgent Germany. The deterioration in the international political atmosphere at that time may be gauged by the fact that at the beginning of 1948 British Foreign Secretary Ernest Bevin argued in the House of Commons that a de facto union was emerging in Western Europe as a result of a series of bilateral agreements between Britain, France, and the Benelux; and that this union ought to be formalized and that further "we shall have to consider the question of associating other historic members of European civilization, including the new Italy, in this great concept."[1]

Ten days after the Communist coup in Prague preliminary discussions on Bevin's suggestion opened in Brussels, which gave its name to the treaty signed two weeks later by the five West European powers. The treaty broke new ground by institutionalizing arrangements for common defense in peacetime; this was to be undertaken by a consultative council composed of the respective foreign ministers and a defense committee composed of the five defense ministers. The latter held its first meeting in London at the end of April 1948 and turned over to its military advisers the task of determining military equipment needs and in particular the amount of supplementary aid that would be required from the United States. By July both American and Canadian experts were joining in their deliberations, for the situation seemed to have deteriorated even more sharply with the initiation of the Berlin blockade in May. By September the Western Union Defense Organization was established with headquarters at Fontainebleau and Field Marshal Bernard Montgomery was

---

[1]Great Britain, Parliament, *Parliamentary Debates* (Commons) 5th series, 446 (1948): 397.

appointed permanent chairman of a committee of land, naval, and air commanders in chief.

The vigor and speed with which the West Europeans revised their security perceptions was impressive, their organizational innovation striking. Even before the signing of the Brussels Treaty, Bevin had asked Secretary of State Marshall for early discussions on the security of the North Atlantic area; Marshall's reply was to embark with Undersecretary Robert Lovett on exploratory conversations with Republican Senator Arthur Vandenberg and Democratic Senator Tom Connally. The outcome was the Vandenberg resolution approved by the Senate on 11 June 1948, a remarkable amalgam of aspiration and realism. While calling upon the president to pursue ways and means of reforming the United Nations so as to ensure the peaceful settlement of international disputes, it more immediately urged the progressive development of regional and other collective arrangements for self-defense and the association of the United States with such arrangements "as are based on continuous and effective self-help and mutual aid, and as affect its national security."[2]

Such a prescription was sufficiently broad to permit the original idea of an association between the United States and the Brussels Treaty powers to be extended to encompass a wider group of countries; discussions began in Washington in July 1948, and the final outcome was the North Atlantic Treaty establishing the Atlantic Alliance, signed in April 1949. The proceedings were enlivened by a band playing selections of popular music, including "I've got plenty of nuthin" from *Porgy and Bess*. The gestation of the alliance was attended with much publicity, including a blistering attack from the Soviet Foreign Ministry reproduced in Soviet newspapers in January 1949:

> The establishment of the Western Union means that Britain, France and the other participant countries have finally abandoned the policy pursued by the democratic states that were the members of the anti-Hitler coalition during the war . . . the new group has been formed . . . with a view to expanding the domineering influence of the Anglo-American ruling circles . . . the aims of the North Atlantic alliance are much more far-reaching than those of the West European grouping, and it is easy to see that these aims are closely interwoven with the plans for the establishment of Anglo-American world supremacy under the aegis of the U.S.A.[3]

[2]U.S., Congress, Senate, *Congressional Record,* 80th Cong., 2d sess., 11 June 1948, pp. 7791–7851.

[3]Soviet Foreign Ministry, statement on the Western Union and the proposed North Atlantic Pact, *Keesings Contemporary Archives 1949,* vol. 7, p. 9770.

THE BRITISH EXPERIENCE

Rhetorical considerations apart, the Soviets still had apparent reason for harping on the Anglo-American nexus within the proposed alliance. France continued to be in the toils of domestic and colonial reconstruction and not entirely reassured concerning its future vis-à-vis Germany; Germany itself at the time had a geographic but not a political existence. Britain had dissolved its Indian empire, extricated itself from Palestine and, with total armed forces of some 800,000 men, some consciousness of being the one European state to be undefeated in the second world war. Not that the British, any more than the Americans, looked forward to the employment of their armed forces; their assertions on this point were borne out by the early history of the alliance itself.

There is a whiff of pedantry in observing that while the North Atlantic Treaty was signed in 1949, it took three years for its organizational structure, the North Atlantic Treaty Organization (NATO), to become operational in the form that has endured for almost thirty years. NATO has become a synonym for the alliance, but there is a difference between the two and it is not without significance, as will be argued later. For the present, suffice it to observe that notwithstanding the prescriptions of the treaty itself, it was not until 1951 that General Eisenhower established Supreme Headquarters Allied Powers Europe (SHAPE) and only in February 1952 did the allies agree to complete the institutionalization of the alliance by appointing a secretary general to head a unified international secretariat and by establishing a council in permanent session in Paris.

It was not that there had been any lack of activity in the first eighteen months of the existence of the alliance; although the first meeting of the North Atlantic Council did not take place until September 1949, it then met three times in four months. These meetings saw the creation of a defense committee, a military committee, and a military standing group as well as five regional planning groups, a defense financial and economic committee, and a military production and supply board; they concluded with the acceptance of the defense committee's recommendations regarding the integrated defense of the North Atlantic area.

All this had a fine martial ring; in fact, it was then alliance policy that priority should go to economic rather than military effort. Thus, the Mutual Defense Assistance Act of October 1949 providing for American assistance to Britain insisted that "economic recovery is essential to international peace and security and must be given clear priority."[4] The point already had been made by Prime Minister Clement Attlee the

---

[4]Mutual Defence Assistance Act, 6 October 1949, *Documents 1949–50* (London: Royal Institute of International Affairs, 1953), p. 295.

previous autumn when he had ensured that reductions in defense expenditure should be included in the massive program of cuts in government expenditure which he had announced as necessary to ward off inflation following devaluation of the pound sterling.[5]

Attlee subscribed to the alliance view that the North Atlantic Treaty served notice on the Soviet Union that any future conflict in Europe would involve the United States from the beginning and that in consequence a moderation in Soviet behavior could be expected. The United States, after all, had an atomic monopoly. It took the outbreak of the Korean War to alter this perception and impel Attlee to initiate a rearmament program that looked to the doubling of the British outlay on defense within three years. At the same time the allies began the active construction of those military and political structures that the treaty had declared as necessary to implement their intention to defend themselves.

The lapse of almost two years between the signing of the treaty and the establishment of SHAPE should occasion second thoughts on the part of those who declared that the alliance was basically aggressive from its inception. It also demonstrates the interaction between defense and economics. As far as Britain was concerned, a general consensus among most writers and commentators was that the adoption of a more and more modest defense posture since the end of the second world war had been due in large measure to the inexorable pressure of economic factors. At least one astute commentator, however, was prepared to question this conventional wisdom and asserted: "Any overview of the British defence effort since 1945 should more properly emphasize 'reshaping': . . . only intermittently have economic imperatives been truly decisive in prompting adjustment . . . the crucial role of the economic constraints in the policy process has been in making governments continuously aware of the necessity for choice—in which respect they have played a constructive part."[6]

Certainly there was nothing parsimonious about the immediate response of the Labour government to the outbreak of the Korean War. Within a month £100 million was added to the defense allocation of £780M; in August a new three-year defense plan was introduced calling for a total expenditure of £3,400M; and in January 1951 following a meeting with President Truman, Attlee announced a further revision upwards, to the dizzy figure of £4,700M over the three-year period.[7]

At a time of abruptly enhanced perceptions of a Soviet threat, Attlee did not hesitate to reimpose austerity upon the country. Speaking to the

[5]Great Britain, Parliament, *Parliamentary Debates* (Commons) 5th series, 468 (1949): 1016–23.

[6]David Greenwood, "Constraints and Choices in the Transformation of the British Defence Effort since 1945," *British Journal of International Studies* (April 1976): 5.

[7]Great Britain, Parliament, *Parliamentary Debates* (Commons) 5th series, 483 (1951): 579–87.

House of Commons a fortnight later, Chancellor of the Exchequer Hugh Gaitskell sought to soften the blow. With respect to home consumption and the standard of living, he stated:

> There must be some absolute reduction . . . it should not be a very large one . . . for some time to come there is no prospect of any rise in the flow of real goods to match the rise in money incomes. So far as manufactured consumer goods are concerned there will be a fall . . . it will be my duty through the budget and in other ways to keep home expenditure down to a level which will be enough . . . to buy only those things we can afford to consume at home.[8]

It was bound to be an unpopular program, and it contributed to the defeat of the Labour party in the general election of October 1951, which brought Churchill back onto Downing Street. Determined to oversee British defense effort, he combined the premiership with that of minister of defense. Churchill slowed down the rate of the rearmament program, since the fear of a Soviet attack in Central Europe had so far proved exaggerated. With the Korean War stalemated and with the death of Stalin in March 1953, he continued his defense program. Speaking in a foreign affairs debate in May, the prime minister referred to the justifiable Soviet concern for security as well as suggesting a summit conference to grapple with the issues dividing East and West. He affirmed his assertions by now vague and cloudy goodwill:

> The Locarno treaty of 1925 has been in my mind. It was the highest point we reached between the wars . . . based on the simple provision that if Germany attacked France we should stand with the French, and if France attacked Germany we should stand with the Germans. . . . I have the feeling that the master-thought which animated Locarno might well play its part between Germany and Russia in the minds of those whose prime ambition is to consolidate the peace of Europe as the key to the peace of mankind.[9]

At a time when the Atlantic allies were anxiously looking to the creation of the European Defense Community and the rearming of Western Germany, it was fortunate that the Soviets chose to dismiss the Locarno system as worthless while welcoming the proposal for a conference of the great powers.

The prospect for such a conference introduces a second aspect concerning the early years of the Atlantic Alliance and one that requires a genuine effort on the part of present-day observers to fully appreciate: the belief that despite the atomic bomb a third world war in Europe would be conducted along the lines of the one only recently concluded. God would

---

[8]Great Britain, Parliament, *Parliamentary Debates* (Commons) 5th series, 484 (1951): 657–58.

[9]Great Britain, Parliament, *Parliamentary Debates* (Commons) 5th series, 515 (1953): 896.

be on the side of the big battalions, supported, sustained, and reinforced from across the Atlantic. The atomic bomb would pile Pelion on Ossa, but the conflict would be laborious and lengthy.

At the time of the signing of the North Atlantic Treaty, Field Marshal Montgomery was at the head of the military planning structures created under the earlier Brussels Treaty. Early West European estimates of the number of divisions that would be required in the event of a Soviet attack were considerably in excess of one hundred; once the North Atlantic Treaty committed the United States to the defense of Western Europe, it was agreed that the earlier estimates could be revised downward. They now called for ninety-six divisions, active and reserve.

Even before the North Atlantic Treaty, the 1948 National Service Act committed British conscripts not only to full-time color service but also to part-time service with the territorial army. After the outbreak of war in Korea, color service was extended, which increased the present army, and 250,000 reservists were called up for refresher training, which obviously tested mobilization procedures.

By 1952 at the Lisbon council meeting of the Atlantic allies, it was agreed that since the Strategic Air Command was locked into the West European order of battle, there remained a need for some fifty divisions "in appropriate combat readiness." Divided amongst the allies, this entailed Britain's providing nine or ten regular and reserve divisions in 1952 and being in a position within a few more years to furnish nine regular divisions immediately and nine additional reserve divisions by D-day plus thirty.[10]

The snag was that even as the Lisbon council was in session the British defense program was being stretched. In April the Conservative government's economic survey declared that the balance of payments position was critical, a major cause for which was the importing of steel for rearmament. Even with reduced defense expenditure, 10 percent gross national product was being absorbed by 900,000 servicemen, and the civilian labor force employed in defense was bound to rise to 2 million. Churchill had been surprised, on assuming the premiership, to find just how far the Labour government had gone in developing the atomic bomb; early in 1952 he was profoundly impressed by briefings in Washington on the role of Strategic Air Command. His chiefs of staff knew that the best they could provide in the way of ground forces were eleven regular and twelve reserve divisions at the cost of heavily burdening the economy; the Lisbon force goals demanded that all but a couple of their regular divisions be committed to Europe. Consequently, there ensued under economic pressure a highly desirable reassessment of strategy.

Now as in the past the United States provided the overwhelming

---

[10] An admirable account of postwar British defense is found in Richard N. Rosecrance, *Defense of the Realm* (New York: Columbia University Press, 1968).

bulk of the nuclear capability of the alliance. Surprising to the Americans, it was the British, impelled by economic factors, who took the first long hard look at allied strategy and advocated increased reliance upon the nuclear deterrent. In Global Strategy Paper 1952 (GSP 1952), the British chiefs of staff advocated that for the future much greater reliance should be placed upon the nuclear weapon than on conventional forces. In particular, they argued that with the deployment of British airstrike forces equipped with atomic weapons not only would the overall deterrent posture of the alliance be enhanced but also British interests could be defended by their use against targets especially important for Britain. Furthermore, they looked to the acquisition of tactical nuclear weapons as a means of achieving the firepower demanded at Lisbon without the disagreeable necessity of achieving the Lisbon force goals. Outside Europe, they envisaged the possibility of reducing British forces as a consequence of a recognition that at least some of the current overseas deployment was conditional upon an obsolete second world-war strategy being applied to a now diminished British Empire. And they forwarded their findings not only to Churchill as prime minister and minister of defense, but also to the American Joint Chiefs of Staff in Washington.[11]

However, their findings met with a cool response. Orthodoxy at both NATO and SHAPE had not envisaged a leading atomic role for Britain, German rearmament within a European army was being feverishly promoted, and reserve forces had to be valorized if the Lisbon force goals were to make sense. In the event, while describing GSP 1952 as a state paper of the highest importance, Churchill did not follow its prescriptions through; nor did the British chiefs of staff who accepted the possibility of 'broken-backed' and therefore extended warfare in Europe. Uncertainty about the duration of a war between the Atlantic allies and the Soviet Union boiled down to a general agreement between the British and American chiefs of staff that it was not necessarily going to be short and sweet.

Indeed, in February 1954 the British defense white paper envisaged a European conflict in uncertain but chilling fashion:

---

[11]Ibid. GSP 1952 is not scheduled to be deposited in the Public Record Office until 1982. This is an improvement on the situation pertaining at the time it was written, when a fifty-year rule applied with respect to nonpublication of official documents. However, its contents and their effect have been established in interviews between key officials, both civil and military, and highly reputable academic commentators. See especially Rosecrance, *Defense of the Realm*, pp. 159–64. L. W. Martin, "The Market for Strategic Ideas in Britain: The 'Sandys Era,' " *American Political Science Review* 56 (March 1962): 23–41 brilliantly demonstrates how to establish the facts when dealing with a period so recent and a system so addicted to secrecy. He refers to GSP 1952 on p. 25 and in fn 11. In the latter he cites a penetrating and witty analysis by the doyen of British strategic studies, the late Alastair Buchan. A minute blemish is Martin's incorrect ascription; it should read: Alastair Buchan: "Their Bomb and Ours," *Encounter* 12 (January 1959): 11–18. Reference to GSP 1952 is on p. 16.

It seems likely that such a war would begin with a period of intense atomic attacks lasting a relatively short time but inflicting great destruction and damage. If no decisive results were reached in this opening phase, hostilities would decline in intensity, though perhaps less so at sea than elsewhere, and a period of 'broken-backed' warfare follow, during which the opposing sides would seek to recover their strength, carrying on the struggle in the meantime as best they could.[12]

Three years or so later, Field Marshal Montgomery envisaged the possibility of broken-backed warfare continuing for as long as two years after the initial nuclear exchange had been *won* by the West.[13]

The readiness of the British chiefs of staff to compromise was occasioned by the objectives they set themselves. Not only had they to consider all-out war in Europe but they also had to plan for limited war outside Europe and particularly in the Middle East, together with the capability for intervention in other parts of the world to defend what might be perceived as British interests. Ironically enough, the advent of General Dwight D. Eisenhower to the presidency and the death of Stalin occasioned not only a reassessment of the likelihood of Soviet aggression but also saw the U.S. Joint Chiefs of Staff looking with a more indulgent eye upon the prescriptions of their British opposite numbers.

In January 1954, Secretary of State John Foster Dulles made his "massive retaliation" speech, but even then strategic bets were hedged. In June 1954, General Gruenther, Supreme Allied Commander Europe (SACEUR), declared:

> If war should take place three years from now we would use atomic weapons. We are working on a philosophy to have a force in being that is the smallest possible and to depend on reserve forces. We feel that it will not hold that long unless we have atomic power to support it. In our thinking we visualize the use of atomic bombs in support of our ground troops. We also visualize the use of atomic bombs in enemy territory.[14]

Economics, strategy, and the rise and fall in the perceptions of a Soviet threat were the first interesting avenues along which to approach the larger European powers in the context of the Atlantic Alliance. Taken together, and they had to be taken together, they would determine whether a politician could be declared a statesman. Concerned about the economic infrastructure of British defense effort, but more drawn to the political and theatrical effect of a summit conference, Churchill longed to leave the political stage with a wreath of olives on his brow.

---

[12]Cmd. 9075 *Statement on Defence* (London: Her Majesty's Stationery Office, February 1954), p. 5.

[13]Field Marshal Viscount Bernard Montgomery, "The Panorama of Warfare in a Nuclear Age," *Royal Institute for Defence Studies Journal* 101 (November 1956): 510.

[14]General Alfred M. Gruenther, *Keesings Contemporary Archives 1954*, vol. 9, p. 13640.

When Sir Anthony Eden succeeded Sir Winston Churchill in April 1955, Harold Macmillan moved to the Foreign Office and became the legatee of the ideas contained in Churchill's speech of May 1953. The following year the government accepted a resolution welcoming "an immediate initiative by Her Majesty's Government to bring about a meeting between the Prime Minister and the heads of the administrations of the USA and the USSR for the purpose of considering anew the problem of the reduction and the control of armaments and of devising positive policies and means for removing from all the peoples of the world the fear which now oppresses them."[15] Macmillan noted that his officials were less than enamored of the idea and favored more traditional diplomacy. However, he had his own ideas:

> I did not believe that a meeting of Heads of Government should be regarded as the end of a negotiation, but the beginning. I envisaged one or two meetings of the four Foreign Secretaries . . . then the meetings of Head of Government—to last a few days (not more than a week)—then more meetings—perhaps in different groups so as to include different powers. . . . I felt we were entering into a period when a whole series of such meetings at different levels might be required.[16]

It was a heady vision and it rested on the belief that Britain was a power still to be reckoned with both within and outside the alliance, because British effort within the alliance at a time when the French were stalling on German rearmament engendered a political intimacy with the United States that reestablished Britain as the major ally of the United States. The charter of the United Nations had elected Britain as one of the five permanent members of the Security Council and, had that organization operated as its founders hoped, Britain would have been confirmed as a great power. The Atlantic Alliance was a substitute structure and as far as British self-estimates were concerned served the same purpose.

The Suez debacle, masterminded by Sir Anthony Eden who saw himself describing full circle twenty years after serving in and resigning from Chamberlain's cabinet of appeasers, dramatically chilled Anglo-American intimacy. It also swept Eden into private life and brought to the premiership a consummate politician, Macmillan, who already had had experience of the great offices of state and was determined to obtain a defense policy capable of defending British interests without straining the economy. Despite the high budgetary cost of maintaining more than three-quarters of a million men under arms, reserves had to be recalled and essential transport had to be hired from civilian organizations. When the invasion fleet finally sailed from Malta, it took longer to reach Alexandria

---

[15]Harold Macmillan, *Tides of Fortune 1945–1955* (London: Macmillan and Company, 1969), p. 584.
[16]Ibid.

than did Lord Nelson 150 years before. Macmillan therefore called upon
Duncan Sandys to formulate, in the light of current strategic needs, a
defense policy that would secure a substantial reduction in expenditure
and manpower.

A quick visit to Washington in 1957 for conversations with Secretary of Defense Wilson preceded some highly acrimonious encounters
with the British chiefs of staff and the enunciation of a new British strategy
for defense that essentially has remained unchanged for a quarter of a
century. Announcing the beginning of the end of conscription, Sandys not
only affirmed increased reliance upon the nuclear deterrent but also
declared it to be an *independent* nuclear deterrent and sought to extend it
at least to the Middle East: "Apart from its own importance, the Middle
East guards the right flank of NATO" and in the event of an emergency
involving the Baghdad pact "British forces in the Middle East would be
made available . . . these would include bomber squadrons based in
Cyprus capable of delivering nuclear weapons."[17]

The independent deterrent was seen as a juju, an amulet that would
restore British self-confidence badly shaken by Suez. It was also a totem
that would reestablish British standing within the Atlantic Alliance and
influence outside. The alliance, in fact, was becoming the sine qua non of
any British evaluation of her great power status. Macmillan held to the
view of both his Labour and Conservative predecessors that Britain stood
at the center of three concentric circles. However, as the fifties advanced
the Commonwealth was beginning to lose its political and even economic
vitality, while the steadfast refusal of all British governments since the war
to be included formally in any but the loosest European institutions had
kept her on the periphery of Europe. There only remained the Atlantic
circle within which British power and status could be demonstrated.

Macmillan, endowed with political skill, leaned heavily on his wartime collaboration with President Eisenhower and obtained less than a
year after Suez the latter's commitment to amend the McMahon Act that
was essential to the British defense program and also singled out Britain
among the Atlantic allies of the United States; it was followed by the joint
effort to develop *Skybolt*. When the latter collapsed, Macmillan transformed a major setback into an asset by obtaining at Nassau in 1962 the
promise of *Polaris*.

These were the calibrators of British political standing within the
alliance, but they also indicated that while status is one thing strength is
another. Notwithstanding the inflow of nuclear information, Britain lacked
the technological infrastructure to deploy her own *Blue Streak* missile or
to proceed with the development of *Skybolt*. The acquisition of *Polaris* off
the American shelf while sustaining strategic policy reduced the pressure
for domestic industrial effort that would have had advantages for

---

[17]Cmd. 124 *Outline of Future Policy* (London: HMSO, April 1957), p. 5.

economic as well as for defense policy. Nevertheless, the Nassau agreement of December 1962 with President John F. Kennedy, which secured British acquisition of *Polaris,* was Macmillan's political apotheosis and for twenty years settled one of the main components of British defense policy. Only now are the alternatives being discussed seriously and openly following the announcement in January 1980 that £1,000M is to be found to prolong the life of the *Polaris* submarine launchers and consideration given to their replacement by new systems whose cost might be £5,000M.

THE FRENCH EXPERIENCE

Meanwhile, the thrust of British policy within the alliance was throwing into relief that of France. Ultimately, the speed with which Anglo-American fences were repaired had a deleterious effect upon French policy toward the alliance as a whole. Accordingly, it is prudent to recognize that from its very inception successive French governments demonstrated their freedom to maneuver within the alliance. Prior to the signing of the treaty it was the French who included the Mediterranean into the political, if not geographical, North Atlantic area by insisting upon Italian membership.[18] Subsequently, in late spring 1951 a semi-official French statement intimated that the government received, "with a certain amount of surprise," an American proposal that Greece and Turkey be admitted, as in its view nothing had changed since the September 1950 meeting of the North Atlantic Council when the Scandinavian members hotly had opposed their membership.[19] The French demurred on political grounds; the United States argued on strategic.

In this event, the United States got its way, just as it did on the far more emotive issue of German rearmament, also raised at the September 1950 council meeting in New York. Press reports spoke of sharp disagreement between Acheson and the other ministers, the secretary of state making the reinforcement of American forces in Europe and the nomination of General Eisenhower as allied commander in chief conditional upon the acceptance of German rearmament. After dispersing to allow for national consultation, the council issued a communique indicating that the principle of German rearmament was on the way to being accepted. At the end of November, Foreign Secretary Ernest Bevin indicated that while the principle might be accepted there was going to be

---

[18]Dean Acheson, press conference, 18 March 1949, *Keesings Contemporary Archives 1949,* vol. 7, p. 9870.

[19]*Keesings Contemporary Archives 1951,* vol. 8, p. 11514.

difficulty over its execution. He also recalled that defense had other aspects as well as the military:

> It is imperative that the free world should not allow itself to be diverted from its first task of strengthening its social, economic and military defences . . . that is why we signed the North Atlantic treaty . . . that is why the Atlantic foreign ministers in New York decided to establish an integrated force under a centralised command, for the defence of Western Europe . . . the USA raised the question of a German contribution . . . His Majesty's government were in agreement . . . we therefore agreed with the Americans that any German contribution must be in the form of units in the integrated Atlantic force. The French government were unable to accept this proposal and the New York meeting had to break up without reaching any final agreement. The French government has now produced its proposals for a European army . . . His Majesty's government do not favour this proposal . . . we fear that it will only delay the building up of Europe's defences. Our first and most urgent need is to set up the integrated force under the Supreme Commander. The next step is to provide for a German contribution to that force.[20]

Thus, early on the French found themselves on opposite sides of the British and the Americans. The acceptance by the latter two countries of the idea of a European army only slightly relieved the nervous tension, because the more closely their allies offered to associate themselves with the European Defense Committee (EDC) the less successive French governments seemed prepared to ratify the EDC treaty. French irritation was further sharpened by Dulles's response to the collapse of the proposed defense community in August 1954: "The French negative action, without the provision of any alternative, obviously imposes on the United States the obligation to reappraise its foreign policies, particularly those in relation to Europe . . . it is a tragedy that in one country nationalism, abetted by communism, has asserted itself so as to endanger the whole of Europe." With gloomy relish, Dulles seasoned his assertion of grievance, his ritual reference to communism, and his veiled threat with a smug expression of superiority: "The tragedy would be compounded if the United States was thereby led to conclude that it must turn to a course of narrow nationalism . . . we are fortunately so situated that we do not need to identify ourselves with what to us seem self-defeating policies."[21]

The way out of the impasse was found by amending the 1948 Brussels Treaty to include "the new Italy" as well as the Federal Republic. Western European Union (WEU) replaced Western Union, whose

---

[20]Great Britain, Parliament, *Parliamentary Debates* (Commons) 5th series, 481 (1950): 1171–73.
[21]John Foster Dulles, 31 August 1954, *Documents 1954* (London: Royal Institute of International Affairs, 1957), p. 21.

military functions already had been absorbed by NATO and SHAPE. Bevin's judgment that the way to strengthen Europe's defenses was first to establish an integrated force under a supreme commander and subsequently to provide for a German contribution was posthumously vindicated.

However, notwithstanding the formal admission of the Federal Republic of Germany to the Atlantic Alliance in May 1955, still another French government sought to avert the unpalatable necessity of assisting in the reemergence of German military power. In March 1956, after a scathing reference to Anglo-American disinterest in Algeria, Foreign Minister Pineau declared his "profound disagreement with the policy pursued by the Western powers during the past few years; we have made a tremendous mistake in thinking that problems of international security were the only problems with which we had to deal."[22] He subsequently accompanied Premier Guy Mollet to Moscow in a final attempt to obtain an agreement on disarmament that would enable the allies to stop thinking of problems of international security and reduce the need for German contingents in the integrated allied forces. They returned convinced that whatever the inadequacies of Western policies, the Soviet Union was not prepared to provide for the security of the West by submitting disarmament proposals that would enable the alliance to stop thinking along military lines. When the Suez episode demonstrated the inefficacy of their military power at the national level, they initiated the programs that were to endow the France of President de Gaulle with its nuclear capability.

Although widely, if erroneously, believed to be the fount of French discord within the alliance, de Gaulle without doubt stamped it with his hauteur. He began as he was to proceed by coolly proposing to Eisenhower and Macmillan in September 1958 an Anglo-American-French directorate of an alliance transformed through a global extension of its scope. To the best of this writer's knowledge his memorandum never has been published, and it was not until 1966 that Senator Henry Jackson obtained a copy of Eisenhower's reply. The State Department took this opportunity to summarize the repercussions occasioned by de Gaulle's dispatch:

> In an endeavour to determine exactly what the French had in mind, two tripartite discussions were held in Washington in December 1958 among the British and French ambassadors and Deputy Under Secretary of State Robert Murphy. The French ambassador indicated that France had in mind an arrangement that would involve joint strategic planning by tripartite combined staffs on a world-wide scale.
>
> At a second meeting with General de Gaulle in Paris in December, Secretary of State Dulles indicated that the United States was ready for a program of consultation round the world, but would

---

[22]Christian Pineau, 2 March 1956, *Keesings Contemporary Archives 1956*, vol. 10, p. 14752.

not go beyond an exchange of views, that it was simply not possible to establish an organic directorate either over NATO or the rest of the world.[23]

De Gaulle's proposals would have had the effect of redrafting the North Atlantic Treaty by introducing two-tier membership with a global purview on the part of the top-tier members. At that time Paul-Henri Spaak was secretary general of NATO, and with studied politeness de Gaulle sent him a copy of his memorandum on a personal basis and arranged for the Italian and German ambassadors to be shown copies. Although none of the other NATO governments saw the memorandum, they had, as Macmillan confided to his diary, "a pretty good idea of its contents and are naturally enraged."[24] Adding condescension to arrogance, if not insult to injury, the French president then turned to the disadvantaged Germans when his proposals were turned down and began to lay the foundations for a Bonn-Paris axis by refusing to truckle with the Soviets regarding the status of West Berlin during the Berlin crisis of 1958–61 when Macmillan, who apparently had the ear of Eisenhower, showed he was at least prepared to discuss the issue with the Soviets in Moscow.

The ideas expressed in General de Gaulle's memorandum, however, were similar to earlier ideas proposed by Macmillan in what he himself half-jokingly called his "Grand Design," a term that one would imagine would not have met with the approval of someone as jealous of the history of France as the general. Throughout his premiership, Macmillan kept floating the idea of more active discussion and cooperation between Britain, France, and the United States, but Macmillan's tripartism was different from that of de Gaulle. During the fifties his mind "was turning more and more to the dangers of Britain remaining outside a community which controlled a central position in what was left of free Europe."[25] To obviate the danger he was prepared to bring pressure upon Eisenhower's successor to support an independent French nuclear force; in return he expected to obtain British entry into Europe, an objective profoundly desired by both Eisenhower and Kennedy. But Kennedy had concluded that as the United States would not initiate an armed attack upon the Soviets "our strategic arms and defense must be adequate to deter any deliberate nuclear attack on the United States or our allies . . . our

---

[23]U.S., Department of State, "NATO and Franco-American Relations 1958–1961," *NATO Letter* 14 (October 1966): 28.
    [24]Harold Macmillan, *Riding the Storm 1956–1959* (London: Macmillan and Company, 1961), p. 453.
    [25]Harold Macmillan, *Pointing the Way 1959–1961* (London: Macmillan and Company, 1972), p. 113.

objective now is to increase our ability to confine our response to non-nuclear weapons."[26] If Macmillan's tripartism ran counter to this objective, then it would remain unfulfilled. De Gaulle's acceptance of tripartism would have served to raise France above her allies, but he decided to veto the British application for membership of the European Economic Community, interpreting the Nassau agreement as proof positive that the Anglo-Saxons wanted whatever primacy there was in the alliance to be theirs and theirs alone.

De Gaulle was certainly the most adept at raising the hackles of his allies. What Churchill once unkindly referred to as "the logic of continental minds" led him to authorize Foreign Minister Couve de Murville to dispel any credibility in the multilateral nuclear force (MLF) proposals earlier introduced by Kennedy, which also effectively undercut proposals for an Atlantic nuclear force (ANF) that were being aired in the House of Commons by the newly returned Labour premier Harold Wilson. Couve de Murville began his demolition at the December 1964 meeting of the North Atlantic Council with a maddening disclaimer of any initial intention to make any contribution to the debate whatever. He observed that the question of nuclear control was being discussed in crisis terms at a time when fear of war had lessened, and he went on to point out that the MLF proposals stressed both nondissemination and the granting of ill-defined rights to non-nuclear allies of the United States. If nondissemination were ensured, such rights would be illusory; if the rights were to be made real, there would be dissemination.[27] It was as neat and as devastating a criticism as could be made at a time when the United States was trying to engage the Soviet Union in a nonproliferation understanding that would signify their joint acceptance of the fact that rivalry notwithstanding they had common interests.

Steps already had been taken by President de Gaulle to progressively withdraw from the integrated command structures of NATO. Subsequently, notice was to be served that all NATO agencies both civil and military were to quit the country. The gap in time between the formation of the alliance and the establishment of NATO and SHAPE supported de Gaulle's contention that France could remain a faithful member of the alliance while yet disengaging herself from its military structures. Painful as it was to the Johnson administration, it had to be recognized that de Gaulle could indulge his idiosyncratic view, because in the final analysis he knew that if his policies ever aroused Soviet ire he could rely upon the support of the United States.

[26]President John F. Kennedy, message to Congress, 28 March 1961, *Documents on American Foreign Relations 1961* (New York: Harper and Row, 1962), pp. 51–56.
[27]Couve de Murville, 15 December 1964, *Keesings Contemporary Archives 1965*, vol. 15, p. 20704.

It was not only the hiatus between the signing of the founding treaty and establishment of NATO and SHAPE that yielded some justification for President de Gaulle's maneuvers, however. As opposed to the provisions of the 1948 Brussels Treaty that bound Britain, France, and the Benelux to render automatically one another military assistance in the event of aggression against any of the parties concerned, the North Atlantic Treaty pledges the signatories *to consult* in case of a threat to any and to regard an actual attack on any as an attack on all. Each country would provide assistance "by taking such action . . . as it deems necessary, including the use of armed force." It is customary for exegists of the treaty to explain this difference by referring to the constitutional position of the president of the United States; but it also reflects the possibility of varying estimates of national self-interest provoking different reactions to an attack upon an ally. It was for this reason that article 6 of the treaty specified the geographical area wherein the provisions of article 4 concerning armed attack were to apply. Some signatories had more widespread interests than others and not to have delineated the area of possible military commitment would have bound the allies to a totally unrealistic and therefore incredible engagement.

More than twenty years after the treaty was signed, Macmillan, in his memoirs, implicitly corroborated de Gaulle's right to determine his policies within the alliance by reference to national considerations: "It is a vulgar but illusory belief that sovereign nations which share the same fundamental principles necessarily pursue in practice a common policy in their international relations."[28] The tone is patrician, which might make the sentiment itself sound more hollow in the ear of the New World. It was precisely because this attitude was the norm of political activity in the Old World that the infant United States was counseled against "entangling alliances." President de Gaulle's independent pursuit of his understandings with members of the Eastern bloc, a concept denoted by the French term détente, became an officially recognized policy of the alliance when the North Atlantic Council accepted the Harmel report in December 1967: "Military security and a policy of détente are not contradictory, but complementary. Collective defense is a stabilizing factor in world politics. It is a necessary condition for effective policies directed towards a greater relaxation of tensions. The way to peace and stability in Europe rests in particular on the use of the Alliance constructively in the interests of détente."[29]

---

[28]Harold Macmillan, *At the End of the Day 1961–1963* (London: Macmillan and Company, 1973), p. 221.
[29]NATO Information Service, "The Future Tasks of the Alliance," North Atlantic Council, December 1967, *NATO Facts and Figures* (Brussels: NATO Information Service, 1969), pp. 333–34.

THE GERMAN EXPERIENCE

If France, once so concerned about defense that it actively collaborated in the supercession of the Brussels Treaty by the North Atlantic Treaty, was yet to develop into the most idiosyncratic of allies, the state which was to become the model member of the alliance hardly had emerged from tutelage in 1949. Divided, its battered economy underutilized and subject to external supervision, the Federal Republic of Germany was circumscribed in regard to foreign policy and relied entirely upon the victorious Western powers for its defense.

Shortly after the establishment of the alliance a formal note passed between East and West protesting German rearmament; it originated from the West and objected to the creation in East Germany of a militarized police force of 50,000 strong. As late as spring 1950 the official stance of the former Western occupying powers was against rearming Germans. The previous autumn both President Truman and his secretary of state had denied knowledge of any discussions within the State Department on the question of recreating an army in Western Germany. This sentiment was echoed by the British Foreign Office, and not long afterward Chancellor Konrad Adenauer insisted:

> I am fundamentally opposed to the rearmament of the German republic . . . we Germans have shed so much blood in two world wars and have also far too few people to allow us to carry through such a project. The allies have disarmed us and the moral and legal duty rests on them to defend us . . . if the allies demanded that we should take part in the defense of Western Europe, I should be in favor not of an independent *Wehrmacht* but of a German contingent in a European force.[30]

It was an adroit speech because it was calculated to arouse feelings of resentment against German nonparticipation in Western defense while indicating a way in which the resentment could be assuaged without provoking fears of the consequences. The fears were real enough. In a foreign affairs debate prior to the dispatch of the Western note on the situation in East Germany, a debate notable for Churchill's expression of support for some German manpower contribution to "a combined system of defense," Foreign Secretary Bevin replied sharply: "I must say to the Right Hon. Gentleman [Winston Churchill] that we have set our face—the United States, France and ourselves—against the rearming of Germany."[31]

---

[30]Chancellor Konrad Adenauer, *Documents 1949–1950* (London: Royal Institute for International Affairs, 1953), p. 310.

[31]Great Britain, Parliament, *Parliamentary Debates* (Commons) 5th series, 473 (1950): 324.

Then came the Korean War. A month later British Minister of Defense Emanuel Shinwell indicated in the Commons that the former opposition was beginning to weaken, provided that priority in the actual supply of arms went to the members of NATO. Two weeks later, speaking at the first session of the Consultative Assembly of the Council of Europe to be attended by the Germans, Churchill made his sonorous plea for the "immediate creation of a unified European army subject to proper European democratic control and acting in full cooperation with the United States and Canada."[32] Things moved rapidly, with Acheson calling at the New York meeting of the North Atlantic Council for ten German divisions to be directly under NATO command.

Bevin ranged himself alongside Acheson, and the French elaborated a counterproposal indicating the nature of the disagreement between the allies. Premier René Pleven's plan was for a unified European army to be responsible to a European minister for defense, who in turn would be answerable to an appropriate political organization. Unprecedented as this was, additional novelty was afforded by the proposal that German contingents should be of regimental size and merged into larger units effectively to prevent the formation of predominantly German divisions. However, time was provided for the novelty to wear off; Pleven's schedule was a lengthy one, beginning with an invitation to Britain and other European countries to consider ways and means of creating such an army. These studies were not to begin until the Schuman plan for coal and steel integration had resulted in a signed agreement: "The French government believed that the realization of the coal-steel plan would accustom people to think in terms of European unity before such a delicate question as that of common defense was broached . . . it now proposes that this question [i.e., German participation in Western defense] should be regulated by the same method and in the same spirit."[33]

The fact that there was disagreement within the Atlantic Alliance concerning the modalities of German rearmament paradoxically enough greatly enhanced the status of the Federal Republic while it still remained a nonmember. Adenauer's aims were simple: he wanted economic and political recovery, security, and reunification. He was to obtain the first because the Western rearmament programs initiated by the outbreak of the Korean War demanded the utilization of the only underemployed economy and the only untapped source of military manpower in Europe. The French solution to their security vis-à-vis Germany—to have recourse to "European" institutions—worked in Adenauer's favor because

---

[32] Winston Churchill, Consultative Assembly of the Council of Europe, Strasbourg, 11 August 1950, *Documents 1949–1950* (London: Royal Institute of International Affairs, 1953), p. 331.
[33] Premier René Pleven, Statement to the National Assembly, 24 October 1950, *Keesings Contemporary Archives 1949–1950,* vol. 7, p. 11037.

his aims accorded entirely with the pressures being brought to bear on him. Acceptance of European economic and military institutions helped resolve the problems of the alliance and obtained German recovery without raising the specter of German nationalism.

German rearmament fell behind German economic rehabilitation as the readiness of the Federal Republic to provide the troops highlighted French procrastination. When EDC was aborted, Dulles not only dressed down the French but also insisted that the West owed it to the Germans to do all it could to restore sovereignty and enable Germany to contribute to international peace and security. Eden's proposed amendment to the 1948 Brussels Treaty and Adenauer's acceptance that rearmament should be supervised by WEU, coupled with the renunciation of atomic, biological, and chemical (ABC) weapons, made the Federal Republic appear the most amendable and conciliatory member of the alliance into which it was formally received in May 1955.

Adenauer obtained his goals of recovery and security without a single German soldier under arms. Indeed, the first units of the *Bundeswehr* passed under NATO command at the same time that the British government announced in the 1957 defense white paper that it intended to renege upon the 1954 pledge to maintain the then existing strength of the British Army of the Rhine (BAOR) and the 2d Tactical Air Force until the expiration of the Brussels Treaty in 1998. Simultaneously, the French were leeching Europe of troops in order to attend to the revolt in what the North Atlantic Treaty referred to as "the Algerian departments of France." This could only increase the standing of the latest recruit to the alliance in the eyes of the U.S. administration, that had been shaken by the demonstration at Suez that its senior allies were not prepared to allow the United States to be the best judge of their interests.

Indeed, the transformation of West German status was such that Adenauer had begun to emulate the British and French. Anxious to maximize his concessions, he delayed the implementation of conscription and then cut down the length of compulsory service. His refusal to make serious offset arrangements for BAOR and the numerous American armies in Germany was made into an additional argument by Britain to cut back her troop deployment in Europe. The onset of the Berlin crisis in 1958, however, dramatically stimulated German readiness to pay for the stiffening of British resolve. The Warsaw Pact invasion of Czechoslovakia in 1968 arrested a similar threat being implemented later, with the result that BAOR has stayed more or less at the same strength for a quarter of a century.

One thing that Adenauer failed to secure was German reunification, despite obtaining allied support for its acquisition as the quid pro quo for German rearmament. For ten years after the accession of the Federal Republic to the alliance, German reunification as the outcome of free elections on both sides of the Iron Curtain, the reunited Germany being free to dispose of herself within the international system as she wished, was a refrain sounded in every communique of the North Atlantic Council. Until 1957, the Soviet Union was prepared to concede reunification and rearmament, but the reunification process offered would have made the East Germans the arbiters of the reunited Germany and isolated it from the Atlantic Alliance and the Warsaw Pact. After 1957, with West German troops fleshing out NATO defenses, First Party Secretary Nikita Khrushchev settled for the existing status quo and declared that East and West Germany had now evolved so differently that reunification was no longer feasible.

Adenauer's critics accused him of selling the German birthright for a mess of Western pottage; his riposte was that the increase in the power of the Western alliance by the rearming of Germany would induce the Soviet Union to concede reunification on alliance terms. He reasoned without Soviet science and technology. Swift Soviet acquisition of nuclear weapons and mistaken perceptions of a missile gap following the successful launching of the first Soviet *Sputnik* in October 1957 allowed the Soviet Union not only to withstand any increase in Western power occasioned by German rearmament but also enabled Khrushchev to attempt forcing the West to accept the division of Germany when he opened the Berlin crisis of November 1958.

Despite appearances the Atlantic allies wished to revise the European status quo. Khrushchev proposed changes in the position of West Berlin, and Berlin had and was to retain a symbolic value disproportionate to any economic, demographic, or other importance it might have for the Federal Republic. However, by the end of 1958 reunification on lines demanded by the allies would have marked a much greater shift in both the real and the apparent distribution of power in Europe. Khrushchev was demanding acceptance of a revision of the position of West Berlin because it entailed acceptance of the status quo in Europe by forcing recognition of the German Democratic Republic.

The political paradox at the end of the fifties was that Khrushchev, who appeared to be forcing the pace, could bring no more power to bear upon his protagonists than they upon him. But he had one advantage—he could afford to forego any change with regard to West Berlin. Pushing the West too far would mean conflict, and conflict over Berlin with nuclear weapons now widely distributed throughout West Germany was far too dangerous a prospect. As for the allies, the existing division of Germany was one that could not be altered without raising similar hazards of conflict. If they accepted the position, however tacitly, the disparity between their declarations and their achievements would gradually redound to their discomfiture.

The Cuban missile crisis dramatically highlighted the risk of East-West confrontation. Yet, the allies continued to maintain confrontation by insisting upon German reunification; it became the albatross hung around the neck of the alliance. The only one of the allies who could remove it without weakening the alliance overall was the Federal Republic, precluded as long as *der Alte* remained the federal chancellor. It required his departure from office before the *Ostpolitik* could be suggested and the incantation on German reunification be dropped from communiques of the North Atlantic Council. When the Social Democrats shook themselves free from the Grand Coalition, the overtures to Poland, Czechoslovakia, and East Germany could be developed within the spirit of the Harmel report and the allied pursuit of détente, because Brandt and his party had nothing to lose in the ultimate acceptance of the division of Germany.

THE NUCLEAR DILEMMA

The growth of Soviet nuclear capability precluded German reunification and thus reinforced the lesson, declaimed by the British and copied by the French, that nuclear capability conferred power notwithstanding inhibitions upon the transformation of such power into force. Indeed, the nonuse of power became the reward for acceptance of the status quo, and the possession of nuclear weapons invested the owner with such strategic power that possession inclined an adversary not to test his political will.

In 1954 the Federal Republic had foresworn ABC weapons as much with an eye to the Western as well as to Eastern susceptibilities. With the onset of the Berlin crisis at the end of 1958, Adenauer was disposed to listen to de Gaulle's insistence that in the very nature of things American and German interests could not always coincide, despite the French memorandum of September 1958 proposing an Anglo-American-French directorate of the Atlantic Alliance.

In order to contain fissiparous tendencies and maintain the cohesion of the alliance, the proposals for a multilateral nuclear force (MLF) were first bruited by Eisenhower as "lame-duck" president at the end of 1960. Taken over by Kennedy, they were supplemented at the end of 1964 by Prime Minister Harold Wilson's Atlantic Nuclear Force (ANF) proposals. Once described in devastating British understatement as "too clever by half," Wilson asserted that his proposals would foster the strength and unity of the alliance by taking account of those non-nuclear members who wanted to exercise greater influence on nuclear planning and policy, and ensure that as far as possible nuclear forces committed to NATO should be under a single unified system "in such a way as to provide an absolute guarantee . . . against the transfer of nuclear striking power from nuclear to non-nuclear powers, a guarantee against the acquisition by non-nuclear powers of a nuclear potential in any shape or form, direct or indirect."[34] At the December 1964 meeting of the North Atlantic Council, Couve de Murville opposed both the MLF and ANF proposals; Secretary of State Dean Rusk in a mealymouthed follow-up declared that the British proposal had stimulated fresh thought and would be studied. The fact was that such a proposal was straining the alliance. Paul-Henri Spaak for Belgium opposed it; Maurice Couve de Murville dismissed it, and only Gerhard Schroeder for the Federal Republic declared his government's continued interest.

Geography, in fact, dictated the interest of the Federal Republic as the one country with an absolute interest in the success of defense policy based on the deterrence afforded by both nuclear and conventional weapons. The Federal Republic was well on the way to fielding its contribution of twelve divisions to the conventional forces of the alliance; its concern focused on the nuclear component of the deterrent. But just as technology helped to preclude German reunification, so it smoothed away the acerbities and anxieties of debate surrounding the credibility of nuclear guarantees, whether American or multilateral. The advent of second-strike capability on the part of both superpowers ushered in the time when war, likely to encompass a nuclear exchange, became not the Clause-witzean continuation of policy but its very negation.

At the meeting of NATO defense ministers in spring 1965, Secretary of Defense McNamara suggested that a select committee of four or five members should study ways of extending nuclear planning and consultation within the alliance. From this "McNamara committee" was to develop the Nuclear Defense Affairs Committee (NDAC) and its executive arm, the Nuclear Planning Group (NPG); the attempt to solve the nuclear problems of the alliance by "hardware" solutions was brought to a halt. By the end of the year, in reporting Chancellor Ludwig Erhard's visit to Washington a little before Christmas, the American press commented upon the demise of the MLF/ANF proposals. The elimination of those issues that kept the Atlantic Alliance and the Warsaw Pact in conflict had become the prime objectives of the foreign policies of both alliances, and in December 1967 when the North Atlantic Council accepted the Harmel report and declared that the objectives of the alliance now encompassed détente as well as deterrence and defense, German anxiety over control of nuclear weapons was eroded as it seemed less and less likely that command and control procedures would be tested.

---

[34]Great Britain, Parliament, *Parliamentary Debates* (Commons) 5th series, 704 (1964): 437–38.

CONCLUSIONS

A cursory view of NATO and the larger European states in the first two decades of the alliance is not confined to the truth of Macmillan's observation about common principles not necessarily entailing common policies. It is those critics of the alliance who try to present it as an instrument for the establishment of American hegemony who ignore the fact that the United States has never found it easy to get its own way.

Consultation has a fine ring and the blandness of the communiques of the North Atlantic Council on occasion presents a misleading impression of allied comity. In May 1956 the council agreed to investigate the whole issue of nonmilitary cooperation and designated three of its members to make recommendations as soon as possible. What robbed the report of the "Three Wise Men" of most of its impact was that between its first drafting in September and its final acceptance in December of the same year there occurred the Suez crisis. Even at the time it could not be maintained that the differences between the United States on the one hand and Britain and France on the other were occasioned by failures in consultation; they were differences of political judgment, differences that received confirmation in the seventies and indeed at the beginning of the eighties. One recalls the cool response to Kissinger's designation of 1973 as the "year of Europe" and the lack of warmth in the late spring of 1980 on the part of President Carter to projected European initiatives in the Middle East.

A further observation might be that as it is structured in NATO, the alliance finds certain agreements too easy and others too difficult. At least one well-qualified critic has suggested that NATO sometimes overburdens itself: "In 1968, at Reykjavik, NATO developed the theory, which I believe is totally wrong, that the alliance is as much an instrument of détente as it is of defense. I think that is simply not correct. NATO is not equipped to be an instrument of détente."[35] From this verdict of Henry Kissinger stems another conclusion: No matter how much President de Gaulle set his allies on edge, in practice his insistence upon the primacy of national assessments of threats to national interests and the corresponding national determination of policies to protect them has been accepted by all the allies.

This is not to imply that the alliance is a facade or a charade. What some critics wrongly regard as sources of weakness were recognized by the founding fathers as characteristics demanding respect. Disparate in power, all members are equal and the treaty, while committing them to the maintenance of common principles, did not and could not enforce any

---

[35]Henry A. Kissinger, "NATO the Next Thirty Years," *Survival* 21 (November/December 1979): 267.

particular prescription of policy. The treaty laid down in article 10 the mechanism that would enable the consultation to take place that was so necessary for the aims of the treaty to be realized. The function of the North Atlantic Council was and remains today consultative. It is not a decision-taking authority but a body seeking to define policy. When policy is defined, the decision on the degree of implementation rests with each signatory state; where policy is undefined, each state is free to determine its own policy and indeed to decide whether it wants a policy at all. The consequence is that the allies sometimes agree, sometimes disagree, and sometimes agree to disagree. A deduction might be that this is a reflection of the vitality of the alliance rather than of its incapacity.

Specifically in regard to the larger European states, one can suggest that the alliance has three considerable and sustained achievements to its credit. Its very existence helped to cushion British adjustment to the realization as the years went by that she was no longer in the front rank of world powers; it provided one of the crucial postwar structures wherein the Federal Republic could develop politically and militarily without sharpening the reservations that her West European neighbors shared, albeit to greater or lesser extents, in the early fifties. Finally, in the primary sense of the word it has contained France since President de Gaulle announced in February 1966 that France would withdraw from the military organizations of the alliance. These were achievements of the fifties, sixties, and seventies, and the alliance is now facing the issues of the eighties with positive confirmation of both its utility and its vigor.

The Alliance Policies of the Smaller NATO Countries

NIKOLAJ PETERSEN

Extensive literature exists on the alliance policies of the larger members of NATO, but this is not the case with respect to the behavior within and toward the alliance of its smaller and presumably less influential member states. General theoretical statements on the NATO policies of the smaller members or on their role in the alliance are very few, as are empirically oriented comparative studies or even individual country studies.[1]

Niels Amstrup has pointed out that by far the larger part of the literature on the foreign policies of small states has concentrated on their security problems, and that much interest has been focused upon what he calls the "small power paradox," the fact that despite their inherent weakness the small powers tend not only to survive but also to proliferate

---

[1]For a look at the roles of small or member countries within the alliance, see Nils Ørvik, "NATO: The Role of the Small Members," *International Journal* 21 (Spring 1966): 173–85. See also Ørvik, "NATO, NAFTA and the Smaller Allies," *Orbis* 12 (Summer 1968): 455–64.

For a comparative analysis of Greece and Turkey (by Willy Andries); Denmark, Norway, and Iceland (by Herman de Fraye); and the Benelux countries (by Frans Govaerts), see Omer de Raeymaeker et al., *Small Powers in Alignment* (Leuven: Leuven University Press, 1974).

For a general comparative analysis of Belgium and the Netherlands, see Jan Deboutte and Alfred van Staaden, "High Politics in the Low Countries: A Study of Foreign Policy-making in Belgium and the Netherlands," in William Wallace and W. E. Paterson, eds., *Foreign Policy-making in Western Europe* (Farnborough: Saxon House, 1978), pp. 56–82. For comparative analyses of various aspects of Nordic security policies, see I.A. Ib Faurby, "Foreign Policy-making in Scandinavia," in *Foreign Policy-making in Western Europe*, 106–34; Nikolaj Petersen, "Danish and Norwegian Alliance Policies 1948–1949: A Comparative Analysis," *Cooperation and Conflict* 14 (1979): 193–210; Egil Ulstein, *Nordic Security*, Adelphi Paper No. 81, International Institute for Strategic Studies (1971); Nils Ørvik, "Scandinavian Military Doctrines," in Frank B. Horton et al., eds., *Comparative Defense Studies* (Baltimore: Johns Hopkins University Press, 1979), pp. 258–72; and Ørvik and Nils Jørgen Haagerup, *The Scandinavian Members of NATO*, Adelphi Paper No. 23, International Institute for Strategic Studies (1965).

For the Netherlands see the analysis in J. H. Leurdijk, ed., *The Foreign Policy of the Netherlands* (Alphen Aan den Rijn: Sijthoff and Noordhoff, 1978). See also L. G. M.

in the modern international system.[2] An important part of small state literature also uses their security predicament as the primary definitional criterion of a small state rather than to measure specific characteristics such as size, or territory, population, economy, etc. This is the case in Robert L. Rothstein's *Alliances and Small Powers* (1968), still the most important theoretical statement on the alliance policies of small states:

> ... a Small Power is a state which recognizes that it cannot obtain security primarily by use of its own capabilities, and that it must rely fundamentally on the aid of other states, institutions, processes, or developments to do so; the Small Power's belief in its inability to rely on its own means must also be recognized by the other states involved in international politics.[3]

This definition implies that the alliance option is one way to solve or at least alleviate the small power's security problem. However, the alliance option has aroused little theoretical interest in the literature compared to neutrality or nonalignment that are the most important alternative options. This situation is especially pronounced with respect to the participation of a number of small states in NATO. Even though Rothstein suggests that participation in a mixed, multilateral alliance such as NATO may be a better solution from the viewpoint of the small power than being part of a bilateral alliance with a larger power or of a regular small-power alliance, he refrains from studying the smaller states in NATO on the basis of the rather facetious claim that their decision to join NATO "has little *theoretical* interest, as they possessed few, if any, viable alternatives."[4] Instead, he concentrates on the problems and advantages of nonalignment as a general foreign policy posture for small states in the present international system.

In conclusion, there is relatively little general knowledge available concerning how the small states behave within NATO and their general alliance behavior. This is evidenced in an analysis by Ole Holsti et al. on a number of theoretical propositions involving all aspects of international alliances.[5] After researching extensive literature the authors arrive at a

---

Jaquet, "The Role of a Small State within Alliance Systems," in August Schou and Arne Olav Brundtland, eds., *Small States in International Relations* (Stockholm: Almqvist and Wiksell, 1971), pp. 57–70. On Denmark and Norway see Johan Jørgen Holst, "Norwegian Security Policy," in Johan Jørgen Holst, *Five Roads to Nordic Security* (Odense: Universitetsforlaget, 1973), pp. 77–126; and Nikolaj Petersen, "Danish Security Policy in the Seventies: Continuity or Change," in Holst, *Five Roads to Nordic Security*, pp. 7–38.

[2]Niels Amstrup, "The Perennial Problem of Small States: A Survey of Research Efforts," *Cooperation and Conflict* 11 (1976): 163–82.

[3]Robert L. Rothstein, *Alliances and Small Powers* (New York: Columbia University Press, 1968), p. 29.

[4]Ibid., p. 244.

[5]Ole Holsti, Terrence Hoppmann, and John Sullivan, *Unity and Disintegration in International Alliances: Comparative Studies* (New York: Wiley Publishers, 1973).

total of 419 such propositions; some 30 of these refer one way or another to small states, but only 2 to their alliance behavior; for example, their policies within the context of an international alliance.

THE SMALLER MEMBERS OF NATO: AN OVERVIEW

It is possible to arrive at the almost surprising conclusion, applying Rothstein's definition to the members of the NATO alliance, that NATO is made up of one larger power (or two counting France) and thirteen or fourteen smaller states. This is hardly a relevant point of departure compared to the more conventional, commonsense view of the alliance as consisting of six larger or medium powers and nine smaller ones, which include Belgium, Denmark, Greece, Iceland, Luxembourg, the Netherlands, Norway, Portugal, and Turkey.

This enumeration is perhaps the most salient characteristic of the group besides their relative small size; namely, their great variety on almost all other dimensions, a major impediment to a comparative analysis of the whole group. First, if Rothstein is correct in suggesting that while great powers ally out of concern for the balance of the entire international system, smaller powers do so because of threats to the local balance,[6] then we have one reason why their policies in the alliance show considerable diversity: relative to their size they are geographically so dispersed that their respective security policy "horizons" may not even intersect; this was one of the reasons why Denmark and Norway were opposed to the inclusion of Greece and Turkey in the alliance in the early 1950s. The Soviet "threat," which however conceived has been and still is the essential raison d'etre of NATO, has significantly different contours when seen from Oslo, Lisbon, and Ankara.

It is even doubtful whether all the smaller states consistently have subscribed to the notion that the Soviet Union and the Warsaw Pact is the most immediate and salient threat to their national security. Certainly, this is recognized by the Benelux countries and Denmark and Norway but not necessarily among the remaining small powers. Since the late 1950s Greece and Turkey have been as much absorbed in their own mutual conflicts over Cyprus and the Aegean Sea as in the East-West confrontation. For many years Portugal's attention was almost entirely focused upon her African adventures, and at least for a period the Icelanders considered the fishing fleets of Grimsby and Aberdeen a greater threat to their national interests than the northern fleet of the Soviet navy.

---

[6]Rothstein, *Alliances and Small Powers*, p. 62.

The most important dividing line within the group undoubtedly exists between the three southern members and the six countries in the north and northwest. Portugal, Greece, and Turkey are economically less developed and have political traditions that set them apart from the rest of the NATO countries. Specifically, they have a tradition of political instability, authoritarianism, and military intervention in politics, which is still very much alive although somewhat less conspicuous now than a decade ago. On the other hand, the Nordic and Benelux members have highly developed and sophisticated economies and firmly entrenched democratic systems based on traditions of antiauthoritarianism and antimilitarism rather than the reverse. In the late sixties and early seventies these differences led to a sharp conflict within NATO between the Netherlands, Denmark, and Norway on one side and the Greek colonels' regime and Salazar's Portugal on the other. The latter conflict threatened NATO cohesion and certainly reduced support for NATO among the former group, although they partially succeeded to have the conflict transferred to other less sensitive arenas such as the Council of Europe.

For these reasons it may be argued that in order to say something specific and meaningful about the alliance behavior of the smaller NATO members one should probably restrict the analysis to a smaller, more homogeneous subgroup, such as the Benelux and Nordic member states. In practice the analysis also will exclude Luxembourg and Iceland, both of which are so small in terms of population that they scarcely make any material contribution to the defense effort of the alliance.[7] Even so many of the following observations are probably to some extent valid for those two countries as well. However, their validity for the southern small states is more questionable.

THE BENELUX AND NORDIC NATO STATES: SIMILARITIES AND DIFFERENCES

The four countries have in common not only relative size but also an advanced capitalistic economic system and a democratic political system. All together these three variables are often viewed as the most potent

---

[7]Luxembourg with a population of 360,000 has an army of 660 and in 1979 had a total military expenditure of about $36 million. *The Military Balance 1979–1980* (London: International Institute for Strategic Studies, 1979). Iceland with a population of 220,000 has no military forces, but this does not mean they do not contribute to the alliance. Iceland always has been considered a vital link in trans-Atlantic communications and as a base for NATO control in the North Atlantic.

source variables for international behavior.[8] However, similarities between them extend beyond this. One is the relatively strong position of the Social Democratic parties. Though it may be difficult to spell out precisely what this may mean for their foreign and defense policies, certain aspects of the Social Democratic "ideology" are clearly relevant such as the notions of international solidarity, peaceful solution of conflicts, arms reduction, and, in several of the parties, traditional antimilitarism. These are ideas that are no longer confined to the Social Democratic parties as such, which predispose the four countries to rather "soft" policies within the alliance, making them less eager to embrace confrontation, tension, and crisis and more likely to support détente and conciliation.

Another common political tradition is that of neutrality. With the exception of Belgium's rather unfortunate alliance with France 1920–36, in itself a reaction to Germany's violation of her internationally guaranteed neutrality at the outset of World War I, all four countries were neutral from the end of the Napoleonic wars until their occupation by Nazi Germany in spring of 1940. In the aftermath of World War I they all had accepted, with some reluctance in the case of the Dutch, the Danes, and the Norwegians, the principle of collective security as embodied in the Charter of the League of Nations. However, faced with the rising threat from Germany and the resulting erosion of the League's authority, they all reverted to a classical nineteenth-century neutrality from 1936 onward and repudiated collective security. For all four countries, joining NATO represented a break with a dominant foreign policy tradition.

There are also several relevant differences between the four. As Table I shows there are important topographical and demographical differences, for instance, Norway is ten times as large as Belgium and more than seven times as large as Denmark. However, with respect to number it is smaller than the rest of the group with a population that is less than half that of Belgium and less than a third of the Dutch population. Norway is one of the least densely populated European countries, while the Netherlands and Belgium are the most densely populated areas. Topographically, the Benelux countries and Denmark are extensions of the North German Plain, highly urbanized, flat and accessible with few natural defenses except the Rhine and the waters around Denmark, while Norway is mountainous, rugged, and relatively easy to defend; its population is concentrated in relatively few regions, mostly in the south and the west.

---

[8]See, for example, James N. Rosenau, "Pre-theory"; and Rosenau, "Pre-Theories and Theories of Foreign Policy," in Barry Farrell, ed., *Approaches to Comparative and International Politics* (Chicago: Northwestern University Press, 1966).

Table 1. Area, Population, and Economy

	1 Area[1] 1000(sq km)	2 Population[2] 1978(mill.)	3 Population per sq km 1975[1]	4 Est. GNP 1978[2] (bn. US $)	5 GNP per head 1978(US$) (4:2)
Belgium	31	10.0	321	97.6	9750
Denmark	44	5.1	117	55.6	10817
Netherlands	41	14.1	334	130.3	9241
Norway	324	4.1	12	39.4	9614

SOURCES: [1] Statistical Yearbook Denmark 1978.
[2] The Military Balance 1979–1980.

The table also shows that there are no important differences in the level of economic prosperity between the four countries, but because of the larger populations of the Benelux nations their total economies are significantly larger than those of the Nordic countries; the Dutch economy is more than three times larger than the Norwegian. This may partially explain why psychologically the Netherlands has been more reluctant to see itself as a small power than the other states. In a famous exclamation Foreign Minister Joseph Luns declared in December 1970 in the Second Chamber: "I have never said that, never, never, never, I have never said that the Netherlands is a small, puny country. The Netherlands is a very important country."[9] Instead, the Dutch often think of their country as a medium power, which she is particularly in economic areas. With her newly found oil wealth Norway also could feel less like a small power in the future than she has until now. On the other hand, Belgium and Denmark consistently have felt (and behaved) as small states.

Geography also creates various differences among the four countries. Belgium's and Holland's security problems are almost entirely tied up with the NATO defense of the North German Plain, although the Dutch also have a separate problem with her flank to the North Sea. Both countries therefore are somewhat sheltered by the forward NATO defense line in Germany to which they contribute with part of their armies and air forces and by having their total defenses firmly integrated in NATO's central region. Their position is further bolstered by having Britain and France behind them.

Norwegian and Danish defense problems are more acute in comparison. Denmark is situated on the northern flank of West Germany and astride the exits from the Baltic. Although the Baltic exits probably have lost some of their former importance to the Soviet naval effort, they are

[9] Alfred van Staaden, "The Role of the Netherlands in the Atlantic Alliance" in J. H. Leurdijk, ed., *The Foreign Policy of the Netherlands*, p. 144.

still important enough to constitute a major defense problem for Denmark that is aggravated by a 4- or 5-to-1 Warsaw Pact preponderance over NATO in the Baltic region. These facts constrain Denmark to seek close military cooperation with the Federal Republic within the Unified Command for Denmark and Schleswig-Holstein under NATO's northern region and to rely heavily on such external reinforcements, primarily from Britain and the United States, which she can obtain in a crisis situation.

Norway's defense problems are sui generis and less tied to the regional balance in Europe than to the central strategic balance between the United States and the Soviet Union. The proximity of north Norway to the Soviet base area on the Kola peninsula where an important part of the Soviet surface and submarine fleets are stationed makes it a strategic area of prime importance for NATO and especially the United States. Since part of Norway is very sparsely populated and lacks certain natural defenses of the rest of the country, she has only a few possibilities for defending herself on her own and therefore has to rely heavily on external reinforcements, especially from the United States and Canada.

Even though the prime defense focus of the four countries differs significantly, these differences should not be exaggerated. The Netherlands has a major naval presence in the North Sea that is potentially important to Norway as well as to Denmark and furthermore contributes to NATO's Standing Naval Force in the North Atlantic (STANAVFORLANT). Together with Belgium she also contributes to NATO's so-called ACE Mobile Force, one of whose primary assignments is the northern flank of NATO—Denmark and Norway. On her side Denmark's security is heavily dependent upon the defense of Western Germany. Even Norway, who in many ways is the most idiosyncratic of the four with her almost total absorption in the problems of the Northern Cape, explicitly recognizes that this preoccupation is predicated upon the security of her southern flank. For example, the defense efforts of Denmark and the Federal Republic were recently revealed by certain undiplomatic comments on the Danish defense debate by the Norwegian defense chief.[10]

Another difference that is almost certain to increase in importance in the 1980s is the fact that the Benelux countries and Denmark are members of the European Economic Community (EEC) and participants in the extra treaty European Political Cooperation (EPC) among the nine, while Norway elected to stand outside when the question was up for decision in 1972. The EPC, which was instituted in the early 1970s following the Davignon report, constitutes one of the few obvious successes of European cooperation in the last decade and has grown slowly and steadily to a point where it constitutes a major element in the foreign policy processes

---

[10]*Berlingske Tidende,* 24 February 1980.

of at least the smaller members of the EPC.[11] Given present trends in the U.S.-European relationship, there is a possibility that the foreign policies of Belgium, Denmark, and the Netherlands will become less Atlantic in their orientation in the future, while Norway is much more likely to retain a pronounced U.S.-oriented policy.

It is clear that even with these differences that the relevant source variables affecting the alliance policies of the four countries are alike enough to allow for a "most similar systems" approach, such as a comparative analysis predicated on the expectation of similar rather than dissimilar NATO policies (the dependent variable).[12] Are the expected similarities in policy due to common domestic variables (size, economic, and political system, etc.) or to mutual emulation and influence? If, for instance, it could be demonstrated that the four countries make up a coherent group within NATO and also in other respects, then this theory might contribute significantly to explaining their behavior.

It is certainly possible to point out cases of cooperation between the group of four or between at least some members of the group, both past and present. The Benelux and Nordic countries have long traditions of cooperation dating back to the nineteenth century and involving a wide field of issues. A more interesting question is how extensive cooperation has been *between* members of either subgroup. In the interwar years the Netherlands, Denmark, and Norway (but not Belgium) belonged to the group of "exneutrals" that cooperated frequently in League of Nations matters, especially with respect to collective security. After 1936 they were joined by Belgium in disengaging from this system. The four also tried to cooperate in fighting the threat to their economic survival posed by the 1929 Depression by signing the Oslo Convention in 1930. However, the convention, which only pledged the signatories to give each other advance notice before raising their tariffs, came to have no significant role in staving off the effects of the slump.

Similar cooperation can be noted from the postwar period. As mentioned below, Belgium and Denmark (later joined by the Netherlands) participated in what became known as the Group of Nine, a forum of smaller NATO, nonaligned, and Warsaw Pact countries that met between 1965 and 1968 to discuss problems of European security and the prospects of détente.[13] The four countries also recently have joined

---

[11]Reinhardt Rummel and Wolfgang Wessels, *Die Europäische Politische Zusammenarbeit* (Bonn: Europa Union Verlag, 1978).

[12]Neil Smelser, "The Methodology of Comparative Analysis," in Donald P. Warwick and Samuel Osherson, eds., *Comparative Research Methods* (Englewood Cliffs, NJ: Prentice-Hall, 1963).

[13]Jeanne Kirk Laux, "Small States and Inter-European Relations: An Analysis of the Group of Nine," *Journal of Peace Research* 9 (1972): 147–60.

together with other north European states in a group of so-called "like-minded" countries that are sympathetic to and in varying degrees supportive of the demands for a new economic world order formulated by the developing countries.[14]

The most striking and clear-cut case of cooperation between the four, however, occurred in 1975 when they joined in "the arms deal of the century," pooling together to purchase 350 U.S. F-16 fighters. Apparently, the four (or at least three) worked together in expressing their hesitation concerning the NATO decision of late 1979 to station new long-range tactical nuclear weapons in Europe, the Theater Nuclear Force (TNF) modernization. Thus, one day in December 1979 Dutch Premier Andreas van Agt, his Norwegian colleague Odvar Nordli, and Danish Foreign Minister Kjeld Olesen descended on Washington to voice the reservations of their governments.[15]

These examples, however, easily may leave a false or exaggerated impression of cooperation between the group of four in NATO. In the TNF case the efforts of the three governments were uncoordinated and to some extent mutually defeating, and the F-16 deal has not been followed by other cooperative ventures in military procurement. In fact, unless the case is one of a specific threat to the influence of the small member states in the NATO policymaking process, they usually prefer to work on their own in lobbying the larger powers rather than engaging in what might be construed by the latter as an attempt at "ganging up" upon them.[16] For all the talk regarding multilateralism, NATO is still what Johan Galtung calls a "feudal" alliance; it is hierarchically (or vertically) ordered with rather limited horizontal interaction, especially among the lower-ranking members.[17]

One significant reservation should be added to the general conclusion that the NATO policies of the smaller members are only to a limited degree interdependent. Important aspects of Danish and Norwegian policies have in fact been interrelated, more often than not by Denmark taking the lead from Norway. Norway's refusal in 1949 to conclude a nonaligned Scandinavian Defense Union and her decision to join NATO was the single most important element in Denmark's decision to accept membership in the Atlantic Pact. Similarly, the Norwegian policy laid down in 1949, which did not permit the stationing of allied troops on her territory in peace-time, contributed significantly to the

[14]Anthony J. Dolman, "The Like-minded and the New International Order," *Cooperation and Conflict* 14 (1979): 57–85.

[15]*Washington Post,* 7 December 1979.

[16]Staaden, "The Role of the Netherlands in the Atlantic Alliance," p. 141.

[17]Johan Galtung, "East-West Interaction Patterns," *Journal of Peace Research* 2 (1966): 147.

formulation of a similar Danish policy in 1953 after efforts to reverse the Norwegian stance had failed.[18] Similar interdependencies between Belgian and Dutch policies undoubtedly exist even though they are hardly as conspicuous as between Denmark and Norway.

JOINING THE ALLIANCE

The failure of neutrality in 1940 forms the common political background to the four countries' policy of alignment after the war. In all of them neutrality became a negatively charged term to be replaced by concepts such as "international solidarity," and "engagement." The problem now was how to translate these concepts into policy, and here differences arose that can be ascribed to the various wartime experiences of the four countries, or rather to their political leaderships. Belgium, the Netherlands, and Norway had governments in exile in London that actively participated in the wartime discussion of the postwar organization of Europe and the world, as there was very little else for them to do. Dutch and Belgian leaders especially became firm believers in the need to supplement or underpin universal organizations (the projected UN system) with regional political and economic organization either in a European or Atlantic framework. The first step in this direction was the signing of the Benelux treaty in September 1944. In contrast, until its dissolution in 1943 the Danish government stayed in Copenhagen almost totally isolated from these discussions and with neutralist Sweden as its only external political contact.

For a while after the war Belgium and the Netherlands shifted toward a more universalist line. However, Belgium continued to be interested in regionalist solutions. When in January 1948 the two countries were approached under the Bevin Plan by Britain and France with an offer of a network of bilateral alliances on the model of the 1947 Treaty of Dunkirk, it was natural for them to counter with a proposal for a more genuinely regionalist, multilateral alliance. This proposal, which was forcefully supported by the United States, was accepted in all essentials by Britain and France and evolved into the Brussels (or Western Union) Pact of 17 March 1948, an important precursor of the Atlantic Pact by demonstrating to the hesitant U.S. administration that the Europeans meant business and were prepared to help themselves. Both Belgian and Dutch leaders clearly saw the pact as a step toward a broader process leading up to a comprehensive Atlantic security scheme.

---

[18]Erik Beukel, *Socialdemokratiet og stationeringsproblemet 1952–53* (Odense: Universitetsforlaget, 1974).

As early as January 1948, Belgian Prime Minister Paul-Henri Spaak had stated that any defense arrangement that did not include the United States would be without any practical value.[19] On this basis the two countries participated actively and effectively in the Washington security talks between the United States, Canada, and the five Brussels powers that eventually led to the signing of the Atlantic Pact in April 1949.

The motives of the two governments for joining the pact were a mixture of military and political considerations. Both shared the view that dominated the Washington talks and claimed that there was a real if not a high threat of a war by mistake or miscalculation, but scarcely a premeditated aggression on the part of the Soviet Union. The main danger was seen as psychological: the possibility that the coup in Czechoslovakia might have a defeatist bandwagon effect in Western Europe that would compromise its economic, social, and political reconstruction, and in conjunction with Soviet military pressure lead to the gradual inclusion of the area in the Soviet sphere of influence. However, there was another, even more political dimension to their decision. At the time the two countries were intimately involved with the ongoing discussions on the organization of Western Europe, especially the six-power discussions on Western Germany and the incipient movement toward European integration. Participation in the Brussels Pact and the Atlantic Pact was seen as part of the same process and as enhancing the influence of the two governments in other arenas as well.

A comparison with the way Denmark and Norway entered NATO reveals important differences. For various reasons the regionalist trend in Norwegian policy came to play only a submerged role during the first two or three postwar years, in which both Danish and Norwegian foreign policy was pointedly universalist, aiming primarily at making the UN system work. In view of both the Danish and Norwegian governments, the best contribution toward this would be a so-called "bridge-building" policy, which in its active aspects involved efforts to further cooperation between the Soviet Union and the Western powers, especially by developing friendly relations with the Soviets as well as with their traditional Western partners, Britain in particular. The passive aspect of this policy was a refusal to become involved in conflicts between the Great Powers. In view of the increasing futility of pursuing the active aspects of bridge-building, only the passive aspects remained, resulting in a policy of neutrality in everything but name. When the failure of bridge-building became too obvious to be ignored and when perceptions of external threat started rising ominously as in the spring of 1948, the regionalist Atlantic trend in Norwegian policy surfaced again and forced the Norwegian government to seek security in an arrangement with the Western powers, while Denmark's first instinct was to seek a nonaligned Nordic defense

[19]U.S., Department of State, *Foreign Relations of the United States 1948*, 3:6.

union. From May 1948 until January 1949 Denmark, Norway, and Sweden negotiated tortuously on the possibilities of concluding a Nordic alliance. It was an attempt, pursued especially by the Danish government, to build bridges between Norway who insisted on certain links between the defense union and the projected Atlantic Pact, and Sweden who saw absolutely nothing of this but demanded that the union be strictly neutral. As Norway could not get her views across, she opted out of the negotiations in order to join the finishing discussions on the Atlantic Pact. Only after that did Denmark decide, reluctantly and *faute de mieux,* to also join the Atlantic Pact.

Danish and Norwegian motives to join the pact were predominantly military in nature. Because of their geographical position and the unfortunate state of their defenses, which had not yet been rehabilitated after the war, both felt much more exposed in a military sense than the Benelux countries who were shielded by the allied presence in Germany. Their threat perceptions were probably also more alarmist than the cool-headed notions that characterized the participants in the Washington talks. Therefore, what they were seeking was primarily a credible military guarantee that Soviet aggression would be met with adequate Western power, especially American. Expectations of military assistance continued to play an important role in the decisions of the two governments, but *political* considerations only played a positive role for the Norwegian government, which saw membership as a means of increasing Norway's international status. The Danish government scarcely saw any such benefits, nor did ideological motivations such as anticommunism contribute significantly to the decisions of the two Nordic governments.

Despite sharing a common background in a tradition of neutrality and its failure, there were important differences in the way the four countries entered NATO. For the Netherlands and Belgium, membership in the alliance represented a continuity of their wartime and postwar policies, while for Norway, and especially for Denmark, alignment represented a discontinuity primarily motivated by acute military insecurity.

ALLIANCE BEHAVIOR: GENERAL ASPECTS

In an article in which he discusses the influence capabilities of small powers in a bilateral alliance, Robert Keohane distinguishes between three general postures from which the small ally can choose and which might be useful in describing the overall roles of smaller powers in a multilateral alliance.[20] First, the small state can play the role of the *loyal*

---

[20]Robert O. Keohane, "The Big Influence of Small Allies," *Foreign Policy* 2 (1971): 161–82.

ally by generally following and supporting the leader of the alliance and trying to mute any differences that may develop. Second, is the role of the *super loyal ally*, the ally who is "more holy than the pope." A typical example is the anticommunism of certain U.S. allies in the Far East. And the third role is that of the *moderately independent ally,* which formulates its policy primarily on its own terms and for which alliance loyalty is only one of several policy determinants. The qualifying term "moderately" should be emphasized, as there are probably limits to how independently the small ally can act before it is "written off" and starts losing the benefits of the alliance relationship. In this and the following section various general and specific aspects of the alliance policies of the four countries will be analyzed with a view toward defining their role within the alliance.

There is no doubt that since 1949 NATO membership has played a dominant role in the formulation of the four countries' foreign policies, despite their somewhat different roads into NATO and their varying enthusiasm about joining the alliance. It is probably also correct to assume that NATO looms larger on their foreign policy horizon than on the horizons of larger members of the alliance. For instance, in the Danish foreign policy "doctrine" membership in NATO (or the Atlantic dimension) traditionally has been conceived as the most important of four "pillars," the others being Nordic cooperation, European cooperation, and UN membership. Any examination of the foreign policy doctrines of the other three countries undoubtedly would reveal similar structures and a similar priority to the NATO relationship. As previously mentioned, this may be changing now to some extent, at least as far as the three European Community members are concerned. First, the threat to the Western democracies is viewed increasingly as economic as well as military. Second, the European Community and the EPC are taking on political functions that at least potentially threaten political cooperation in NATO.

Contradictions between an Atlantic and a European orientation have constituted a central problem for the Benelux countries during the whole lifetime of NATO. Their traditional response to it, especially evident in Dutch policy, has been to work for increasing compatibility between the two by having the United States and Britain participate as much as possible in European affairs. When incompatibility has been unavoidable, the Atlantic orientation usually has been given top priority. For instance, the Netherlands were initially rather hesitant about the EDC proposal of the early 1950s. They were relieved when it was defeated in the French National Assembly and subsequently replaced by the less exclusively Continental WEU arrangements, in which Britain participated. From the late 1950s the Netherlands and Belgium became firm proponents of Britain's membership in the Common Market, at least partially to relieve the increasing contradictions between European and Atlantic cooperation after the rise of de Gaulle. In the beginning of the 1960s both the Dutch and the Belgians were firmly opposed to those aspects of the Fouchet Plan for increased foreign policy cooperation in Europe, which they saw as a French attempt to organize Europe politically against the United States.

Only after France had accepted British membership in the European Community in 1969 was it again possible to discuss political cooperation in Europe, which resulted in the institutionalization of the EPC in 1971–72. Until recently EPC discussions have concentrated mostly on issues that are not central to NATO consultations, such as the coordination of European policies toward the European Conference on Security and Cooperation, in which the United States took only a moderate interest. Therefore, participation in the EPC has not been a major problem for the smaller member states who value both the limited influence it gives them and the information they derive from it. Nevertheless, with the globalization of political issues and the resulting trend toward policy rifts between Europe and the United States as recently witnessed in connection with the Iran and Afghanistan crises, the smaller countries are increasingly likely to find themselves in a loyalty conflict between Europe and the United States.

Participation in the EPC was a *conditio sine non* of Denmark's accession to the EEC in 1973. Even more than the Benelux countries she has tried to stress the "functional division" between European and Atlantic cooperation by insisting that all matters pertaining to defense and national security affairs should be discussed in NATO but not in the EEC-EPC frameworks. To date no serious challenge to this policy has arisen, but as for the Benelux countries the problem of balancing European and Atlantic commitment may become less amenable to easy solutions in the future.

Norway, who remained outside the EEC-EPC, is not placed in a similar dilemma and has, if anything, reacted to this situation by cementing its links with the United States and Canada.

In all four countries support for NATO membership has been firm both at the level of public opinion and at the parliamentary level. In all four membership is opposed by the parties to the left of the dominant Social Democratic parties, this opposition has had no significant parliamentary strength. A more important element is the fact that there has been or still is scepticism toward the alliance based on neutralist premises in parts of the Belgian, Dutch, and Danish Social Democratic parties, but only to a very limited degree in the Norwegian Labor party. The most conspicuous exponent of this trend is the Dutch Labor party that came to power in 1973 under the leadership of Joop den Uyl on a program that the Netherlands should consider leaving NATO if the alliance did not try to achieve security and détente in Europe. Furthermore, the Netherlands demanded a denuclearization of Dutch territory and ultimately of Europe and a reduction in defense expenditures. In recent years the Dutch Labor party has expressed itself quite firmly on the question of the neutron bomb and TNF modernization in Europe. However, as the actual policy of the den Uyl cabinet (1973–77) and Foreign Minister Max van der Stoel showed, critical attitudes are only to a moderate degree converted into oppositional policies in the alliance, let alone concrete considerations of actually leaving the alliance.[21]

The salient fact as Danish Social Democrats critical of NATO usually argue, is that at the present there is no viable alternative to NATO. This attitude is also reflected in the small but influential Danish Radical party, which perhaps more than any other non-Socialist party within the NATO alliance embodies traditional neutrality doctrines. A Danish government study in the early 1970s took up this question and concluded that the only alternative to NATO membership that Denmark freely could choose was that of neutrality and then went on to present so many arguments against that course that the status quo became a foregone conclusion.[22]

Status quo thinking also characterizes the views of the four countries on the present structure of the alliance, especially the balance between the United States and Europe. They were all unanimous in rejecting de Gaulle's bid in 1966 to radically change the alliance. In the 1970s they all have participated in the work of the Eurogroup in NATO, of which the Netherlands is an especially active member, but have no desire to develop the group into an autonomous entity in the alliance.[23] Their general support for U.S. leadership in the alliance implies, as Alfred van Staaden has made clear in the case of the Netherlands, is that the small powers do not try to act as balancers or mediators in the alliance. Whatever influence they may have has been used to bolster the status quo of American predominance.[24]

In certain respects support for NATO is today firmer and criticisms weaker in the four countries than a decade ago. The end of the American involvement in Vietnam and the fall of the Greek and Portuguese dictatorships removed severe strains in the alliance loyalty, especially of the Nordic countries and the Netherlands. A still more important change was the redefinition or broadening of NATO's official role that took place in the late 1960s and which meant that NATO was coupled onto the general search for détente in Europe. When NATO was founded its sole function was seen as that of political and military deterrence. Since this was what the four countries were seeking at the time, they subscribed wholeheartedly to this purpose even though the Nordic countries soon became uneasy at

---

[21]Jerome L. Heldring, "Rhetoric and Reality in Dutch Foreign Policy," *The World Today* 34 (October 1978): pp. 409–16.

[22]Denmark, *Problemer Omkring Dansk Sikkerhedspolitik* (Copenhagen, 1970). This document usually is called the Seidenfaden report.

[23]North Atlantic Treaty Organization, "The Eurogroup," in *The Atlantic Community Quarterly* 14 (1976–77): 76–88.

[24]Staaden, "The Role of the Netherlands in the Atlantic Alliance," p. 147.

some aspects of NATO's "policy of strength" vis-à-vis the Soviet Union in the 1950s.

In the 1960s when East-West tensions began to abate, deterrence was increasingly believed to be an inadequate foundation of NATO. Belgium and Denmark became the leading exponents within the alliance of the view that NATO had to rejuvenate itself by including détente as one of its main objectives besides continued deterrence, the necessity of which no one disputed. As mentioned, the two countries, which were joined by the Netherlands in 1967 were members of the Group of Nine in the mid-1960s. As early as 1965–66 Denmark came out as a supporter of the idea of a European security conference, provided it was duly prepared and provided the United States and Canada participated in the conference.

Denmark also was actively involved when the question arose in 1966–67 on how to define or redefine NATO's role in the wake of de Gaulle's challenge to the organization and in view of the fact that even the United States and the Federal Republic were cautiously starting to evolve policies of détente toward the East. Norway played an active role in these alliance discussions, but the main effort probably was made by Belgium, whose foreign minister, Pierre Harmel, became chairman of the NATO committee set up to discuss the question. The Harmel committee's report on "The Future Tasks of the Alliance" (December 1967) concluded that:

> [T]he Atlantic Alliance has two main functions. Its first function is to maintain adequate military and political solidarity to deter aggression and other forms of pressure and to defend the territory of member countries if aggression sould occur . . . its second function [is] to pursue the search for progress towards a more stable relationship in which the underlying political issues can be solved. Military security and a policy of détente are not contradictory but complementary.[25]

This formula, based on a joint Danish-Norwegian draft, went a long way toward neutralizing growing criticisms of NATO as an impediment to détente and so contributed to the reaffirmation of alliance bonds that took place in at least three of the countries in 1968. The Danish case is perhaps especially illustrative in this respect.

The malaise of the mid-1960s, resulting from among other things a perceived tension between the official government policy of détente and the traditional NATO doctrine, was perhaps more pronounced in Denmark than in other NATO countries. While there was never any real probability that Denmark would choose to leave NATO after the lapse of its initial twenty-year duration in 1969, the "1969 problem" was widely discussed with the press and among the political parties, especially the Radical party which was eager not to close the option. One of the

---

[25]North Atlantic Treaty Organization, *NATO Facts and Figures* (Brussels: NATO Information Service, 1969), pp. 333–34.

possibilities of the situation was that membership would be reconfirmed but only on a conditional basis depending upon developments in NATO and internationally, and that in this way the membership problem would become a permanent political issue. However, nothing like that happened. In early 1968 parliamentary elections led to the rather surprising formation of a non-Socialist coalition government consisting of the skeptical Radicals and two staunchly pro-NATO parties, the Conservatives and the Liberals, which in its government declaration confirmed that Denmark would stay in NATO past the 1969 deadline with explicit reference to the recently adopted Harmel Report. Without the report it is difficult to see how the decision to stay, which was a sine qua non of government formation for the two NATO parties, could have been made without a protracted and agonizing public debate.

The general aspects of alliance policy that have been discussed so far are not necessarily specifically small-power policies. For instance, the smaller members of the alliance have no monopoly on détente, and in many respects their general NATO policies have many similarities with those of Canada and more recently the German Federal Republic. It also may be noted that among the four the Dutch were relatively latecomers to détente. However, there are at least two traits that may be called typical small-power characteristics. One is the moralistic tenor of their foreign policy. The smaller countries may be short on traditional material power elements but not necessarily on moral values; in fact, most people in these countries seem convinced that they have more than others and that having succeeded in creating "the good society" this gives them not only the right but also the duty to try and expand the basic values of their society abroad.[26]

The propagation of these values has created problems vis-à-vis the alliance. First, the propagation of democratic values led in the late sixties and early seventies to sharp criticisms of the regimes in Athens and Lisbon as well as of what was perceived as Washington's leniency toward the two regimes. Even though the campaign against Greece was primarily conducted in other forums than NATO, it led to the temporary exclusion of Greece from the Council of Europe; for instance, the nature of the two regimes undoubtedly affected public support for NATO in a negative sense.

Another political value that has created problems vis-à-vis alliance partners is anticolonialism. French and Portuguese colonial policies have been widely criticized in the four countries and very often linked to their status as NATO members. The greatest challenge to alliance loyalty, however, arose from the U.S. role in Vietnam, which created a host of

---

[26]These remarks apply primarily to the Netherlands and the Nordic countries. The Belgian policy tends to be more pragmatic and compromising than the Dutch. See Deboutte and Staaden, "High Politics in the Low Countries: A Study of Foreign Policy-making in Belgium and the Netherlands," pp. 56–57.

troubles for pro-NATO politicians in the four countries. By and large, they refrained from criticizing the U.S. policy too openly but at the cost of domestic support. Still another typical small-power trait is their interest in furthering political consultation within the alliance. Consultation can be used to solve two problems inherent in smallness: 1) the difficulty in acquiring relevant foreign policy information through own efforts; and 2) of finding a forum for influencing the policies of larger powers. For these reasons small countries often prefer to work in multilateral settings like the UN, the EEC, or NATO rather than in bilateral relationships. In NATO the smaller countries always have been highly supportive of efforts to enhance the consultative mechanisms of the alliance, provided that consultation is based on equality. In the 1950s they supported the efforts of the "Three Wise Men" to increase alliance consultation, while they were strongly critical of de Gaulle's efforts in 1958 to create a great power directorate in NATO. An illustrative case was the original Dutch opposition to McNamara's 1965 proposal to establish a five-power group in NATO to discuss nuclear consultation within the organization. It was instrumental in creating the present consultation mechanism in which all member states who wish to can participate.[27]

The smaller countries, as a general rule, value highly the benefits of information and influence that the present consultative procedures in NATO give them. There are some snags, however. Influence can go both ways, and consultation can be used in efforts to line up the smaller countries on questions where they might have preferred to remain sitting on the fence. In view of the limited, local, or regional perspectives of the smaller countries, this problem especially arises in connection with questions outside the NATO area, such as Afghanistan. Efforts by the larger members to extend the geographical scope of NATO are likely to be viewed with some concern by the smaller members as soon as the process extends beyond the mere sharing of information.

ALLIANCE BEHAVIOR: SPECIFIC ASPECTS

The single most divisive issue within the alliance during its lifetime undoubtedly has been the role of nuclear weapons. The credibility of the American deterrent has been at the heart of the French-American dispute and has been central in U.S.-German relations. Although nuclear strategy also has been a central issue in the alliance policy of the smaller countries (if for no other reason than they have been forced to take stands in the discussions between the larger powers), their perspectives have been

---

[27]See Robert W. Russell, "The Atlantic Alliance in Dutch Foreign Policy," in J. H. Leurdijk, ed., *The Foreign Policy of the Netherlands*, p. 174.

rather different from those of the larger powers. First, the smaller countries basically have accepted that the NATO strategy is based upon nuclear deterrence, and, with the possible exception of the Netherlands, they have shown no greater enthusiasm than the larger European countries for strategies that would make the alliance less dependent upon nuclear weapons. Second, in contrast to at least some of the larger members they have never expressed doubts as to the credibility and availability of the American guarantee. Third, and as a consequence of this, they have been quite content to leave nuclear deterrence exclusively under U.S. auspices and have been skeptical, if not outright hostile, toward efforts to broaden nuclear control.

A pertinent example of this attitude is their policy toward the MLF-proposal in the mid-1960s, which was designed to still the nuclear anxieties of the Federal Republic. Norway, Denmark, and Belgium all refused to participate in talks over the proposal, while the Dutch were slightly more positive but only out of alliance loyalty than out of any conviction of the necessity or even usefulness of the project. All four countries heaved a sigh of relief when the MLF scheme was abandoned and replaced by a consultative scheme, especially as they succeeded in giving the smaller countries a satisfactory representation in such consultative organs as the Nuclear Defense Affair Committee (NDAC) and the Nuclear Planning Group (NPG). From their viewpoint, the problem of nuclear sharing received the best possible solution, one that has been highly valued ever since.

This does not mean, however, that nuclear questions have ceased to be problematical, domestically as well as in relation to the alliance. As the recent discussion over the TNF modernization reveals, the people in all four countries are highly sensitive to anything nuclear, a sensitivity that is shared by parts of the political elite extending into the Social Democratic parties.

Furthermore, on the nuclear question one can speak about a limited independence on the part of the two Nordic members in so far as they always have refused to have nuclear weapons stationed on their territories, whether tactical or strategic. This policy nominally applies only to "present" circumstances, but in reality it has become a fixed dogma in both countries and was laid down as early as 1957 before the start of the antinuclear movement in Europe. The reasons for this nuclear restriction should be viewed in the specific circumstances of the two countries at the time as well as in conjunction with another voluntary, self-imposed restriction; namely, the refusal to accept foreign bases on their territories in peacetime. In the case of Norway this goes back to 1949, while the Danish policy, which does not apply to Greenland, was laid down in 1953. Norway and Denmark also have imposed restrictions on the movement of allied units in especially sensitive areas—Finmark and Bornholm.

If neither Belgium nor the Netherlands have formulated similar restrictions, a large part of the explanation may lie in the different strategic positions of the two pairs of countries. The Benelux countries lie sheltered behind Federal Germany, both geographically and politically, and the Soviets never have been particularly interested in or sensitive to the way they have formulated their security policies. On the other hand, Denmark and Norway have highly exposed flank positions, and they both face overwhelming local Soviet military superiority against which no conceivable effort of their own can protect. Additionally, the Soviets are obviously sensitive to the formulation of their policies.

In this situation the Norwegian and Danish overall security policy response has been a posture that combines military deterrence with a political strategy of minimal provocation and even reassurance vis-à-vis the Soviet Union. The basic aim is to minimize regional tension in order to retain the Nordic area as the traditionally quiet corner of Europe. On the whole these policies have been quite successful. The Soviet Union appears reasonably assured of the peacefulness of Norwegian and Danish policy, and their NATO allies gradually have come to accept them as relevant strategies. They are sometimes seen as constituent elements of the so-called Nordic balance, which on the Eastern side is believed to be reciprocated by a specially lenient policy toward Finland. They represent national strategies on the part of the two countries aiming at maximizing national rather than regional security.

The Nordic balance presently seems to have two prescriptive functions. One is that the security policies of the Nordic countries of NATO should take into consideration the interests of the other Nordic countries; the other is that nothing should be done to alter its basic configuration. In this way the concept becomes and is used as an argument for the status quo, including Danish and Norwegian membership in NATO.

The base and nuclear policies of Denmark and Norway frequently have been seen as representative aspects of a "minimum" alliance participation on their part. However, in certain respects this characterization seems unfair. First, it should be stressed that these restrictions are self-imposed and conditioned upon the prevalence of low tension; they can therefore be lifted unilaterally if the two governments deem it necessary. Second, what were undoubtedly significant restrictions in the 1950s are hardly so today. There is no pressure from the alliance to allow the stockpiling of nuclear weapons on Danish or Norwegian soil, and in any event they could be introduced rapidly in a crisis situation. The base restriction may be more politically salient today in view of the very short warning time in modern warfare. On the other hand, during these years the two governments continued to negotiate arrangements such as prestocking of heavy material and earmarking of specific allied reinforcements that went a long way in alleviating these problems.

Forthcoming reinforcement arrangements will make the defense efforts of the Northern flank countries even more dependent on and interwoven with the overall alliance defense effort and reduce the relative defense autonomy that always has been characteristic of NATO's northern region. In the future Norway and Denmark will be more closely integrated in the common alliance defense, not as intimately as Belgium and the Netherlands but more so than recently has been the case.

The charge of minimum participation is more relevant in connection with the defense efforts of the four countries. In an intriguing article, Mancur Olson and Richard Zeckhauser have linked the distribution of defense efforts in an alliance to the theory of collective goods. They argue that the benefits of any action taken by a nation to provide a common good to others does not necessarily mean they have the incentive to provide optimal amounts of such goods. There especially will be a tendency for the larger members, who supposedly place a higher absolute value on the public good, to bear a disproportionate share of the burden, while the smaller nations lack the incentives to shoulder "their share" of the burdens of alliance defense.[28] As shown in Table 2 this theory seems to contain plausibility. During the entire lifetime of NATO, the smaller countries typically have allocated lower percentages of their GDP to defense than the larger European members or Sweden, which at least for the Nordic members is the most natural country of comparison among the European neutrals. The table also shows noteworthy differences within the group that supply further confirmation to the argument presented by Olson and Zeckhauser. Until recently the Dutch defense effort has been slightly higher than that of Belgium and the Nordic member states, which may have resulted from her larger economic resources. However, during the 1970s the Dutch defense effort has dropped relative to Belgium's so that the two countries now contribute almost equal percentages to defense. Among the Nordic countries Norway always has contributed more in relative terms than Denmark, a fact that cannot be explained by the Olson-Zeckhauser model but rather deals with domestic parliamentary factors and the prevailing public attitudes toward defense. A more complete picture emerges when comparing absolute defense expenditures and expenditures per head (See Table 3), which shows that in absolute terms the Dutch contribution to NATO is nearly 50 percent higher than Belgium's and more than three times that of Norway and Denmark. It also reveals that Belgium, the Netherlands, and Norway spend almost exactly the same amount per head, while Denmark spends about 15 to 20 percent less.

---

[28]Mancur Olson, Jr., and Richard Zeckhauser, "An Economic Theory of Alliances," *The Review of Economics and Statistics* 47 (1966): 266–79.

**Table 2. Defense Expenditures of Certain European Countries
1954–79 as Percentage of GDP (Gross Domestic Product)**

	1958	1964	1968	1974	1977
Belgium	3.7	3.4	3.1	2.8	3.1
Denmark	2.9	2.8	2.8	2.4	2.4
Netherlands	4.7	4.3	3.7	3.3	3.5
Norway	3.5	3.4	3.6	3.1	3.1
Federal Republic of Germany	3.0	4.6	3.6	3.6	3.4
France	6.8	5.3	4.8	3.7	3.9
United Kingdom	7.0	6.0	5.4	5.1	4.9
Sweden	4.7	4.1	3.7	3.7	3.4
Switzerland	3.2	2.8	2.4	2.1	2.1
Austria	1.5	1.5	1.2	1.0	1.1

SOURCE: World Armaments and Disarmament. SIPRI Yearbook 1979. (SIPRI, 1979).
Tables 1A.4 and 1A.10.

Table 3. Defense Expenditures of Certain European Countries

	$ mill.	$ per head	% gvt. spend.	% of GNP
Belgium	3,143	315	9.2	3.5
Denmark	1,317	258	7.2	2.4
Netherlands	4,323	309	9.6	3.3
Norway	1,254	308	9.1	3.2
Federal Republic of Germany	21,366	347	22.9	3.4
France	15,225	285	17.0	3.3
United Kingdom	14,090	252	10.5	4.7
Sweden	2,946	355	8.5	3.4
Switzerland	1,552	275	18.1	1.9
Austria	718	95	3.9	1.2

SOURCE: The Military Balance 1979–1980. (IISS, 1979).

At the present time the main issue in defense contributions is the NATO decision confirmed at the Washington summit of May 1978 to increase defense budgets with 3 percent yearly in real terms over a given period. Both Norway and the Netherlands have taken steps to comply with the decision, while Belgium and Denmark have not. On this account Denmark, and to a lesser degree Belgium, was criticized sharply at the recent meeting of NATO defense ministers in Brussels in May 1980.[29]

In the case of Denmark the question is presently at the heart of ongoing discussions on the preparation of new defense legislation. The NATO recommendation of a 3-percent yearly increase is supported by the non-Socialist opposition parties (except the Radicals), some of whom argue for even higher increases but are up against the governing Social Democratic party and the Radicals who oppose any expansion of the defense budget at a time when cuts are being made in many other sensitive parts of the government budget such as social welfare and education. In this situation the government attempted to open parliamentary negotiations with a proposed "zero solution," which failed to rally sufficient support among the other parties. In view of the parliamentary necessity of reaching a compromise with the prodefense non-Socialist parties, the end result might be a solution that entails some increase in real terms of the Danish defense budget but probably not enough to stave off criticism from NATO and the leading alliance partners.

CONCLUSIONS: THE FOUR AS LOYAL ALLIES?

In summary, there are three possible roles for the small state in an alliance—loyalty, super loyalty, and moderate independence. None of the four have been super loyal toward NATO; it is probably very difficult for democratic states with attentive public opinions to follow a course of super loyalty. However, what about the other patterns? In an article on the role of the Netherlands in the Atlantic Alliance, van Staaden describes the faithful ally by the following behavioral patterns:

a) giving unconditional or almost unconditional diplomatic support to any actions undertaken throughout the world by the leader of the alliance;
b) a marked identification with aims and interests of the alliance as a whole;
c) the desire to give a good example to the other allies;

---

[29]*Politiken,* 14 May 1980.

d) making efforts to reinforce the military integration and the political cooperation of the alliance; and
e) conscientiously keeping any promises it has made.[30]

Van Staaden concluded that to a great extent the Dutch policy has conformed to this ideal type. The author argues that despite the lower alliance profile of Belgium and her more moderate defense efforts her policy can be described as that of a loyal and faithful ally. But what about the Nordic countries that certainly have taken special positions on a number of occasions? Even on this point it can be argued that moderate independence may be too strong of a term to describe their NATO policies. For example, there has never been any doubt regarding their support for the central aspects of the Atlantic Alliance, including the traditional American-European balance. Second, these deviations from the common NATO line are rather marginal and of decreasing importance as well as fully arguable from an alliance viewpoint. Their policies therefore also appear to fall within the boundaries of the category of the loyal ally.

This evidence then apparently contradicts the conclusion of Nils Ørvik.[31] Ørvik's argument was that because of the imbalance in the contributions of the larger and the smaller members and because the original contribution, mainly territory, of the smaller states was losing in importance, it was difficult to point to any specific area where the needs of the larger powers of NATO can be met more effectively today by a small ally than by a small neutral state. This argument probably has never been correct in a military sense, and it ignores the potential political importance of the smaller members. At times they may slow down the speed of the boat, but they have never rocked it the way that France has. In an alliance where any disagreement has a tendency to be viewed as a symptom of crisis or malaise, it is surely important to have at least some members who do not question its central tenets and features.

---

[30]Staaden, "The Role of the Netherlands in the Atlantic Alliance," pp. 152–53.
[31]See fn. 1.

NATO IN THE WORLD

The Warsaw Pact, USSR, and NATO: Perceptions from the East

ROBERT W. CLAWSON AND GLEE E. WILSON

This study surveys the record of Soviet and other Warsaw Pact members' image of the Atlantic Alliance as a military and political coalition. Against the background of the development of both alliance systems, it is concerned primarily with tracing the complex evolution of Soviet bloc perceptual reactions to NATO and its policies.[1]

A discussion of Warsaw Pact images of NATO based mainly on published Soviet and East European sources perforce runs substantial risks and raises important questions. For instance, is the often protested threat from the West really perceived as such, or is it merely an excuse for taking measures that would be unpopular at home or in the Third World if not tied to some external imperialist threat? Are the Soviets actually convinced that NATO always has been an aggressive alliance? Or do they use threat imagery as a convenient bogey to manipulate their Soviet and East European populations and to mislead Western military policy-makers? Are their histrionic protestations simply smoke screens for domestic and Third World consumption?

These questions are sufficiently complex to warrant careful answers. Clearly, part of the Soviet and East European NATO imagery is propaganda of a most primitive nature.[2] Campaigns such as the "peace

---

[1]For a detailed theoretical discussion of the role of perception in relations between nations, see Robert Jarvis, *Perceptions and Misperceptions in International Politics* (Princeton, NJ: Princeton University Press, 1976), pp. 409–10. Significant literature on Soviet perception is beginning to emerge; for example, see Morton Schwartz, *Soviet Perceptions of the United States* (Berkeley, CA: University of California Press, 1978); Nikolai V. Sivachev and Nikolai N. Yakovlev, *Russia and the United States: U.S.-Soviet Relations from the Soviet Point of View* (Chicago, IL: University of Chicago Press, 1979); U.S., Senate, Committee on Foreign Relations, *Perceptions: Relations Between the United States and the Soviet Union* (Washington, DC: Government Printing Office, 1978). See also Coit Dennis Blacker, "The Soviet Perception of European Security," in Derek Leebaert, *European Security: Prospects for the 1980s* (Lexington, MA: Lexington Books, 1979), pp. 137–61.

[2]Typical of those Soviet organs that specialize in semihysterical anti-NATO propaganda are the (English versions) *New Times* and *Moscow News*. The Novosti Press Agency

109

movement" of the early 1950s, the antineutron bomb exercise of the late
1970s, and many others are easily identifiable illustrations of Soviet
penchant for crude but energetic hyperbole designed to attain specific
political and military objectives and echoed faithfully by most of the
fraternal allies. Even with this category of publicists, however, the often
hysterical tone and obvious fabrication does not necessarily mean that the
Soviets see no threat. On the contrary, they would be unlikely to
undertake such large-scale efforts if no real fear existed. However, it may
be a fear whose exact nature and origin are obscured to the outsider. To
provide effective insights, the analyst must discover the source of that
anxiety. In aid of that purpose, Soviet bloc publicists are often remarkably
indirect and unhelpful; they rarely say precisely what they mean.

It is possible to identify a second category of material from which to
glean images of NATO. The political leaderships of the USSR and other
bloc states frequently address the topic.[3] While it seems clear that
leadership statements have sometimes been used for strategic military and
political deception, those instances generally become detectable with the
passage of time. Again, it is the analyst's task to determine the target and
desired effect. It also is likely that a position taken by a political leader in
public is one that he will avoid with some reluctance as opposed to the
propagandist who may express an opinion and suddenly adopt the exact
opposite. Thus, if the general secretary of the Communist party of the
Soviet Union indicates a particular public position on NATO, it is
relatively safe to regard it as an important reflection of Soviet policy
although not necessarily to be taken at face value. For the concerned
scholar attempting to analyze President Jimmy Carter's image of the
Soviet threat after the occupation of Afghanistan, it is perhaps not so
important to establish whether or not the president actually believes all
that he publicly expresses. It is the speech itself as well as the programs
that inevitably flow from it that largely determines policy. Much the same
theory appears to be true in the Soviet bloc.

A third source of perceptual images comes from the Soviet and
Warsaw Pact military leadership and press.[4] Soviet bloc analysts of

---

Publishing House issues numerous small propaganda pamphlets for widespread international
distribution. The nations of Eastern Europe also publish multilanguage sources, the most
informative of which are the Romanian weekly newspaper *Lumea* (English version) and the
monthly *Romanian News.*

[3]The daily newspapers *Pravda* and *Izvestia* regularly carry leadership statements.
TASS prepares special releases for added emphasis or specific targets. Also speeches and
articles by the Soviet leadership are printed in specialized newspapers and journals,
depending on where they were given originally or what topic is being addressed. Therefore,
an important speech by Brezhnev, touching on international affairs, may be printed in the
Soviet trade union newspaper *Trud* [Labor] because it was given to a trade union meeting
somewhere.

[4]Basic public policy documents relevant to Soviet defense and the Warsaw Pact are
published regularly in such sources as *Pravda* and *Izvestia* as well as in the ministry of
defense daily newspaper *Krasnaya zvezda* [Red star]. Increasingly valuable for the analyst

military affairs mainly consider developments, especially in weapons and strategy, based on a "worst case" mode. Common in the West, such policy analysis is based on the principle that a defense establishment should be prepared to stand up against the worst that could possibly happen: that all the opposition's weapons will work as they were designed; that their communications will serve them optimally; and that their troops fight up to their potential. It is also a way of thinking that apparently includes the assumption that the potential enemy will, at some indeterminable time, choose to fight it out. Considering the nature of their system, the public Soviet bloc military writer's image of NATO is probably an accurate reflection of at least a significant portion of that group's reasoning.

A fourth segment, comprised of more serious academic and journalistic specialists in international affairs, devotes an extraordinary amount of time and print to a continual reexamination of the political and military complexion of the Atlantic Alliance.[5] Apparently, they feel compelled to start an article or book with a ritualistic assumption that NATO, like the European Economic Community (EEC), is about to come unstuck due to internal contradictions. However, once this obligation has been fulfilled, they often address themselves to issues that can reveal a great deal about the basic assumptions of serious analysts. The academic specialists, especially historians within these ranks, seem to have increasingly free access both to selected archives and the works of Western specialists. They generally present regime approved versions of each historical event or period, but presently there appears to be room for personal or professional interpretation of the data.

Although it is a fact that the other individual members of the Warsaw Pact have been far from puppets in the hands of Soviet masters, especially on matters related to role and mission, this study will make specific and detailed reference, in addition to the USSR, only to Romania. As expected on virtually every significant issue of importance to the focus of a study on "perceptions of NATO," East European and Soviet-published attitudes correspond to each other with no significant variation. The only exception is Romania's constant and largely public mischievousness.

of postwar Soviet military assumptions and the perceptions behind them are: *Voyenno-istoricheskiy zhurnal* [Journal of military history]; and *Kommunist vooruzhennykh sil* [Armed forces Communist].

[5]The foremost journal (English version) in this field is *International Affairs* published by the All-Union *Znaniye* [Knowledge] Society. Newspapers such as *Literaturnaya gazeta* [Literary newspaper] also may carry articles by specialists as well as providing additional vehicles for leadership statements. For analyses of the role played by the specialists, see William Zimmerman, *Soviet Perspectives on International Relations 1956–1967* (New York: Columbia University Press, 1969); and W. W. Kulski, *The Soviet Union in World Affairs: A Documented Analysis 1964–1972* (Syracuse: Syracuse University Press, 1973). See also Richard B. Remmek, *Soviet Scholars and Soviet Foreign Policy* (Durham, NC: Carolina Academic Press, 1975).

The principal portion of this research focuses on four periods: first, from 1945 through the formation of NATO, the accession of West Germany, and the creation of the Warsaw Pact; second, from the Warsaw Pact to the invasion of Czechoslovakia; third, from the Czech invasion to the Helsinki Conference of 1975; and fourth, from the Helsinki Accords to the Soviet invasion of Afghanistan.

FROM 1945 TO THE FORMATION OF THE
WARSAW PACT IN 1955

The Soviet perception of a Western threat in 1945 had been conditioned by a persistent distrust of the United States and the West dating back to the allied intervention during the earliest days of Lenin's Soviet state, and only modestly reduced by the uneasy wartime alliance.[6] Citing immediate security needs at the time, the USSR took a number of steps designed essentially to extend its frontiers in Europe and thereby reinforced a similarly persistent Western fear of Soviet expansionism in the Tsarist tradition. The American reaction appeared to confirm the basis of Stalin's mistrust.[7]

Although the U.S. recollects its postwar military withdrawal from Europe as "immediate," the Soviets remember that phenomenon as "prolonged." At the same time the sudden cancellation of U.S. lend-lease

---

[6]For Stalin's view of the allied intervention many years later, see M. Gorky et al., *The History of the Civil War in the USSR* (New York: International Publishers, 1936). Present-day commentary has changed very little in tone. See S. S. Lototskiy et al., *Armiya Sovetskaya [The Soviet Army]*, English version (Moscow: Progress Publishers, 1971), pp. 46–52, 74–80. See also A. A. Grechko, *Vooruzhyonnye sily Sovetskogo gosudarstvo [The Armed Forces of the Soviet State]*, English version (Moscow: Progress Publishers, 1977), pp. 27–30.

For the period of the wartime alliance, see Vojtech Mastny, *Russia's Road to the Cold War* (New York: Columbia University Press, 1979). Mastny presents a comprehensive view of Soviet fears and ambitions. For additional dimensions of Soviet suspicions and anxieties, see Graham Lyons, ed., *The Russian Version of The Second World War* (Hamden, CT: Archon Books, 1976).

[7]The Western literature on Soviet policy in Eastern Europe and Germany in the days immediately following the expulsion of the Nazis is voluminous. The Soviets did not focus scholarly attention on that period until the latter years of the 1960s, when limited archival material evidently became available to certain specialists. See, for example, A. Beryozkin et al., *Istoriya vneshney politiki SSSR [History of the Foreign Policy of the USSR]*, English version (Moscow: Progress Publishers, 1969), pp. 469–89. See also I. A. Kirilin, ed., *Istoriya mezhdunarodnykh otnosheniy i vneshney politiki SSSR, tom tretiy 1945–1967 gg* [History of the international relations and foreign policy of the USSR, volume 3, 1945–1967] (Moscow: Mezhdunarodnaya otnosheniya, 1967), pp. 6–9. For understandable reasons, little East European material of quality exists on this period.

in April and the termination of deliveries in August 1945 seemed to be additional evidence of increased U.S. hostility. If the Soviets ever had hoped for U.S. aid in their postwar reconstruction, this action, in addition to numerous examples of American and British bad faith concerning the wartime aid program, must have helped convince them of the basic unreliability of the West.[8] The U.S. possession of the atom bomb, along with Truman's apparent willingness to use its existence for political leverage against the USSR in Eastern Europe, undoubtedly also contributed to Stalin's perception of U.S. power as a hostile strategic threat.[9]

The slow Soviet demobilization, the creation of "people's armies" in the Soviet-dominated East European buffer states, the blustering sword-rattling of their strategically inferior armed forces, as well as the sporadic but continued agitation of the Communist parties in France, Italy, and Greece may well have been designed to mask and protect the USSR critically weakened by the war against Nazi Germany.[10] However, if it were all a bluff the U.S. reaction—the Truman Doctrine, the Marshall Plan, and the genesis of NATO—convinced the Soviets of Western hostility and of the need to take additional security measures.[11]

Although the USSR had been able to consolidate its Western line of European defense at a great distance from its borders, including by 1948 the establishment of a people's democracy in Czechoslovakia, it found itself at a disadvantage against what appeared to them to be a rearming Western Europe and an American program to create long-range air forces

---

[8]Soviet postwar attitudes toward lend-lease are featured in such "official" histories as G. A. Deborin, *Vtoraya mirovaya viona* [The second world war] (Moscow: Voennoe izdatelstvo, 1958), esp. pp. 138, 139, 148, 172, 200, 239, 414. See also Institute of Marxism-Leninism's *Istoriya velikoi otechestvennoi voiny Sovetskogo Soyuza 1941–1945*, 5 vols. [History of the great patriotic war 1941–1945] (Moscow: Voennoe izdatelstvo, 1960–63), esp. 2:179–90, 188–90, 363–65. The famous "lost" $6-billion loan application for U.S. postwar reconstruction aid to the USSR perhaps should be added to the list of Soviet-perceived transgressions.

[9]Cf. Gar Alperovitz, *Atomic Diplomacy* (New York: Simon and Schuster, 1965). Although a controversial book, the portrayal of Stalin's attitude toward the atomic bomb and its use apparently is accurate.

[10]For an "approved" Soviet version of their "defensive" and "protective" relationship with the "People's Democracies" in Eastern Europe, see Kirilin, *Istoriya mezhdunarodnykh otnosheniy III*, pp. 10–26. The creation of the "people's armies" is covered country by country in A. V. Antosyak et al., *Zarozhdenie narodnykh armiy stran—uchastnits Varshavskogo dogovora 1941–1949* [The origin of the people's armies of the Warsaw Pact members] (Moscow: Nauka, 1975).

[11]A. Y. Bovin, "Europe's Three Epochs," in G. A. Ponamarov, ed., *Europa na putyakh razryadki [Europe on the Road to Détente]*, English version (Moscow: Progress Publishers, 1978), pp. 14–15. See also Soviet comments on the Truman Doctrine from *Izvestia* (13 March 1947); the initial Moscow statement on the proposed Marshall Plan (29 June 1947); and Andrey Vyshinsky's speech on the Marshall Plan to the UN General Assembly (18 September 1947). Translated and reprinted in Alvin Z. Rubinstein, *The Foreign Policy of the Soviet Union* (New York: Random House, 1960), pp. 230–35.

based in North America and Europe.[12] Caught in an increasingly inferior strategic position, the Soviets responded with a massive agitation and propaganda "peace and disarmament" campaign designed to weaken European resolve sufficiently in order to buy time for the creation of their own nuclear forces and to modernize their conventional military.[13] A principal target of their enormous propaganda effort was the Atlantic Alliance. The Soviets considered NATO the newest form of aggressive capitalism that could only perpetuate itself by embarking on new and ever more threatening imperialist ventures.[14]

The fanatical energy of that essentially defensive campaign as well as other related Soviet foreign policies shocked the Western political leadership into further measures designed to check Soviet foreign policy initiatives. And the war in Korea added impetus. By the mid-1950s the Western response included the development of modernized and massive Anglo-American strategic nuclear air fleets, accompanied by the doctrine of massive retaliation, a rapid expansion of U.S. overseas bases, and the inclusion of a rearmed West Germany in NATO.[15] These vast undertakings were seen as an even greater threat to the very existence of the USSR. The inclusion of West Germany in the NATO system was accepted as evidence of U.S. willingness to encourage virulent anti-Soviet forces again to prosper in Western Europe. One element of the Soviet counter reaction was the establishment of the Warsaw Pact in mid-1955.[16]

While a dangerous military threat was attributed to NATO especially following German accession, Soviet political commentators, from the very beginning, predicted the alliance's breakup due to internal contradictions. NATO was originally portrayed as a vehicle to help ensure Anglo-American domination of a reluctant Europe and to strengthen unstable and reactionary governments there; it was a mission that was sure to fail.[17]

---

[12]The giant U.S. six-engined B-36 that flew in 1946 was deployed in the summer of 1948. Truly intercontinental in range, it could deliver atom bombs to any target in the USSR and return. The Soviets at that time had no adequate defense against this growing armada. Christopher Chant et al., *The Encyclopedia of Air Warfare* (New York: Thomas Y. Crowell, 1975), p. 157.

[13]Cf. Marshall D. Shulman, *Stalin's Foreign Policy Reappraised* (New York: Atheneum, 1966), esp. pp. 80–103.

[14]"Memorandum of the Soviet Government on the North Atlantic Treaty," 31 March 1949, printed in *New York Times*, 1 April 1949, and reprinted in Rubinstein, *Foreign Policy*, pp. 265–69.

[15]Edwin H. Fedder, *NATO: The Dynamics of Alliance in the Postwar World* (New York: Dodd, Mead and Company, 1973), pp. 29–52.

[16]P. I. Efimov et al., *Boevoy soyuz bratskikh armiy* [The fighting alliance of fraternal armies] (Moscow: Voennoe izdatelstvo, 1974), pp. 12–15. See also A. M. Aleksandrov, ed., *Nash soyuz boevoy* [Our fighting alliance] (Moscow: Voennoe izdatelstvo, 1975), pp. 4–5.

[17]"Memorandum of the Soviet Government. . . ." See also Shulman, *Stalin's Foreign Policy*, pp. 63–64, 94–95.

However, their analyses of the military threat was usually more cautious and more complex.

FROM THE WARSAW PACT TO THE
INVASION OF CZECHOSLOVAKIA, 1955–68

Rapid German rearmament and the possibility of nuclear weapons in German hands generated a whole spectrum of Soviet reactions from threats of intervention to a concerted effort to detach West Germany from the alliance.[18] Despite a post-Stalin thaw in the Cold War, the major anti-Soviet rebellions in East Berlin, Poland, and Hungary threatened to compromise the Soviets' conventional defense system, while the USSR remained strategically vulnerable to the Anglo-American nuclear air forces.[19] The unrest and uprisings in Eastern Europe were seen to be fed, if not directly instigated, by Western efforts through Radio Free Europe, Radio Liberation, and CIA covert operations.[20] The ferocious Soviet reactions inevitably caused a major increase in Western perception of Soviet threat. The alliance, while implicitly recognizing postrebellion Eastern Europe as a permanent Soviet sphere of influence, pushed rapid West German rearmament as a critical element of an upgraded NATO defense. The Soviets were increasingly galvanized by visions of a possibly nuclear-armed Germany, manipulated by the West and bent inevitably on revenge.[21]

Painful but steady Soviet efforts to modernize their military capabilities resulted in a reduction of the Soviet conventional army. By the early 1960s, however, the program also produced the beginnings of a long-range rocket force, and for the first time seemed to threaten the West's overwhelming strategic superiority.[22]

---

[18]Rubinstein, *Foreign Policy*, pp. 292–93.

[19]Raymond L. Garthoff, *Soviet Strategy in the Nuclear Age* (New York: Frederick A. Praeger, 1962), p. 132.

[20]Harry Rositzke, *The CIA's Secret Operations: Espionage, Counterespionage, and Covert Action* (New York: Thomas Y. Crowell Company, 1977), pp. 156–58.

[21]N. S. Khrushchev, speech at the Twenty-first Congress of the CPSU, 27 January 1959, in Rubinstein, *Foreign Policy*, pp. 308–10. The following quotation illustrates the point: "West Germany is turning into NATO's main atomic and rocket base. In this aggressive bloc, West Germany is already beginning to play a leading role. Apparently some Western politicians think of directing the point of the German menace to the East this time also . . .

"A situation is being created in which German militarism can for a third time drag mankind into a world war . . . now everyone can see that militarism and revanchism in West Germany has reared its head and is threatening peace-loving peoples."

[22]Cf. *The Communist Bloc and the Western Alliance 1961–62* (London: Institute for Strategic Studies, 1962).

Although the Soviets noted that NATO in the early 1960s was plagued by internal political division and flagging resolve—with the French eventually departing from the military framework—the perceptions of serious analysts were of a continually strengthening NATO military capability.[23] The loss of France as viewed by Soviet observers using "worst-case" analysis was seen mainly as a technical absence.[24] Western spending on arms and weapons technology apparently increased at a steady, if not intermittent, pace.

Their own new missile capability, as the Soviets well knew, was technically primitive, unreliable, and unsupported by alternate strategic systems.[25] In the mid-1960s Soviet conventional forces, having been the target of Khrushchev's budgetary axe, made a dramatic and conclusive return to high priority under Kosygin and Brezhnev. However, by Soviet standards the years of neglect had left their ground army undermanned and poorly equipped.[26] The USSR again saw itself slipping into a position of strategic and qualitative inferiority and it once more began to turn to negotiations. Diplomatic and economic initiatives were designed, in part, to buy time until it could assure its ultimate security through the traditional means of military strength.[27]

Politically, the key to the puzzle of Western European intentions continued to elude the Soviets. They first saw the new EEC as the economic wing of NATO built to bind Europe closer to the United States through economic domination; their immediate response was that the EEC was bound to fail due to obvious contradictions.[28] Following French

---

[23]F. Fyodorov, "NATO and the Demand of the Times," *International Affairs,* no. 2 (February 1964): 38–41.

[24]Kirilin, *Istoriya mezhdunarodnykh otnosheniy III,* pp. 401–5. See also Kulski, *Soviet Union in World Affairs,* pp. 95–104. Naturally, the Soviets slowly built a campaign to secure better Franco-Soviet relations. Soviet commentators largely refrained from talking about possible French reentry or collaboration until the early 1970s. See L. Vidyasova, "France in December," *International Affairs,* no. 3 (March 1971): 80–85.

[25]Arnold L. Horelick and Myron Rush, *Strategic Power and Soviet Foreign Policy* (Chicago: University of Chicago Press, 1965–66), esp. pp. 162–207.

[26]Thomas W. Wolfe, "The Warsaw Pact in Evolution," *The World Today* 22, no. 5 (May 1966): 191–98. Soviet appreciation of the changes in U.S. strategic planning toward the "flexible response" idea added to their anxiety. For a detailed analysis of the Soviet interpretation of the changes, see Wolfe, *Soviet Strategy at the Crossroads* (Cambridge, MA: Harvard University Press, 1964), pp. 243–57.

[27]The Soviets under Khrushchev had held out a variety of possibilities for various kinds of détente to the Europeans. How serious they were is very difficult to assess. They would have given a great deal to keep Germany out of the alliance, but they were also prone to combine their offers with the kind of bullying that the West Germans would never accept. Under Khrushchev's successors, Western Europe once again became the target of a wide variety of Soviet diplomatic initiatives. See Rubinstein, *Foreign Policy,* pp. 308–10 for a summary of earlier Soviet offers.

[28]Marshall D. Shulman, "The Communist States and Western Integration," *International Organization* 17 (Summer 1963): 649–62.

withdrawal from NATO, many Soviet political commentators also predicted the imminent political collapse of the alliance. As the American preoccupation with Asia belatedly became noticed by Soviet analysts, the possibility of separating Western Europe from the United States looked increasingly realistic.[29] Thus, a new multipronged Soviet political offensive was launched; disarmament, foreign troop withdrawal, demilitarization, increased trade, and détente were all offered to Western Europe while the United States became increasingly bogged down in Southeast Asia.[30]

Until the founding of the Warsaw Pact, the armies of Eastern Europe were directly dominated by Soviet advisers and instructors. Only after 1955 did the various forces slowly begin to assume national characters. This corresponded in some cases with limited experience in exercising national sovereignty in the areas of foreign and defense policies. However, the only long-lived and public example of this phenomenon has been displayed by Romania.[31]

Romania, behind the buffer of fraternal socialist allies, had no direct fear of West Germany or NATO. Events in Hungary in the autumn of 1956 confirmed to the Romanian leadership the real purpose of the pact and demonstrated a "Khrushchev Doctrine" with respect to deviation and autonomy in the socialist camp.

Gheorghiu-Dej cooperated with the Warsaw Pact in the suppression of the counterrevolution in Hungary in order to maintain control in Romania, stabilize the situation in the former Hungarian possessions in Transylvania, and maneuver for the future. Having proven reliable and helpful in the Hungarian situation, Romania could capitalize on Khrushchev's other problems to promote "patriotic" and "national" socialism at home.[32]

---

[29]V. Khostov, "The USSR and European Security," *International Affairs*, no. 2 (January 1968): 3–7. In the same issue Major General A. Slobodenko saw the principal benefits of French withdrawal going to West Germany. A. Slobodenko, "NATO 'Reorganizes,' " pp. 36–41.

[30]Cf. Karl Birnbaum, "Ways Towards European Security," *Survival* 10 (June 1968): 193–99.

[31]The Romanian position with respect to NATO and the Warsaw Pact in the period between 1955 and the invasion of Czechoslovakia in 1968 should be seen in the context of Romanian national aspirations. Romania has a long history of struggle for survival, territorial integrity, and autonomy. It always has been surrounded by powerful and expansive neighbors and disputes over territory such as Bessarabia, Bucovina, Transylvania, and the Dobruja have continued into the post-World War II era. Romania has developed a tradition of tightrope diplomacy and whenever possible has promoted her internal objectives and territorial claims, often against dismal odds. See, for instance, Stephen Fischer-Galati, *New Rumania: From People's Democracy to Socialist Republic* (Cambridge, MA: MIT Press, 1967); Fischer-Galati, *Twentieth Century Rumania* (New York: Columbia University Press, 1970); and Paul Lendavai, *Eagles and Cobwebs, Nationalism and Communism in the Balkans* (New York: Doubleday and Company, 1969).

[32]Fischer-Galati, *New Rumania*, pp. 52–53, 57.

In 1958 as NATO forces were being strengthened and nuclear weapons deployed in Western Europe, Romania played on emerging Sino-Soviet problems and bargained for the removal of Soviet troops from Romanian territory.[33] Gheorghiu-Dej, taking advantage of the official Moscow line of peaceful coexistence, continued to open contacts with the West, Yugoslavia, and China.[34]

In the early 1960s worsening Soviet relations with China and the crises in Berlin and Cuba also were exploited by Gheorghiu-Dej who remained firmly in control in Romania despite certain misgivings in Moscow. Far from being hostile toward the West, he saw it as a counterforce to Soviet political, military, and economic aims in the region. Economic ties in the 1960s were established with Italy, France, and with both West Germany and the United States.[35]

The Romanian position against all supranational organizations was announced in an April 1964 statement.[36] This could have been perceived as provocative by the USSR, but the attack on all such blocs probably forestalled any overreaction. Typically, Romania did participate in Warsaw Pact maneuvers in 1962, 1963, and 1964. However, in late 1964 the term of military service was unilaterally reduced to sixteen months, apparently without consultation with the Soviets.[37]

Furthermore, to emphasize its unique position, in 1965 Romania declared that it had advanced itself a stage on the road to communism and would in the future be called the Socialist Republic of Romania.[38] Following Gheorghiu-Dej's death in March of 1965, his young successor, Nicolae Ceaușescu, pressed ahead playing on the Soviets' post-Khrushchev uncertainties. He skillfully took advantage of the continuing Sino-Soviet rift to further promote Romanian sovereignty.

In 1966 Ceaușescu reiterated and reemphasized the 1964 declaration by attacking all military blocs, bases, and troops on the territory of other states. He labeled them anachronistic and inconsistent with normal

---

[33] Ibid., p. 70.

[34] Ibid., p. 71.

[35] Mircea Malita, *Romanian Diplomacy* (Bucharest: Meridiane Publishing House, 1970), p. 180. By 1970 Romania maintained relations with 97 states, double the number of ten years before.

[36] In an address entitled "Statement of the Rumanian Workers' Party Concerning the Problems of the International Communist and Working-Class Movement," a revised English translation is found in William Griffith, *Sino-Soviet Relations, 1964–1965* (Cambridge, MA: MIT Press, 1967), pp. 269–96.

[37] A. Ross Johnson, "Soviet-East European Military Relations: An Overview," in Dale R. Herspring and Ivan Volgyes, eds., *Civil and Military Relations in Communist Systems* (Boulder, CO: Westview Press, 1978), p. 249.

[38] In June 1965, Ceaușescu announced the renaming of the Romanian Workers' party to the Romanian Communist party and in the same month changed the name of the country from the Romanian People's Republic to the Socialist Republic of Romania. Fischer-Galati, *Twentieth Century Rumania*, pp. 184–85.

relations among independent and sovereign states.[39] By 1967 he was strong enough to recognize West Germany (the first Warsaw Pact state to do so, after the Soviet Union) and refused to conform to the official bloc line during the Mid-East crises.[40]

When the USSR drew the line on independence in Czechoslovakia during August 1968, Romania responded to the Brezhnev Doctrine by refusing to participate in what Ceaușescu termed a "misuse" of pact forces.[41] The Romanians undoubtedly got some satisfaction when in late August President Lyndon Johnson warned the USSR to stay out of Romania, apparently forcing the Soviets vigorously to deny that they had any untoward intentions in the area.[42]

Warsaw Pact forces intervened in Czechoslovakia in August 1968 under the aegis of the Brezhnev Doctrine, specially created after the fact, to restore Socialist orthodoxy and ensure Soviet control.[43] It was an unusual situation in which the Soviets fabricated a propaganda image— strictly for public consumption—of NATO and its allies that they knew to be completely false; that is, British and German agitation and covert activities were responsible for the situation in Czechoslovakia, hence the pact was forced to intervene to save one of its own.[44]

In 1968, bearing in mind the lessons of the Hungarian revolution, Czech reformers, as well as those promoting less spectacular changes in other East European countries, never really challenged their countries' roles in the Warsaw Pact, even to the extent of the Romanian model. Nevertheless, there is evidence that the Soviet image of NATO during this period was not universally shared even among the militaries of a number of East European states.[45]

---

[39]Fischer-Galati, *New Rumania,* p. 115. Marks the forty-fifth anniversary of the founding of the party.

[40]Fischer-Galati, *Twentieth Century Rumania,* pp. 187, 200.

[41]Ibid., p. 207. See also especially the text of Ceaușescu's speeches such as 29 June 1968 and the 120th anniversary of the 1848 revolution, on 14 August to the 1968 graduating class of the military academy and the special session of the Grand National Assembly, on 22 August in N. Ceaușescu, *Romanian Achievements and Prospects, July 1965–February 1969,* selected texts (Bucharest: Meridiane Publishing House, 1969).

[42]*New York Times,* 2 September 1968.

[43]Robin Alison Remington, *The Warsaw Pact: Case Studies in Conflict Resolution* (Cambridge, MA: MIT Press, 1971), pp. 94–112.

[44]For a typical earlier and awkward example of this very extensive ad hoc campaign, see the 15 August 1968 issue of *Izvestia.* Better constructed versions, broadened to include the Bonn-NATO linkage, were published later. See, for instance, *Pravda,* 17, 20 September 1968; and *Izvestia,* 30 November 1968. A detailed explanation of the extent of the Soviet fabrication of NATO and West German involvement is contained in Ladislav Bittman, *The Deception Game: Czechoslovak Intelligence in Soviet Political Warfare* (Syracuse, NY: Syracuse University Research Corporation, 1972), pp. 167–215.

[45]Johnson, "Soviet-East European Military Relations," pp. 243–66. See also Andrzej Korbonski, "The Warsaw Pact," *International Conciliation,* no. 573 (May 1969): 5–73, esp. 57–59, 61. For a review of post-Czech invasion attitudes from the individual East European members, see Peter Bender, "Inside the Warsaw Pact," *Survey,* no. 74/75 (Winter–Spring 1970): 253–68.

FROM THE INVASION OF CZECHOSLOVAKIA TO THE HELSINKI CONFERENCE, 1968–75

As the shock of the Warsaw Pact invasion of Czechoslovakia quickly wore off, the West European allies seemed particularly willing to respond to persistent Soviet overtures for the reduction of East-West tensions.[46] By the end of the 1960s, with their China border increasingly insecure, the world Communist movement little more than a hollow memory, and the Warsaw Pact itself in disarray, some accommodation with Western Europe and the United States must have seemed essential in spite of the conflict in Southeast Asia. If in the process Europe could be separated from the United States and NATO dissolved, so much the better.[47]

At about that same time the Soviet leadership appears to have concluded that it needed to secure still another infusion of Western technology, and it was evident that it could only hope to obtain the necessary quantity if there were a substantial "thaw" in the cold war.[48] Already deeply involved commercially with East Europe, the European NATO allies met the new Soviet initiatives with an enthusiasm that eventually made American reluctance economically costly and by the early 1970s politically burdensome.[49] Belatedly, Nixon and Kissinger accepted the Soviet initiatives and quickly signed SALT I, a preliminary trade agreement, and a promise of most favored nation status. Such actions must have reassured the Brezhnev leadership that Western technology would be forthcoming and that Soviet conventional military capability could be brought safely to a healthy level of superiority along

---

[46]Many of the Soviet "European security" initiatives had been part of their diplomatic stock and trade for at least a decade. However, while earlier they had left the impression that their proposals were invented largely for propaganda effect, their new energy and apparent willingness to negotiate seriously, at a time when American foreign policy interest was focused elsewhere, convinced many in Europe that the Soviets were finally serious in their desire to reduce tensions. For a synoptic review of the situation, see Pierre Hassner, *Change and Security in Europe, Part I: The Background* (London: Institute for Strategic Studies, 1968). Typical of the Soviet campaign at the end of the 1960s is the article by N. Yuryev, "European Security: A Dictate of our Time," *International Affairs*, no. 8 (August 1970): 3–7. Countless similar articles and pamphlets were written; many were translated and distributed throughout Western Europe.

[47]Bender, "Inside the Warsaw Pact," pp. 253–54. See also Walter Clemens, Jr., "The Changing Warsaw Pact," *East Europe* 17 (June 1968): 7–12; Clemens, "The Future of the Warsaw Pact," *Orbis* 11 (Winter 1968): 996–1033; and A. Ross Johnson, *The Warsaw Pact "European Security" Campaign* (Santa Monica, CA: Rand, 1970), R-565-PR.

[48]Connie M. Friesen, *The Political Economy of East West Trade* (New York: Frederick A. Praeger, 1976), pp. 22–25.

[49]Robert W. Clawson, "East-West Trade," in Harold W. Berkman and Ivan R. Vernon, eds., *Contemporary Perspectives in International Business* (Chicago: Rand McNally College Publishing Company, 1979), pp. 333–46. See also Herbert S. Levine, "An American View of Economic Relations with the USSR," a paper prepared for the Strategic Studies Center of the Stanford Research Institute, 30 April 1974.

with parity in strategic nuclear weapons.[50] By the early 1970s determined efforts were being made to give the Soviet armed forces an overwhelming deterrent edge in Europe and an adequate in-depth defensive capability on the Chinese border. Simultaneously, they were developing air and sea capabilities that would enable them for the first time in Soviet history to develop, augment, and protect more distant interests in the Third World.[51]

The Soviet image of the NATO military threat during the early 1970s seemed to be little changed. If Britain no longer played a central role, West Germany, on the other hand, had assumed a larger dimension. Soviet analysis of the Federal Republic in the first few years after the Czech occupation was colored by what they felt were sure signs of German nuclear ambitions accompanied by the continued influence of revengeful ex-Nazis in important positions. NATO was seen as giving "rear-cover" for a new German imperialism. Only after the signing of a series of trade and friendship treaties did the tone become less bellicose.[52]

Along with a generally realistic recognition of intra-NATO problems and the U.S.-Asian preoccupation, serious Soviet analysts of the military threat posed by NATO pointed out that defense expenditures continued to rise and that especially in advanced technology NATO was continuing to strengthen its capabilities.[53] The apparent permanent absence of France from the military structure, although counted as a

---

[50]Lawrence Freedman, *U.S. Intelligence and the Soviet Strategic Threat* (Boulder, CO: Westview Press, 1977), esp. pp. 153–76.

[51]Cf. W. Scott Thompson, *Power Projection: A New Assessment of U.S. and Soviet Capabilities* (New York: National Strategy Information Center, 1978). See also John E. Moore, *The Soviet Navy Today* (New York: Stein and Day Publishers, 1975), pp. 29–37.

[52]For articles illustrative of this continued and massive campaign, see N. Glazunov, "Militaristic Fever in Federal Germany," *International Affairs*, no. 2 (February 1969): 20–26; N. Palyanov, "Bonn's Challenge to Europe," *International Affairs*, no. 1 (January 1969): 21–28; Y. Grigoriev, "Anglo-West German Nuclear Cooperation," *International Affairs*, no. 1 (1970): 122–23; and *Pravda*, 10 May 1970. As the Soviet initiatives toward the Federal Republic began to gain plausibility, the Soviet analysis of the situation changed dramatically. See O. Sayanov, "Europe and the USSR-FRG Treaty," *International Affairs*, no. 8 (August 1971): 45–47; P. Tolmachev, "Treaties with the FRG—Important Contribution to the Easing of Tension," *International Affairs*, no. 8 (August 1972): 95–97; and *Izvestia*, 1 June 1972.

However, the ink was scarcely dry when the Soviets again noticed fascism and "NATOism" growing. See, for example, *Izvestia*, 7 September 1973; and *Pravda*, 21 November 1973. The Soviets were reluctant to sustain an attack with their previous vigor.

The tone of Soviet commentary generally was moderated during the mid-1970s to reflect the growing commercial interrelationship. See "USSR-FRG Five Years of the Moscow Treaty," *International Affairs*, no. 9 (September 1975): 30–31.

[53]A. Gorokhov, "Entering the 1970s," *International Affairs*, no. 1 (January 1970): 3–10; and Y. Gavrilov, "Military Expenditures of NATO Countries," *International Affairs*, no. 12 (December 1973): 115–16. Cf. V. G. Mityaev, *Yadernaya politika S.Sh.A. v NATO* [The nuclear policy of the USA in NATO] (Moscow: Mezhdunarodnaya otnosheniya, 1973); N. S. Nikitin, *Otdelenie i vzvod y boyu (po inostrannym armiyam)*

significant political liability to the alliance, was not perceived as a serious military disadvantage; it had to be assumed that the French would fight alongside NATO forces in any major conflict in Europe, despite the various friendship and trade agreements worked out between France and the USSR.[54]

In the first half of the 1970s rapidly warming relations between China and Western Europe were seen as endangering Soviet long-term strategy; they had hoped to keep the two problem areas separated and treat them in radically different ways. Equally as disconcerting were the international relationships that Romania was developing.[55]

Optimistic political forecasts were still focused on NATO disarray and potential disintegration, despite whatever the "worst case" analysts were concluding during this period. The political commentators were encouraged in their work by numerous Western and neutral sources writing about the future after NATO. For the Soviets the political separation of Western Europe from the United States naturally was viewed to be more possible because of EEC development trends that now seemed to be in direct conflict with American economic interests. Soviet analysts could scarcely project the ultimate resolution of the chaos that they and many in the West predicted, but they saw the growing contradictions as creating a panic that inevitably would drive the United States to respond to the same military and political détente pressures that apparently worked so well in Western Europe. Though struggling against it, eventually America also would be forced to deal seriously with Soviet

---

[Squad and platoon in battle (with foreign armies)] (Moscow: Voennoe izdatelstvo, 1974); P. I. Sergeev, ed., *Sukhoputnye voyska kapitalisticheskikh gosudarstv* [The ground forces of the capitalist states] (Moscow: Voennoe izdatelstvo, 1974); V. Matveyev, "NATO at the Time of Changes," *International Affairs*, no. 8 (August 1975): 85–92; *Pravda*, 22 October 1974; *Pravda*, 13 March 1974; *Izvestia*, 23 September 1975; *Pravda*, 24 June 1975; and *Pravda*, 19 September 1975.

[54]T. Ievleva, "In Opposition to European Interests," *International Affairs*, no. 4 (April 1970): 122–24; K. Lavrov, "Soviet-French Cooperation," *International Affairs*, no. 4 (April 1969): 24–30; Georges Cogniot, "Leninism and the Destiny of Europe," *International Affairs*, no. 5 (May 1970): 29–34; Maurice Schuman, "Franco-Soviet Relations," *International Affairs*, no. 12 (December 1975): 79–85; *Pravda*, 13 January 1975; and *Pravda*, 6 December 1975.

The military literature is substantial. See, for instance, V. Drobkov, *Kommunist vooruzhennykh sil*, no. 1 (January 1974), in Joint Publications Research Service (JPRS), no. 61271; and V. Mikhaylov and Yu Khudyakov, *Kommunist vooruzhennykh sil*, no. 16 (August 1975), JPRS, no. 65785.

[55]*Literaturnaya gazeta*, 11 August 1971. See also V. Borisov, "Peking and Détente," *International Affairs*, no. 12 (December 1973): 31–35; V. Pavlov, "Europe in Peking's Plans," *International Affairs*, no. 3 (March 1972): 15–20; and Y. Agranov, "Peking's Great-Power Policy and Western Europe," *International Affairs*, no. 4 (April 1974): 23–27, 34. For a further treatment of the subject, see A. I. Stepanov, *FRG i Kitay (K istorii otnosheniy, 1949–74 gody)* [The FRG and China (on the history of relations, 1949–74)] (Moscow: Mezdunarodnaya otnosheniya, 1974).

initiatives on European security, troop withdrawals, demilitarization, and strategic arms limitations.[56]

It was against this background that the USSR signed the Helsinki Final Act, ensuring at least a short-term mutual accommodation in Europe.[57] A number of unsettled political issues resulting from World War II were seemingly resolved. Along with the U.S. withdrawal from Southeast Asia, the Soviets felt they had succeeded in militarily, and to some extent, politically reducing the principal threats to the homeland itself and to their careful expansion of influence overseas. Many West Europeans believed that the USSR finally seemed convincingly committed to a nonmilitary means of conducting foreign policy.[58]

From the Romanian viewpoint, the period following the Czech occupation brought both opportunities and obstacles. Ceauşescu was careful not to provoke the Soviets with any issues that could give them a pretext for similar action in Romania. However, in September of 1969 the Romanian armed forces were reorganized into the nucleus for a people's resistance movement: a potential 20 million-strong guerrilla army.[59] Ceauşescu reiterated that the Warsaw Pact was defensive in nature and its forces only should be used against imperialist aggressors.[60] In the spring of 1970 he stressed that Romania's armed forces had no aggressive ambitions and were essentially defensive in character; that the country would remain free and independent and never tolerate outside interference. In addition, Romanian armies would be commanded only by Romanians. Typically, these statements were made after the reaffirmation of Soviet-Romanian friendship in the treaty belatedly signed in July 1970.[61]

When Ceauşescu visited China in June of 1971 few observers could misunderstand the meaning of Chou En-lai's reference to "imperialists"; Romanian-Chinese ties were strengthened.[62] Similarly, when President Nixon visited Bucharest and Ceauşescu visited the United States in return, Romania was continuing to strengthen a web of protective political

---

[56]Y. Zhukov, "NATO: What Now?" *International Affairs*, no. 7 (July 1969): 84–89; L. Vidyasova, "Shifts in the Alignment of Forces in the Imperialist Camp," *International Affairs*, no. 10 (October 1970): 22–25; V. Repnitsky, "The Military-Technological Revolution and Inter-Imperialist Contradictions," *International Affairs*, no. 11 (November 1970): 48–53; and W. Stankiewicz, "The Contradictions of Military-Industrial Integration in Western Europe," *International Affairs*, no. 7 (July 1972): 28–34.

[57]Ponamarov, *Europa*, p. 23.

[58]Stephen J. Flanagan, "The CSCE and the Development of Détente," in Derek Leebaert, ed., *European Security*, pp. 189–232. For a comprehensive review of Soviet objectives in the European security talks, see Blacker, "Soviet Perception of European Security," ibid., pp. 137–61.

[59]*Scinteia* (daily organ of the Central Committee of the Romanian Communist Party, Bucharest), 25 September 1968.

[60]*Scinteia*, 7, 13 May 1970.

[61]Ibid. 27, 28 September 1970.

[62]Ibid., 9 June 1971.

relationships, although they could not have had any illusions about actual military support from China or the West.[63]

By the early 1970s Romania was developing a modest domestic armaments industry as well as acquiring weapons from outside the bloc. Small arms production had begun in 1967 and was expanded to include ammunition and artillery.[64] Support and maintenance facilities were provided for the home-produced equipment that now included land vehicles as well as sea and river craft. In 1975 production of military goods was up 106 percent over 1965 and Romania was producing 60 percent of its own needs. In the early 1970s contracts for arms were made with Israeli, French, British, and Yugoslav suppliers.[65] The cost was high but the upgrading added a combined practical and psychological advantage in Ceaușescu's nationalistic campaign; it surely received a positive response from the Romanian military leadership. The equipment would not be under Soviet control nor would it conform to the Warsaw Pact weapons integration scheme. Finally, the Defense Law of December 1972 further emphasized national objectives and determination; it bound all leaders to resist any invader and made it illegal to cede any Romanian territory to an enemy.[66] Thus, a call for Soviet "assistance" by some obscure personage was made even more dangerous than it might have been elsewhere.

Romania also went so far as to refuse the Soviets passage through the Dobrudja in order to participate in maneuvers in 1971, and in 1974 they vetoed a proposed Odessa-Varna (Bulgaria) railway line that was part of a regional defense transport scheme. Still, Romania did participate in Warsaw Pact exercises in 1973.[67]

At the Helsinki preparatory talks in 1972 the Romanian delegation irritated the Soviets by proposing that each country should participate on its own, free from any bloc attachments. All relationships, they argued, should be based upon the principles of independence and sovereignty. Romania insisted that it be a full member on the issue of military security of Europe, at Helsinki or elsewhere.[68]

---

[63]President Nixon visited Romania in August 1969. In turn, Ceaușescu came to the United States in October 1970 and again in December 1973. For an informative summary of these and other aspects of U.S.-Romanian relations, especially the commercial aspects, see "Perspectives on East West Trade: Rumanian's Trading Policy in Context," *Tower International Newsletter*, no. 16 (January 1974). The newsletter is distributed from Tower International headquarters in Cleveland, OH.

[64]Aurel Broan, *Romanian Foreign Policy Since 1965: The Political and Military Limits of Autonomy* (New York: Praeger Publishers, 1978), p. 169.

[65]Ibid.

[66]*Scinteia*, 27 December 1972.

[67]F. Stephen Larrabee, "The Romanian Challenge to Soviet Hegemony," *Orbis* 17 (Spring 1973): 230.

[68]Viktor Meier, "The Political Dynamics of the Balkans in 1974," chapt. 2 in *The World and the Great Power Triangles*, ed. W. E. Griffiths (Cambridge, MA: MIT Press, 1974), p. 44.

In the spring of 1973, Ceauşescu argued that Romania should be involved in the mutual and balanced force reduction talks at Vienna and proposed a nuclear-free peace zone for the Balkans; he made it clear that Romania blamed both sides for the arms race.[69] Moscow was again defied when Romania refused to adopt the Soviet line in the Arab-Israeli crisis of 1973. In fact, Romanian relations with Israel were strengthened as a result of Foreign Minister Abba Eban's visit to Bucharest during that same year.[70] Both China and the United States helped the Romanian position considerably during this period by exercising their restraint in not making an issue of this deviant image. The rest of Eastern Europe looked on with curious interest.

FROM HELSINKI TO THE SOVIET
INVASION OF AFGHANISTAN, 1975–80

While détente flourished briefly in the mid-1970s the Soviets continued their diplomatic efforts for MBFR and other schemes to reduce tensions on the Western borders.[71] However, the rapidly growing power of the Soviet conventional armed forces stationed in other Warsaw Pact countries, the expansion of Soviet naval capabilities, and the continuous Soviet strategic buildup, became increasingly troublesome for both West Europeans and Americans.[72] The USSR's military involvement in the Third World, greatly expanded in the latter 1970s through new long distance air and naval deployment capabilities, created an additional reaction in the West.[73]

---

[69]Ibid., p. 78.

[70]Shortly before the 1973 Middle East war Romania had played host to Israeli Prime Minister Golda Meir.

[71]A. P. Sheetikov, *Evropeyskaya bezopasnost i sotrudnichestvo: predposylki, problemy, perspektivy [European Security and Cooperation: Premises, Problems, and Prospects]*, English version (Moscow: Progress Publishing, 1976), pp. 161–94. See also A. Chernyshov, "Peace and Security for the Indian Ocean," *International Affairs*, no. 12 (December 1976): 42–50; D. Proektor, "Military Détente: Primary Task," *International Affairs*, no. 6 (June 1976): 35–43; *Izvestia*, 24 July 1976; *Pravda*, 8 June 1977; and *Pravda*, 9 June 1978.

[72]Peter H. Vigor, "The Strategic Balance Sheet, 1976," in David R. Jones, ed., *Soviet Armed Forces Review Annual* (Gulf Breeze, FL: Academic International Press, 1978), 2:1–5; Jacquelyn K. Davis and Robert L. Pfaltzgraff, Jr., *Soviet Theater Strategy: Implications for NATO* (Washington, DC: U.S. Strategic Institute, 1978), USSI report 78-1; General H. F. Zeiner-Gundersen, "The Balance of Forces and Economic Problems," *NATO Review*, no. 5 (October 1979): 3–7; Helmut Sonnenfeldt and William G. Hyland, *Soviet Perspectives on Security* (London: International Institute for Strategic Studies, 1979), Adelphi Papers, no. 150, esp. pp. 13–21.

[73]Lee Aspin and Jack F. Kemp, "Realities of Soviet Power: Two Views," *AEI Defense Review* 2 (1979). For a comprehensive treatment of the Angola intervention, see

Soviet analysts were feeling slightly more secure by the late 1970s. NATO was still a threat, but it no longer was seen to have the capability, nuclear or conventional, to intimidate the Eastern bloc. The "correlation of forces" had shifted in the Warsaw Pact's favor.[74] However, as new NATO weapons and technical programs got underway, Soviet observers agreed that the issue was not permanently settled. The Eurogroup's joint projects, as well as U.S. programs for European deployment of the neutron bomb, *Pershing II,* and the cruise missile, were convincing evidence that the West was bent on entering a new and even more dangerous round of the arms competition.[75] While Western specialists were pointing to the enormous gap between the conventional forces of NATO and the Warsaw Pact, Soviet "worst case" analysis was concluding that the West had "sacrificed the present for the future." The Soviets saw the possibility of entering into a period when they would once again be vulnerable to NATO weapons and forces, perhaps as early as the mid-1980s.[76] Additionally, even the slightest progress toward NATO standardization and interoperability—to NATO planners an almost impossible task—had been taken seriously as an important military variable.[77]

The tone of Soviet analysis grew increasingly overwrought as cooperation between China and various members of NATO expanded. In February of 1978, General Alexander Haig was quoted in the Soviet press as having stated: "It is not at all illogical to say that China is the 16th

---

Carl G. Jacobsen, "Angola and the Evolution of Soviet Theory and Capability for Intervention in Distant Areas," in David R. Jones, ed., *Soviet Armed Forces Review Annual,* 2:351–64; and Patrick J. Rollins, "The USSR and Black Africa," *Soviet Armed Forces Review* 3: 134–43. For the naval and air dimension see Paul J. Murphy, ed., *Naval Power in Soviet Policy* (Washington, DC: Government Printing Office, 1978), esp. pp. 259–97; Bradford Dismukes and James M. McConnel, eds., *Soviet Naval Diplomacy* (New York: Pergamon Press, 1979), pp. 336–56; Paul H. Nitze and Leonard Sullivan, Jr., et al., *Securing the Seas: The Soviet Naval Challenge and Western Alliance Options* (Boulder, CO: Westview Press, 1979); and Robin Higham and Jacob Kipp, eds., *Soviet Aviation and Air Power: A Historical View* (Boulder, CO: Westview Press, 1977).

[74]*Pravda,* 30 January 1977; *Izvestia,* 23 February 1978. See also Lewis Allen Frank, *Soviet Nuclear Planning: A Point of View on SALT* (Washington, DC: American Enterprise Institute, 1977).

[75]A. Migolatyev, "Who is Speeding Up the Arms Race and Why," *International Affairs,* no. 11 (November 1977): 89–95; *Pravda,* 27 December 1978; V. Leushkanov, "The Arms Race and the NATO Eurogroup," *International Affairs,* no. 3 (March 1978): 115–21; *Krasnaya zvezda,* 18 March 1979; E. Kamenskiy, "NATO v 1978 g," in *Mezhdunarodnaya ezhegodnik* [International yearbook] (Moscow: Izdat. Politicheskoy Lit., 1979), pp. 144–52.

[76]Keith A. Dunn, "Soviet Perceptions of NATO," *Parameters* 8 (September 1978): 53–69. See also A. Antonov and G. Ziborov, "NATO: Escalating the Arms Race," *International Affairs,* no. 8 (August 1978).

[77]*Krasnaya zvezda,* 8 July 1976.

member of the North Atlantic alliance."⁷⁸ The willingness, indeed enthusiasm, with which the European members of NATO were bidding to
supply modern weapons to China shocked Soviet observers who seemed
to be protesting a "betrayal."⁷⁹ Their Eastern border defense strategy was
dependent on Chinese weaponry remaining obsolescent for the foreseeable future; a significant and a rapid change in Chinese military technology would have a profound effect on the entire Soviet security scheme.

The French also provided certain unpleasant developments for the
Soviets, who had so carefully endeavored to neutralize and permanently
separate them from NATO. Not only was France among those offering to
upgrade Chinese military capability but also it became involved militarily
and covertly in the Third World, most directly contrary to Soviet interests
in Zaire. Added to these transgressions, the French armed forces continued to increase their level of "informal" participation in NATO
military affairs. Soviet analysts now virtually had to disregard the formal
separation.⁸⁰

Most of the new anxieties facing Soviet defense policymakers have
been pinpointed by their analysts as originating in a fresh wave of right-
wing hysteria. Especially in the NATO countries, reactionary circles have
been gaining influence, with Soviet style détente its principal victim.⁸¹
According to the Soviets, right wings of NATO have dishonestly built
their reactionary campaigns on the "myth" of a Soviet military "threat."
Gullible publics have been all too willing to be diverted from their own
considerable national economic problems. Soviet analysts note, however,
that in the past this particular charade has not withstood the test of time.⁸²

The Soviets continue to point out contradictions within the alliance,
despite the high degree of pessimistic realism that marks their commentary
concerning security problems in the late 1970s. However, a better

---

⁷⁸Quoted in *Kurs, Khaos i voyna [Heading for Chaos and War]*, English version
(Moscow: Novosti Press Agency Publishing House, 1978), p. 46.

⁷⁹I. Alexeyev, "Peking's European Policy," *International Affairs*, no. 1 (January
1976): 58– 65; *Pravda*, 14 May 1978, 17 June 1978, 5 August 1978; *Selskaya zhizn*, 5
February 1978; *Izvestia*, 18 May 1978; V. Vladimirov, "Peking Looks for Arms,"
International Affairs, no. 3 (March 1979): 142–43.

⁸⁰*Pravda*, 9 June 1976; *Izvestia*, 25 February 1977; *Pravda*, 13 April 1977; *Pravda*,
23 May 1978, 23 June 1978; *Izvestia*, 5 July 1978. See also "Zayavlenie TASS v svyazi s
sobytiyami v Zaire" [statement by TASS in connection with events in Zaire], 18 May 1978;
and "Zayavlenie Sovetskogo pravitelstva v svyazi s rostom napryazhennosti na afrikanskom
kontinente" [statement by the Soviet government in connection with the growth of tensions of
the African continent], 23 June 1978. Both are included in *Vneshnyaya politika Sovetskogo
soyuza i mezhdunarodnaya otnosheniya* [Foreign policy of the Soviet Union and international relations] (Moscow: Mezhdunarodnaya otnosheniya, 1979), pp. 73, 102–7.

⁸¹*Pravda*, 20 November 1976; *Krasnaya zvezda*, 24 January 1976; and *Pravda*,
16 July 1978.

⁸²*Pravda*, 19 March 1978, 26 November 1978, 2 August 1979.

informed analysis characterizes the more recent Soviet work. They continue to foresee NATO's demise; the event is no longer cast as imminent.[83]

During the latter half of the 1970s Romania stood out as the only significantly independent member of the Warsaw Pact. Official statements make it clear that Romania continued to be critical of both blocs—NATO and the Warsaw Pact—as examples of the "spheres of influence" mentality and a source of tensions reminiscent of the Cold War.[84]

Romania maintained its recalcitrant position as the Warsaw Pact neared its twenty-fifth anniversary. At the 1976 pact meetings Ceauşescu was outspoken in his proposal to restructure the alliance along political lines, instituting a Council of Foreign Ministers that would give the member states a greater voice.[85] In 1978, stressing economic problems, Romania refused to raise its contribution to pact expenses. Ceauşescu was unwilling to waste money on an alliance he could not fully support. In a series of speeches to the army and the Central Committee of the party, marking the sixtieth anniversary of the creation of Greater Romania, Ceauşescu repeated his objection to the idea of Romanian troops under foreign command.[86]

Romania also took substantially divergent steps toward weapons procurement. Arguing that they were always last in line on the Warsaw Pact weapons chain, accelerated efforts were made to replace obsolete equipment. Following arrangements made earlier in the 1970s, aircraft engines were obtained from Great Britain, helicopters from France, and a fighter bomber was produced in cooperation with Yugoslavia. In addition, modern attack vessels were purchased from China. Military exchanges with China, Great Britain, Italy, France, and the United States were continued as well.[87]

---

[83]N. Turkatenko, "Inter-Imperialist Contradictions and the Strategy of 'Atlanticism,' " *International Affairs*, no. 2 (February 1976): 82–91; "Spartak" Beglov, "The West in Search of a Coordinated Policy," *International Affairs*, no. 5 (May 1977); G. Vorontsov, "The U.S. and Western Europe: Rivalry and Partnership," *International Affairs*, no. 3 (March 1978): 32–40; and V. Nekrasov, "Insoluble Contradictions," *International Affairs*, no. 9 (September 1979): 21–31. Also compare G. A. Vorontsov, *SShA i Zapadnaya Evropa: novy etap otnosheniy* [USA and Western Europe: a new stage of the relationship] (Moscow: Mezhdunarodnaya otnosheniya, 1979).

[84]Speech by Ceauşescu at the plenary meeting of the Central Committee of the Romanian Communist Party, 29 November 1978, Agerpres, Romanian News Agency, no. 48, November 1978, Bucharest, Romania.

[85]Broan, *Romanian Foreign Policy Since 1965*, pp. 110–11.

[86]Speech by Ceauşescu to representatives of the army and ministry of the interior, 27 November 1978, Agerpres, Romanian News Agency, no. 46, November 1978, Bucharest, Romania.

[87]Walter M. Bacon, Jr., "The Military and the Party in Romania," in Herspring and Volgyes, *Civil and Military Relations*, p. 169.

Ceauşescu continued to stress that Romania would fulfill all War-saw Pact defense obligations in Europe without giving any ground on the question of national sovereignty. He has repeated his proposals to turn the Balkans into a nuclear-free zone of peace and suggested that the same positive approach should be applied to the Danubian countries.[88]

The Soviet invasion of Afghanistan once again raised the specter of similar intervention in Romania. Soviet actions in Asia confirmed all of Ceauşescu's worst fears concerning his own foreign policy and further impressed him with the need for Socialist orthodoxy at home. But again Romania felt secure enough to publicize its disapproval by choosing to be absent at the time of the UN vote on the Afghan issue. When the Romanian ambassador returned, following the vote, he spoke out against the Soviet action as a threat to peace, a violation of national sovereignty, and interference in another nation's internal affairs. He called for a withdrawal of all foreign troops from Afghanistan.[89] In the foreseeable future, Romania is likely to remain as a unique quantity within the pact. Under Ceauşescu leadership Romania will be conservative and national-istic at home and realistically aggressive abroad.

During the latter half of the 1970s the Soviet Union has been able to ensure effective control of the Warsaw Pact's collective image of NATO except in Romania. However they view the Atlantic Alliance's strengths and weaknesses, the Soviets appear to have become increasingly in-sensitive to Western reactions as the West's military capabilities have diminished in relation to those of the Warsaw Pact.

By the end of the 1970s, as NATO began to respond militarily to the Soviet-Warsaw Pact buildup, the USSR found itself facing an increasingly unified Western arms and technology program that threatened once again to place it in a strategic and perhaps conventional position of qualitative inferiority.[90] However, with parity closer than ever before, the USSR has viewed Western attempts to link further détente with changes in Soviet domestic or foreign policy—outside Europe—with relative disbelief.[91]

---

[88]Speech by Ceauşescu at the joint session of the central Committee of the Romanian Communist Party, the National Council of the Socialist Unity Front, and the Grand National Assembly marking the sixtieth anniversary of Romanian unification, *Romanian News,* supp. no. 38, 1978.

[89]*Lumea,* 18 January 1980, p. 9.

[90]Kamenskiy, "NATO," esp. p. 147. See also "Vneshnyaya politika SSSR i mezhdunarodnye otnosheniya v 1978 g" [Foreign Policy of the USSR and International Relations in 1978] in the same volume, pp. 19–20. In addition, see Vorontsov, *SShA,* pp. 174–216. Typical of this analysis is A. Yeremov, "NATO: Old Wine in New Bottles," *International Affairs,* no. 11 (November 1976): 59–65. Indicative of the contemporary Soviet military reaction is V. Kuznetsov, "Pentagon's Eurostrategy Plans," *Soviet Military Review,* no. 2 (February 1980).

[91]*Ekonomicheskaya gazeta,* no. 31 (July 1977); *Pravda,* 12 March 1978, 20 July 1978.

They apparently believe that they never again would have to rely solely on the flimsy tools of diplomacy and commerce in order to safeguard modern Soviet interests.

The postdétente military competition, fueled first by the Soviet buildup and the Western reaction followed by events in the Middle East, was given additional impetus by the Soviet military occupation of Afghanistan in December 1979.[92] A new round of the cold war greeted 1980, tempered this time by a Western appreciation of how close the Soviet Union and Warsaw Pact were to having comprehensive military superiority.

SUMMARIZING THE WARSAW PACT VIEWPOINT

Stephen P. Gibert, using Soviet perception data mainly from the first half of the 1970s, has offered a number of valuable generalizations regarding Soviet grand strategy that seem to be confirmed in this study.[93] A 1978 article by John Erickson has provided additional insights and refinements.[94]

There is a great deal of evidence to suggest that the Soviets and even some Eastern Europeans actually have become convinced (not just for the purposes of strategic deception) that the "correlation of forces" has shifted in their favor and nuclear parity, or even advantage, has been reached. Consequently, the Soviets seem to have decided that they could extend their global influence and exploit worldwide trends without substantial risk to the homeland or to fraternal allies. As they have carried out their projects, especially in Asia and increasingly in Africa, the Soviets have anticipated that some Western nations might become desperate, finally realizing that history is against them. They might be tempted to use military means to turn back the clock as they did in Cuba and Vietnam. However, because the Soviet armed forces have grown in strength and capability, the West's military alternatives have been steadily reduced. For the same reason, the USSR and its allies need no longer refrain from employing the military instrument in aid of their Third World interests.

However, what seems to be a relatively advantageous situation has

---

[92]TASS, *On Events in Afghanistan: Leonid Brezhnev's Replies to a Pravda Correspondent* (Moscow: Novosti Press Agency Publishing House, 1980); *Pravda*, 23 December 1979; K. Mikhailov, "Provocatory Campaign Over Afghanistan," *International Affairs*, no. 3 (March 1980): 97–100.

[93]Stephen P. Gibert, *Soviet Images of America* (New York: Crane Russak and Company, 1977).

[94]John Erickson, "Soviet Military Policy in the 1980s," *Current History* 75 (October 1978): 97–138.

been made less so in Soviet eyes by certain inherent instabilities. They clearly have decided that steadily increasing military might is necessary to maintain their position, because as the West grows more frenzied the Capitalist elites become easy prey to the simple but irrational military solutions offered by "reactionary circles." Warsaw Pact military superiority has been viewed as an ultimate necessity to convince the West that it cannot win. Only with the absence of world war and an end to the stalemate in Europe can peaceful coexistence safely provide conditions for increasing Soviet involvement in the Third World.

This attitude has led inevitably to an ambivalent view of Western military power at the end of the 70s. Soviet analysts in particular have tended to perceive NATO armed forces as dangerous and menacing, partly from a realistic appraisal that they are not yet that advanced and partly from an obvious concern on behalf of the military managers that they continue to receive a very large slice of the Soviet domestic budget. At the same time it has been both realistic and ideologically sound to recognize that the West continues to be frought with contradictions rooted in its Capitalist mode of production.

These seemingly conflicting assumptions appear to be widely shared among Soviet and bloc leaders and serious analysts alike. Given such images they apparently have drawn a number of conclusions specifically about the NATO alliance and the future of the East-West struggle.

First, from its inception NATO consistently has been taken seriously by the Soviets, sloganized predictions of imminent disintegration notwithstanding. While encouraged by every sign of friction within the alliance, Soviet and bloc analysts increasingly have noted a fundamental stability in the system, although there is a significant variation in how crucial developments are perceived. For instance, the Soviets and even some East Europeans have been slow to appreciate the many facets of the newly emerging European identity within the alliance and in Western Europe as a whole.

Second, it is evident that to a greater extent than their East European colleagues Soviet analysts never have seen any reason for NATO's existence if passive defense is its only rationale. U.S. nuclear weapons on West European soil have been taken as the leading prima facie evidence of aggressive intent, either for actual warfare against the Warsaw Pact, or for political leverage in the region or elsewhere. Those Atlantic forces are all the more dangerous as the "correlation of forces" shifts to the Warsaw Pact and the NATO allies become desperate while possibly subject to domination by reactionary political leaders.

Third, there is apparently an emerging Soviet assumption that in the 1970s the alliance had "sacrificed the present for the future," so that by the mid-1980s a new U.S. fleet, a modernized and highly integrated NATO air defense system, new U.S. and European armor, a vastly improved ability to move extremely large numbers of combat troops long distances, along with matured NATO-Chinese cooperation, may place the USSR once again on the military defensive in the European theater and possibly on their Eastern borders as well.

Fourth, Warsaw Pact perception of the role of the German Federal Republic has been slowly modified over the years. Hysterical bombast has been replaced by a moderated tone, and the role of the Federal Republic in NATO and the EEC now seems to be the object of much more detached and realistic analyses. The fact that a rearmed Germany has not emerged as the sole important military and political influence on the European continent finally appears to have dawned on Warsaw Pact analysts. While the Soviets and several key East and West European states still view the possibility of German control over nuclear weapons with trepidation, they see it as less important than they once did.

Finally, the chronic Soviet attribution of hostile intent to NATO's actions feeds a habitual set of antagonistic Western assumptions, and vice versa. The relationship between the two cannot accurately be termed mirror image; the nature of the responses and counterresponses depends too much on various differences between the perceptions held by each. Some NATO analysts tend to view all Soviet military policy as emanating from a naturally aggressive Soviet dictatorship with certain almost biological impulses such as an urge to warm water ports. To others it seems that the Soviets are so paranoid that almost any action NATO takes is viewed as hostile; that every defensive reaction is exaggerated. From Moscow, however, Western reactions to Warsaw Pact and Soviet foreign policy initiatives appear not so much from paranoia as a result of an increasingly desperate scheme for reversing the forces of history to ensure the continuation of imperialist domination.

NATO and the United Nations in American Foreign Policy: Building a Framework for Power

THOMAS M. CAMPBELL, JR.

WOULD NATO SUPERSEDE THE UNITED NATIONS?

As America moved to consider the newly signed North Atlantic Pact in the spring of 1949, an impassioned Henry A. Wallace warned an audience: "The clear intention of the pact is to take the place of the United Nations . . . the one hope for peace. . . . Now is the time for the American people to act. The United Nations was born at San Francisco in 1945. The supreme question is: 'Shall it die in Washington in 1949?' "[1] The threat NATO posed to the United Nations was a familiar theme in the critics' arsenal of attacks against the Atlantic Pact at the time it was being debated in the Senate. The idea that the United Nations had failed, and therefore NATO became necessary in order to buttress Western security, is a common view shared by the treaty founders and various scholars.[2] While it has some validity, if its central point is to be sustained it must be agreed that the United Nations had failed to keep the peace among the great powers. This criticism does injustice to the United Nations on two counts. First, however fragile the peace seemed it was intact. Second, the founders of the United Nations had acknowledged from the start that this untried international body could not ensure peace among the so-called permanent powers; its successful functioning would depend on cooperation and amity among the Big Five founding powers.[3] It will be argued in

---

[1]*New York Times*, 28 March 1949, p. 5.
[2]Escott Reid, *Time of Fear and Time of Hope: The Making of the North Atlantic Treaty* (Buffalo, NY: McClelland and Stewart, 1977), pp. 29–33; Arthur H. Vandenberg, Jr., and Joe A. Morris, eds., *The Private Papers of Senator Vandenberg* (Boston: Houghton Mifflin, 1952), pp. 340–41, 400–1; Hans Kelsen, "Recent Trends," *The Law of the United Nations: A Critical Analysis of Its Fundamental Problems* (New York: Praeger, 1951), p. 922; Ben T. Moore, *NATO and the Future of Europe* (New York: Harper and Row, 1958), pp. 115–16.
[3]Inis L. Claude, Jr., *Power and International Relations* (New York: Random House, 1962), pp. 155–65.

this study that rather than detracting from the United Nations, NATO complemented its mission and perhaps even helped the United Nations to survive.

AMERICA'S BROADENING GLOBAL VIEW

With the onset of the Great Depression in 1929, events moved with such shattering rapidity that the period between 1929 and 1949 can accurately be said to constitute a revolutionary epoch in world affairs. World War II, however harrowing an experience, also presented the U.S. government with a unique opportunity to extend the influence of American institutions on a global scale.[4] Prior to the 1940s there either had been strong nations to limit their ambitions or the American people had not desired to undertake the commitments necessary for the nation to play the role of a world superpower. With the crushing defeat the allies administered to Japan and Germany in World War II and the relative weakness of our allies, including the Soviet Union, there was no nation in 1945 capable of blocking America's ascendency. Furthermore, the majority of American citizens had undergone a significant change in attitude about the importance of the United States taking a leading role in international affairs.[5] The seminal factor in this new reasoning was the bitter experience of war itself—the realization that it had been partly because the United States had stood aloof in the twenties and thirties that Fascist powers had been able to threaten our vital interests. During the war public opinion makers had emphasized a constant theme that Americans must accept the responsibilities of active leadership in order to prevent a new, even more devastating, cycle of war in the future.

This greater sophistication in the public's mind regarding the United States acting as a world power was but one ingredient in the changing potpourri that made up America's foreign policy. Equally important was the economic might that had continued to develop despite the depression. The country's economy was global in dimension, anticipating the expansion of world markets in the context of a stable international financial community. Technology had brought the nation to the point that by air and through new manufacturing processes we would of necessity be geared into the world community. U.S. readiness for leadership also was reflected in Congress, where a belief in an active American presence in world

---

[4]Thomas M. Campbell, *Masquerade Peace: America's UN Policy, 1944–1945* (Tallahassee: Florida State University Press, 1973).

[5]Robert A. Divine, *Second Chance: The Triumph of Internationalism in America During World War II* (New York: Atheneum, 1967), pp. 98–155.

matters had become a common assumption among many congressmen of both parties. This readiness also was apparent in the educational institutions, churches, press, and public forums of America, as literally hundreds of topics pertaining to our world activities provided the themes of discussion.[6]

A UNIVERSAL OR REGIONAL APPROACH TO SECURITY?

Underlying the intense popular interest in postwar world issues was the difficult question of how the nation could give institutional expression in its foreign policy to the new commitment to activism. The creation of both the United Nations and NATO provided two major answers and brought into sharp contrast an ongoing dilemma in U.S. foreign policy: could national security be entrusted to universal organizations or to more limited regional systems, the latter being in essence a new expression of the age-old balance of power system. What was new in revolutionary tides of the mid-twentieth century, lay primarily in the areas of man's destructive capabilities and in the political order. There was really little new in the ideas discussed regarding the organization of humanity's future collective security. Americans had entered the war with their ideas unformed about future organizations of peace. Many ideas emerged during the war years with respect to the postwar world. While a smattering of voices called for world government and stressed the "one world" theme that Wendell Willkie and Henry Wallace popularized, such views never were shared by the mass of citizens. The majority of Americans favored creating a new international organization akin to the League of Nations but free of its defects. Under the guidance of Secretary of State Cordell Hull and the State Department, which devoted a great deal of their energy and time to planning for the United Nations, the public evidenced strong support for following this route to assure the nation's future security. Congress demonstrated that, unlike in the Wilson era, it would provide more support than opposition to the planning; and in the fall of 1943 through the Fulbright and Connally resolutions both houses of Congress went on record favoring American participation in a postwar peace-keeping organization.

In the nation there was considerable debate over the proposed organization's parameters of power. One very strong school of advocates

---

[6]Ibid.; William A. Williams, *The Tragedy of American Diplomacy,* rev. ed. (New York: Dell Publishing, 1962), pp. 160–229; Thomas G. Paterson, *Soviet-American Confrontation, Postwar Reconstruction and the Origins of the Cold War* (Baltimore: Johns Hopkins University Press, 1973), pp. 1–33.

favored the regional approach to collective security. Such influential Americans as former Undersecretary of State Sumner Welles and columnist Walter Lippmann argued for the wisdom of granting great powers wide latitude to enforce peace within their own spheres. Regional blocs should have only a limited responsibility to the global international organization. The regional approach found favor among those who wanted to safeguard the sanctity of national sovereignty and to allow the great powers broad latitude in assuring their individual security requirements. Generally cordial to the regional security idea were the military branches and conservative congressmen.[7] By the spring of 1944, British Prime Minister Winston Churchill favored each major wartime ally policing its own postwar sphere. These regions of strength would form the foundation upon which a supreme council would be founded and have authority to act in cases involving disputes among great powers.[8]

Churchill never resolved the issue of how much autonomy the regional bodies should have, but he was not alone in his indecision. Roosevelt had expressed his notions concerning the Four Policemen acting as gendarmes in their respective regions of the world, but he came around by 1944 to accept the universalist blueprint that Hull presented as the State Department tentative draft for an international organization. The president wavered on a number of basic UN issues and often reverted to a position that his key advisers already had dismissed. His only consistency in this field lay in his belief that justice for great and small nations should be as equal as possible in the UN, and to this end he favored creating a forceful organization. Stalin concurred that a strong UN was worthy, but he was interested largely in the five permanent powers controlling decisions. Unity of action was the central Soviet demand. Dissension over a permanent power's right to veto Security Council proceedings took an inordinate amount of time in the eleven months prior to signing the UN Charter and symbolized the rising tensions racking the Grand Alliance.

The high point of the universalist cause came during the Dumbarton Oaks conference, where it was agreed that the UN Security Council should have first jurisdiction over all matters pertaining to disputes among nations that entailed the use of sanctions or force. Some critics have maintained that the Dumbarton conferees met in an atmosphere unrelated to the realities of battles and the high stakes of territorial and other ambitions that already were undermining allied unity, and therefore the deliberations had little basis in the realities of the time. That view is incorrect. In fact, there was widespread support, particularly among

---

[7]Divine, *Second Chance*, pp. 178–82; Thomas M. Campbell, "Nationalism in America's UN Policy, 1944–1945," *International Organization* 27 (Winter 1973): 25–44.

[8]Thomas M. Campbell and George C. Herring, eds., *The Diaries of Edward R. Stettinius, Jr., 1943–1946* (New York: New Viewpoints, 1975), pp. 51–54 (hereafter referred to as *Stettinius Diaries*).

Americans, for making the United Nations as strong and independent as possible, and the negotiators at Dumbarton Oaks were reflecting that general attitude.[9]

Through the winter of 1944–45 and into the spring the hopes of the universalists remained high as the U.S. government flooded the country with a massive information program on what the Dumbarton Oaks proposals meant and the public's mind turned expectantly toward the Golden Gate city where the United Nations would be forged. Even such a close observer of the Soviet scene as Ambassador Averell Harriman could argue that the imperatives of continued close relations with Russia outweighed those actions that caused the West frustration. As for President Franklin Roosevelt, when pushed by anxious congressmen in mid-January 1945 about the prospects of an amicable peacetime association with Russia, he responded that the early establishment of the machinery of the United Nations was the best course to assure this goal.[10] Roosevelt's references to his faith in the United Nations became more frequent in the final two months of his life, reminiscent of Woodrow Wilson's own appeals for support on the grounds that the League of Nations could remedy defects of the Versailles Treaty.

COLLECTIVE SELF-DEFENSE AT THE U.N. CONFERENCE

Roosevelt sensed the decay that was now becoming more apparent in allied relations, and he drew comfort from ephemeral hopes. The winter of 1944–45 saw the British and Russians moving in Europe to consolidate their own national advantage. The momentary euphoria of the Yalta conference was dashed within a month, and by mid-March of 1945 the Big Three were exchanging accusations of treachery regarding Romania, Poland, and the surrender of German forces in Italy. Outside of the European sphere traumas also shook allied solidarity. In the Middle East, French efforts to reassert mandate rule in Syria and Lebanon resulted in armed resistance from the populace and a blunt desist warning from the British government. Around the globe in Southeast Asia, removed from the spotlight, the de Gaulle government proved more successful when it won U.S. approval for reimposing French authority after the defeat of

---

[9]See Keith Barton, "The Dumbarton Oaks Conference" (Ph.D. diss., Florida State University, 1974) for the most extensive study on this important meeting.

[10]W. Averell Harriman and Elie Abel, *Special Envoy to Churchill and Stalin, 1941–1946* (New York: Random House, 1975), pp. 431–32, 440–41, 448; Harriman to Stettinius, 13 February 1945, Papers of Edward R. Stettinius, Jr., Alderman Library, Charlottesville, VA; *Stettinius Diaries*, pp. 214–15.

Japan.[11] Within the Western Hemisphere allied partners of the United States worried about Argentina's potential for aggression unless it were reconciled to the region's family of nations. Dissatisfied with what most Latin American leaders regarded as a cavalier treatment of their interests in planning for the United Nations and wanting to present a united front at the San Francisco conference, their governments attended the Charter conference in a demanding mood.

The proceedings of the United Nations Conference on International Organization (25 April—26 June 1945) offer an important strand of evidence for the view that the Cold War was already in its formative stages. It is to be found in the triumph of the regionalist case for collective security. The political and territorial rivalries that wracked the globe like a series of seismic tremors in the spring of 1945 were prominently on the minds of the framers of the UN Charter. With numerous signs of a troubled international climate ahead of them, a number of delegations searched for mechanisms to give expression to the rising nationalism that was undercutting their commitment to a strong international organization.[12] Out of this milieu came the shift away from having the Security Council enjoy the wide authority over regional organizations that the Dumbarton Oaks blueprint had specified.

Having won a U.S. pledge in March at the Mexico City Conference on Problems of War and Peace in an attempt to continue wartime hemisphere mutual defense commitments through a postwar regional security treaty,[13] Latin American delegates attended the UN conference determined to extend the concessions they recently had won. Their spokesman was Colombia's Foreign Minister Alberto Lleras Camargo. A zealous and eloquent man, he played on the sympathies of Assistant Secretary of State Nelson Rockefeller and Senator Arthur Vandenberg in order to gain favorable consideration within the U.S. conference delegation of a Charter article that would give broad latitude to regional defense arrangements to take enforcement action.[14] At one point in a meeting of

---

[11]Herbert Feis, *Between War and Peace, The Potsdam Conference* (Princeton: Princeton University Press, 1960), pp. 132–35; U.S., Department of State, *Foreign Relations of the United States: The Conference of Berlin, 1945,* 1:959-61 (hereafter cited as *FRUS,* followed by the appropriate year); George C. Herring, "The Truman Administration and the Restoration of French Sovereignty in Indochina," *Diplomatic History* 2 (Spring 1977): 97–117.

[12]Campbell, "Nationalism in America's UN Policy," pp. 35–44.

[13]Final act of the inter-American conference, resolution 8, Act of Chapultepec, U.S., Department of State, *Report of the Delegation of the United States of America to the Inter-American Conference on Problems of War and Peace* (Washington: Government Printing Office, 1946), pp. 74–75.

[14]Lleras Camargo's leadership in championing the cause of collective defense for the hemisphere at this time was a major factor in his being selected in 1948 as the first secretary general of the OAS.

the Latin American delegation chairmen with Secretary of State Edward R. Stettinius, Jr., Lleras Camargo bluntly warned that their nations expected Russia to seek to spread its influence into the Western Hemisphere after the war. He stated that the Latin American countries would vote against Russia's desire to obtain its bilateral treaty with France exempted from UN jurisdiction unless a similar exception was granted to the inter-American system.[15] At the UN conference he took advantage of Rockefeller's long-term interests in Western Hemisphere affairs and role as assistant secretary for Latin American affairs as a means to influence Rockefeller to approach Vandenberg. The senator's forceful letter of 5 May 1945 to Stettinius set the stage for a lengthy debate within the U.S. delegation on the issue of universal versus regional security.[16]

It has been argued that had it not been for the Latin American campaign on behalf of regional security the authority of the Security Council would have emerged stronger in the Charter.[17] This view, however, overlooks the eager zest with which the great powers took up the quest to construct a regional escape clause as a safety valve from the strictures of a too powerful international organization. While intense debate occurred within the U.S. delegation over the virtues of the universalist position and initially aroused concern among the British,[18] the common denominator that quickly developed out of Western great power conversations was how they might find a formula to allow their countries to build an alliance system at some future unspecified time against the predatory, expansionist ambitions of the Soviet Union.[19] The answer that covered these anticipated events became enshrined in the Charter as article 51 of chapter VII: "Nothing in the present Charter shall impair the right of individual or collective self-defense if an armed attack occurs against a Member of the United Nations, until the Security Council has taken measures necessary to maintain International peace and security."[20] It is particularly noteworthy that article 51 was included at the end of chapter VII on Action with Respect to Threats to the Peace, Breaches of

---

[15] This was the Soviet-French treaty of 22 December 1944, which provided mutual defense guarantees against any future German resurgence.

[16] *Stettinius Diaries*, pp. 349–56.

[17] Lawrence D. Weiler and Anne Patricia Simons, *The United States and the United Nations: The Search for International Peace and Security* (New York: Manhattan Publishing, 1967), pp. 79–83.

[18] Leo Pasvolsky, special assistant to the secretary of state and the most knowledgeable American expert on international organization matters, argued the universalist case most forcefully. He articulated the views of former Secretary of State Cordell Hull, whose illness prevented his attending the conference proceedings.

[19] *FRUS, 1945*, 1:672, 675, 698–703.

[20] Ruth B. Russell, *A History of the United Nations Charter: The Role of the United States, 1940–1945* (Washington: Brookings Institution, 1958), pp. 1043–44.

Peace, and Acts of Aggression and immediately followed by article 52 of
chapter VIII on Regional Arrangements, in which "nothing in the present
Charter precludes the existence of regional arrangements or agencies for
dealing with such matters are appropriate for regional action. . . ."[21]
Together, these portions of the Charter acted as brakes on the authority of
the embryonic Security Council, reduced the potential power of the
United Nations, and became the basis for the alliance system that soon
came to dominate Cold War international relations.

The crisis over regionalism was soon overshadowed by a lengthy
and bitter controversy concerning veto power. One major interpretation
about the significance of this question argues that ". . . the insertion of the
veto provision in the decision-making circuit of the Security Council
reflected the clear conviction that in cases of sharp conflict among the
great powers the Council ought, for safety's sake, to be incapacitated."
There was a consistent realization among the delegates and their governments that the United Nations could have little effect in forcing a great
power to desist from an act of unilateral aggression.[22] What should be
added is the Western permanent powers, and the Americans, in particular,
went to great lengths during the San Francisco negotiations to insist that
Russia accept the so-called Yalta voting formula. This argument was not
finally decided until Stettinius orchestrated a direct appeal to Premier
Stalin through Harry L. Hopkins, who had gone to Moscow to try to break
the impasse over organizing the Polish government. The American
success in obtaining agreement for veto-free discussions on procedural
questions in the council was soon followed by a similar Russian concession that the General Assembly should be allowed to discuss any issues its
members deemed pertinent. This insistence on the right to bring matters
before the United Nations reflected a growing Western appreciation that it
might be able to use the organization as a favorable public relations
sounding board in any future conflicts with the USSR.[23]

The exact scope and nature of an East-West showdown could not be
readily projected in the period in which the statesmen completed their
drafting of the UN Charter. When President Harry S Truman arrived in
San Francisco for the signing ceremonies, the mood of the city was
festive—even triumphant. For millions of casual observers it appeared as
if the tedious deliberations had achieved a long, frustrated political
millenium. Citizens in America and many abroad wanted to believe that
the Charter somehow would assure peace in the foreseeable future, and
even though spokesmen in both the Roosevelt and Truman administrations
carefully had hedged these prospects with admonitions that UN success

---

[21] Ibid., p. 1044.
[22] Claude, *Power and International Relations,* pp. 158–62.
[23] Campbell, *Masquerade Peace,* pp. 176–90.

depended on close cooperation among the great powers, the cautions were swept aside in the mood of ebullience. Truman's nationwide address on 26 June emphasized the positive prospects that the Charter harbored for humanity's future.[24]

There can be little doubt that the president expressed expectations that he genuinely hoped would achieve fruition. In his public career, Truman frequently had expressed support for international cooperation to preserve or achieve peace, but it stretches Truman's depth of commitment to claim that he had become an "internationalist."[25] Historians have long debated the motives of Truman and his close associates during the early years of the Cold War, creating a broad spectrum of arguments in trying to "prove" whether the Americans or Soviets bear the great onus for subsequent tragedies. A favorite theme of New Left critics was that Truman tried to utilize the atomic bomb to force a "showdown" with Stalin and win a postwar settlement favorable to the West by the use of "atomic diplomacy." Proponents of this notion could offer no hard evidence of specific cases where the administration had employed the bomb as a lever.[26]

NATIONAL INTEREST SPURS RELIANCE
ON REGIONAL SECURITY

The initial two years of Truman's presidency defy neat categorization. Through the first nine months the president and his foreign policy experts wrestled with the options of accommodation and confrontation. Within the State Department, to which the inexperienced president paid close attention, Soviet affairs expert Charles H. Bohlen put together a detailed policy review by mid-December 1945, which emphasized the advantages in general, conciliatory approaches to Moscow.[27] The high point of the soft line in dealing with Russia came at the Moscow foreign ministers conference. Secretary of State James F. Byrnes went beyond the

---

[24]Stettinius, San Francisco conference diary, 25, 26 June 1945, Stettinius Papers; *New York Times,* 27 June 1945, p. 1.

[25]Wilson D. Miscamble, "The Evolution of an Internationalist: Harry S. Truman and American Foreign Policy," *Australian Journal of Politics and History* 23 (August 1977): 268–83.

[26]Gar Alperovitz, *Atomic Diplomacy and Hiroshima and Potsdam* (New York: Simon and Schuster, 1965). A stinging rebuttal was provided by Robert J. Maddox, *The New Left and the Origins of the Cold War* (Princeton: Princeton University Press, 1973), pp. 63–78.

[27]Bohlen was special assistant to Secretary of State Byrnes. See "The Bohlen-Robinson Report," *Diplomatic History* 1 (Fall 1977): 389–99.

president's intentions when he made concessions to Molotov regarding Eastern Europe. Upon his return to Washington, Truman privately rebuked Byrnes and never again relied as closely on his secretary's judgment. Truman's personal anger was a small part of his closer orientation to the hard-line assessment of Soviet intentions, which came to the forefront within the administration by way of George F. Kennan's policy recommendations that reached Washington on 22 February 1946. Over the next eighteen months Kennan's containment ideas gained wider attention within the administration, while the Bohlen alternative path of accommodation went unheeded.[28]

Gradually during this period advocates of containment increased their power within the Washington hierarchy. Dean Acheson moved from assistant secretary to undersecretary of state when George C. Marshall took over as secretary of state in January 1947. Acheson left the State Department briefly in 1948 but remained an influential voice and returned as secretary in 1949. Both men were firmly admired by the president and exerted great influence as Truman developed his blend of nationalism and regional security. However, none of the American policymakers were ready to abandon the new institutions of the United Nations. Instead the United States used the issue of Russia's continued troop presence in Iran to great advantage by public and private pressure in the United Nations, receiving a Soviet withdrawal pledge in March 1946 that was widely applauded as a major victory for the United Nations.[29] In the wake of the Iranian crisis, which has been touted as the West's first success in the Cold War showdown, Stettinius soon resigned as permanent representative to the Security Council after personally and privately charging Truman and Byrnes with abandoning assurances that they would back the United Nations as the centerpiece in American foreign policy formulation.[30] By the end of the year most of those who shared the Roosevelt-Hull vision of a postwar world built on cooperation between East and West had long since departed their government posts.[31]

Events allowed little time for respite. Despite reluctant congressional approval of a massive U.S. loan to shore up Britain's nearly bankrupt

---

[28]Robert L. Messer, "Paths Not Taken: The United States Department of State and Alternatives to Containment, 1945–1946," *Diplomatic History* 1 (Fall 1977): 304–17.

[29]*FRUS, 1946*, 7:346–47, 563–67; *Newsweek* 27 (15 April 1946): 40–41; *Time* 47 (1 April 1946): 26–27; Gary Hess, "The Iranian Crisis of 1945–1946 and the Cold War," *Political Science Quarterly* 89 (March 1974): 117–46.

[30]*Stettinius Diaries*, pp. 403–4, 419, 429–30, 459–60, 469–75. The former secretary of state publicly hid his differences with the president about his true reasons for leaving government service. He privately had thought that Truman was pursuing policies all along that emphasized confrontation with Russia and undermined the potential effectiveness of the United Nations.

[31]Some of the most prominent were Henry Morgenthau, Stettinius, Henry L. Stimson, Harry L. Hopkins (deceased), and Henry Wallace.

economy, the Labour government informed the State Department in February 1947 that it could no longer maintain Western interests in the eastern Mediterranean. The administration responded with alacrity; less than three weeks later the president addressed a joint session of Congress, outlining in stark terms how freedom in Greece and Turkey were menaced by outside totalitarian forces. His Truman Doctrine called for immediate assistance to the two nations and went on to claim that the time had arrived for free people everywhere to rally to the defense of democracy.[32] Securing congressional approval of funds in short order, Truman and Marshall raised the curtain two months later on an even more spectacular plan: American underwriting of Europe's economic recovery.

The administration launched the Marshall Plan as its chief economic fusillade and moved to protect the nation's southern flank by convening the Rio conference in August 1947.[33] Truman personally attended in order to underline the importance that the United States attached to achieving the first priority of the meeting, a mutual defense treaty aimed at halting the Soviet Union from spreading international communism into the Western Hemisphere. The ensuing treaty pledged that an attack on one party would be construed as war on all. By a two-thirds vote the signatories considered what collective action to take. The appropriate mechanism was the Organization of American States created by the Pact of Bogota in 1948.[34]

The triple U.S. riposte of 1947 embraced each of the major elements of Truman's Cold War strategy: ideological commitment of the Truman Doctrine; foreign aid through the Marshall Plan; and pledges of aid against aggression by means of a regional defense treaty. Within the broad parameters of the president's world there was still ample room for assuring that each of America's initiatives blended with the goals of the United Nations. Indeed, the U.S. government could point with alarm to Soviet bullying and negative behavior in casting vetoes in the Security Council as clear evidence that America and its allies supported peace while the Soviets were boorishly bent on obstructionism and insidious expansion. In every instance the administration skillfully manipulated public opinion to believe that it was faithful to the tenets of the United Nations, even when it encountered persistent queries on this score from skeptical friends of the UN Charter.[35] One reason that the U.S. government was so careful to pay

---

[32] *Public Papers of the Presidents of the United States: Harry S. Truman, 1947* (Washington, 1963), pp. 178–80.

[33] Officially entitled the Inter-American Conference for the Maintenance of Continental Peace and Security.

[34] Roger Trask, "The Impact of the Cold War on United States-Latin American Relations, 1945–1949," *Diplomatic History* 1 (Summer 1977): 271–84.

[35] Thomas G. Paterson, "Presidential Foreign Policy, Public Opinion, and Congress: The Truman Years," *Diplomatic History* 3 (Winter 1979): 1–18 presents the case that "... public opinion and the Congress proved malleable, compliant, and permissive. President Truman successfully grasped more than once the opportunity to free himself from

homage to the United Nations arose from Truman's appreciation that the nation lacked the powerful military muscle it had possessed only several years earlier. As the Cold War intensified, the United States needed more than ever to utilize the legitimate existing institution of the United Nations rather than depend on conventional military manpower.

Whatever mainsprings moved men to action in the Kremlin, two Soviet policies in the first half of 1948 seemed to prove that the USSR was the bête noire alarmists had warned against for nearly three years. In late February a Communist coup suddenly removed Czechoslovakia from its perch as a portal to the West through the Iron Curtain. Less than four months later Soviet authorities imposed the Berlin blockade. As war scares reverberated through the Western countries, the Truman administration intensified its search for ways to assure European security while respecting American sensitivity on the score of entangling alliances. The Czech crisis provided a strong spur to the behind the scenes deliberations of Undersecretary of State Robert Lovett and Vandenberg, now Republican majority leader of the Senate.[36] The senator's role was crucial in two respects. He had the political power vital to the administration's plan to win Senate approval of a resolution favoring American participation in a regional and collective security arrangement. Second, he had taken the most direct part of any senator in active negotiations involving the United Nations and the birth of the Organization of American States (OAS). After a full partnership role with the State Department for four weeks, Vandenberg introduced Senate Resolution 239 on 11 May and shepherded it through passage a month later by the lopsided margin of 64 to 4.[37]

This unprecedented turn of events occurred at a period when leading American diplomatic and military officials already had been at work for several months on how to correlate U.S. and European interests on general security matters. Well before the grim events in Prague, British Foreign Secretary Ernest Bevin was pressing Secretary of State Marshall on the need for the United States to take more than an economic role in

---

political and constitutional restraints so that he could define and carry out his foreign policy preferences." Lawrence S. Kaplan, "Isolationism, the United Nations, and the Cold War," in Morrell Heald and Lawrence S. Kaplan, *Culture and Diplomacy: The American Experience* (Westport, CT: Greenwood Press, 1977), pp. 217–28 takes a somewhat different perspective by pointing out that administration officials " . . . underestimated the meaning the United Nations had acquired for many Americans. . . . Belatedly, they were compelled to respect the fact that newly educated elites sympathetic with the abandonment of the older isolationism during World War II required appeasement of their devotion to the United Nations before they would follow the seminal changes implicit in the containment policy of the late 1940s."

[36]*FRUS, 1948,* 3:82–118; Vandenberg, *Private Papers,* pp. 399–408.

[37]U.S., Congress, Senate, Subcommittee on the United Nations Charter of the Committee on Foreign Relations, Final Report, *Review of the United Nations Charter,* Senate Report 1797, 8th Cong., 2d sess., 1956, p. 184.

European recovery. Bevin envisioned "some sort of union in Western Europe . . . a Western democratic system . . .," which would embrace the region from Scandinavia through Turkey and include Spain and Germany "as soon as possible."[38] While Bevin and his activist colleagues shortly concluded the fifty-year Brussels Pact that embraced Britain, France, Belgium, the Netherlands, and Luxembourg, the Americans were still unwilling to plunge so intimately into European affairs. Marshall supported the concept of a pact that was based on the collective self-defense rights and regional authorization articles of the UN Charter.[39] He preferred caution at this time. The Vandenberg resolution had not yet been introduced, and several proposals were buffeting Congress concerning the reform of the United Nations. Cool heads around the president appreciated the necessity for a step by step process.[40]

The year between the Brussels Treaty and the much more impelling commitments undertaken by America joining her European partners in creating NATO brought forth the Berlin blockade and airlift. The world came close to war. Gradually, the people grew used to the bravery of pilots ferrying west Berliners their economic lifeblood. They watched Truman win against all odds in an election where the president worried very little about Republican criticism of his handling of European matters.[41] The administration could not wait for the uncertainties of an uphill election before proceeding on a European collective alliance. The president and his advisers were not sure exactly how much time the West had before Russia might explode its first atomic bomb. Already three years had passed, and the early estimates of five to seven years were much closer by the end of 1948. National Security Council estimates in this period projected no likelihood of a Soviet attack against Western Europe or into the Middle East. But action to unite the United States and Western Europe seemed imperative before Soviet technology could change perceptions and willingness to act. As Truman moved the country toward the NATO commitment, he also saw to it that the United States worked to solidify its hold on raw resource materials around the world for the nuclear weapons power that the alliance would have to possess.[42]

Once committed to the principle of a major American-European security organization, the Truman administration faced the challenge of

---

[38]*FRUS, 1948,* 3:4–6.

[39]Ibid., 3:26–29, 33–34.

[40]Lawrence S. Kaplan, "Toward the Brussels Pact," *Prologue* 12 (Summer 1980): 73–86; Central Intelligence Agency, "Review of the World Situation," 16 March 1949, in *Declassified U.S. Government Documents* (Washington: Carrolton Press, 1978), pp. 77–281A.

[41]Robert A. Divine, *Foreign Policy and U.S. Presidential Elections, 1940–1948* (New York: New Viewpoints, 1974), pp. 226–76.

[42]*FRUS, 1948,* pt. 2:617–32, 655–74; and "Foreign Policy Aspects of United States Development of Atomic Energy," ibid., pp. 677–798.

persuading the public that NATO posed no threat to the United Nations. This task was made more difficult by the unrelenting attacks from isolationists and advocates of the United Nations. Isolationists again unfurled the banner of Washington's Farewell Address and warned of the perils of "entangling alliances." They made two major charges. First, they argued that the United States was overextending itself and draining its resources, which would weaken rather than strengthen its position. Their second argument was constitutional in nature. Pointing to the pledge under article 5 of the NATO treaty where each state would assist a member attacked by an aggressor, isolationists claimed this would made a mockery out of the power of Congress to declare war. Article 11 of the treaty supposedly guarded our constitutional procedures by providing that we would act only in accordance with established law, but the chance that an attack would confront any Congress with a *fait accompli* made the isolationist point a valid one. Nonetheless, in the mood of national apprehension over the aims of the Soviet Union, the isolationist appeal made little headway.

The most effective critics of the NATO agreement were the pro-United Nations advocates. Indeed, the greatest part of the debate centered over the United Nations and the relationship of NATO to it. Republican Senator Robert A. Taft, who preferred the guarantees of congressional restraint that he saw in the UN Charter, went on national radio to question whether the NATO alliance was legal under article 51. Taft claimed that NATO exceeded the limits set by the article, especially concerning the idea of a "temporary" response to aggression. Former Vice-president Wallace charged that NATO was created to replace the United Nations, which remained as it had been when established in 1945 the best hope for world peace. He saw NATO commitments as a potential drain on the economic assistance that Congress had promised to provide Europe under the Marshall Plan.[43]

To counter these pro-United Nations arguments, the Truman administration launched a massive public relations campaign during the early part of 1949. Warren R. Austin, U.S. representative to the United Nations, praised NATO. "The North Atlantic pact is an historic move toward peace taken within the concept of the United Nations. It clearly recognizes that the obligations contained in it are subject to the overriding obligations of the United States as a member of the United Nations." Austin then vigorously defended the defensive nature of the pact. He called it "armor but not a lance; it is a shield but not a sword."[44] Likewise, Bohlen, counselor of the State Department, argued that NATO was not a

---

[43]Justus Doenecke, *Not to the Swift: The Old Isolationists in the Cold War Era* (Lewisberg, PA: Bucknell University Press, 1978), pp. 153–69; Kaplan, "Isolationism, the United Nations, and the Cold War," pp. 231–37; *New York Times,* 31 March 1949, p. 3.
[44]*New York Times,* 19 March 1949, p. 2.

substitute for the United Nations. The United Nations was still the "primary organ" for peace.[45] The campaign intensified on 18 March 1949, with a nationwide radio address by Acheson, who stressed that the pact was "carefully and conscientiously designed to conform in every particular with the Charter of the United Nations." Acheson also reasserted that it was the Soviets who forced this response through their misuse of the veto power. Fortunately, he said, the United Nations Charter was a "flexible instrument" that permitted the formation of limited associations like NATO. "The Pact," he insisted, "did not bypass the United Nations."[46]

The public relations campaign supporting NATO was by no means limited to the Truman administration. Bevin, one of the principal architects of the North Atlantic Pact, praised NATO as "the most powerful bulwark yet erected against the spread of revolutionary communism."[47] He stressed the defensive nature of the pact and its legality within the UN framework. Likewise, Lester B. Pearson, Canadian secretary of state for external affairs, stated that "peace and freedom can be secured only if those who love both peace and freedom pool their resources and stand together."[48] He also emphasized the legality of NATO within the structure of the United Nations, and concluded that Soviet intransigence made such action unavoidable. The leaders of the other NATO nations similarly fell in line.

The test of Truman's public relations campaign began on 4 April 1949 when the pact was signed in Washington by the twelve members of the North Atlantic Committee. After ninety-six witnesses testified over a three-week period, the committee issued a favorable report, and on 21 July 1949 the Senate ratified the NATO treaty by an impressive majority of 82 to 13. Truman's campaign had been a smashing success. The dissidents had been crushed by an avalanche of bipartisan support.[49]

NATO BRINGS STABILITY TO THE UNITED NATIONS

The fears of those who protested that NATO would be a death knell for the United Nations proved groundless. In the retrospect of thirty years the Atlantic Pact actually proved a saving benefit for the United Nations.

---

[45]Ibid., 30 March 1949, p. 18.

[46]Ibid., 19 March 1949, p. 1; Chester Bowles, *Ambassador's Report* (New York: Harper and Row, 1954), pp. 236–38.

[47]Lord Ismay, *The Memoirs of General Lord Ismay* (New York: Viking Press, 1960), p. 354; *New York Times*, 19 March 1949, p. 1.

[48] Lester B. Pearson, "Canada and the North Atlantic Alliance," *Foreign Affairs* 27 (April 1949): 372, 370–74.

[49]*New York Times*, 22 July 1949, p. 1.

It provided a supplemental security framework which, when joined by the Warsaw Pact six years later, created a much needed structure for stabilizing international relations. Thus, NATO actually reinforced the potential of the United Nations. First,the bitter and potentially explosive Soviet-American rivalry was removed from the UN arena, whose powers were insufficient to offer solutions acceptable to both sides. Second, by creating an institutional framework into which confrontation could be channeled, the alliance lessened the prospects of a world war. Third, the United Nations gained freedom to focus on matters where it might achieve relative success. This was to be seen particularly in cases of disputes among emerging nations and in the fields of social and economic issues, such as world health where the United Nations was to achieve a record of meritorious service.

With the creation of NATO and the United Nations earlier, the United States completed the most sweeping revision of its foreign policy in the nation's history. Well into the 1950s American leaders were absorbed with European issues and the mechanics of fleshing out the Atlantic Pact, especially integrating Germany. By the time of the Suez crisis of 1956, as non-European global questions required more attention, it was clear that the strong European focus of U.S. policy provided little support for America's effort to cope with Third World controversies. Gradually, the United Nations became more representative of global matters. For all its international character, the United Nations was still a European-American dominated organization, whose Security Council recognized a "permanent" power order that inadequately reflected the interests of Africa, Latin America, or South and Southeast Asia. NATO seemed to be an increasingly static element in a world shaped more and more by events not directly related to the issues of the superpower Cold War. However, both the Americans and Soviets were so absorbed with European matters involving their respective pacts and satellites that the leaders lacked energy and resources to handle problems elsewhere around the globe.

NATO remains a necessary deterrent against the temptation that Soviet leaders might want to move militarily into Western Europe; Soviet leadership still has not developed a military preponderance of power. In today's world, however, it is the United Nations that has come through over the past thirty years with greater potential than NATO has to solve the global problems of the last decades of the twentieth century. The potential has not been fulfilled—and may not be—even if American leaders should pay more attention to making the United Nations a focus of its diplomacy. The stabilizing presence of NATO is still required to handle the issues of Soviet-American relations peculiar to the European arena.

The United States, NATO,
and the Colonial World

SCOTT L. BILLS

It may or may not be true, as V. I. Lenin once observed, that the "masses" do not read diplomatic history, but the statement has an air of reality.[1] As a corollary, one might suggest that diplomatic historians often have neglected to read the masses; for example, they have failed to integrate fully the movements of the colonized into their policy studies. Historian Steven Sapp, noting that the Cold War era "is fast becoming one of the most profusely studied subjects in American history," has urged scholars to move beyond further and unnecessary examination of the Soviet-American rivalry and points of pertinent historiography.[2] There is also a Eurocentric bias to be overcome, one that reflects the identical geopolitical priorities of American policymakers in the postwar period.

Certainly, the roots of U.S.-Third World contention and alienation extend further back than 1945. For instance, the dynamics of capitalist economy, the role of national and racial myths, the methods of manifest destiny, and zeitgeist might be explored. The immediate postwar era, however, contained within it the source of many contemporary problems that inhibit American policy formation toward the "national liberation" struggles and modernization efforts that have so animated the societies of former colonial areas in recent years.

American policymakers in the critical period after World War II assumed almost without question that the United States was an inherently anticolonial power, even when its actions were inconsistent with that belief. As John Hickerson, former director of the Office of European Affairs, has commented: "We won our independence against a colonial power and we have always tended to sympathize with people trying to achieve independence."[3] The United States, after all, had long advocated

---

[1]V. I. Lenin, "Secrets of Foreign Policy," *The National Liberation Movement in the East* (Moscow: Foreign Languages Publishing House, 1962), p. 194. This essay was first published in *Pravda,* 23 May 1917.

[2]Steven P. Sapp, "The United States, France and the Cold War: Jefferson Caffery and American-French Relations, 1944–1949" (Ph.D. diss., Kent State University, 1978), p. iv.

[3]Personal interview with John D. Hickerson, 26 June 1979, Washington, DC.

the opening of restrictive, essentially mercantile, imperial trade systems. On the whole it had not embraced the extensive overseas land expansion of European colonialism nor devised the complex colonial administrative doctrine and establishment to supervise large foreign populations. Still, the economic expansion implicit in the Open Door Policy, combined with strategic imperatives, propelled the United States toward both a formal and informal empire.

The relationships between the United States and dependent areas would have been far from certain even if no Cold War had existed. The policy complications engendered by Soviet-American polarization undermined whatever sentiment previously had existed in support of American anticolonialism. The apocalyptic Cold War vision—a death struggle waged against an immoral, ruthless, and insidious power—left little room for an anticolonialism that had no base in pragmatic considerations. The rhetorical component did not waver and certainly many of the expressions were genuine. The emerging contradictions between actions and words gave rise to what Julius Pratt termed a "distressing dilemma" in policy formation.[4]

In a lecture delivered in October 1946, John Carter Vincent, director of the Office of Far Eastern Affairs, spoke out against American support for the status quo in the Pacific, favoring the adoption of "progressive policies" and avoidance of "short-term expedients."[5] Philip Jessup, appointed U.S. ambassador at large in March 1949, was fond of the obstetrical metaphor, referring to the postwar years as the "natal stages" for dependent peoples.[6] In a letter of October 1949 to Joseph Ballantine of the Brookings Institution, Jessup mentioned the need for an "imaginative sympathy" with Asian peoples, "looking at their problems from their point of view rather than ours." He concluded: "Clearly a policy which approached the problem of the Far East from any other direction would have little chance of succeeding."[7] Comparable statements could have been made of Africa or the Middle East. Both statements were accurate assessments of the situation, but neither one represented what later became the realities of American foreign policy.

Relations between the U.S. government and the nations and peoples of the Third World steadily deteriorated in the years after 1950. The

[4]Julius W. Pratt, "Anticolonialism in United States Policy," in *The Idea of Colonialism*, ed. Robert Strausz-Hupé and Harry W. Hazard (New York: Frederick A. Praeger, 1958), p. 133.

[5]John Carter Vincent, "Our Far Eastern Policies in Relation to our Overall National Objectives," in *America's Future in the Pacific*, ed. John Carter Vincent et al. (New Brunswick, NJ: Rutgers University Press, 1947), pp. 5–6.

[6]Philip C. Jessup, *The Birth of Nations* (New York: Columbia University Press, 1974), p. 2.

[7]Jessup to Joseph Ballantine, 14 October 1949, Papers of Philip C. Jessup, General Correspondence 1919–58, Box 47, Library of Congress.

alienation of emergent areas was an indirect result of policy decisions made by American leaders in the period 1945–49, capped by the formation of the North Atlantic Treaty Organization. Many of the ideas and considerations influencing U.S. policymakers reflected forces of longstanding import in American affairs. However, actions in the period of global upheaval following the defeat of the Axis powers were taken or not taken in a milieu of newness and fresh opportunity, and thus had a heightened impact for the ensuing decades.

THE MIDDLE LANDS

In his opening remarks for a series of joint talks between the United States and Great Britain on Middle East affairs beginning 16 October 1947, Lord Inverchapel commented: "There lies between the western countries and the countries which are Communist or Communist controlled, a kind of crescent of middle lands stretching from Scandinavia through Europe, the Middle East and South East Asia to the Far East, whose orientation will either be towards Western ideas or towards Communism."[8] For the most part, these "middle lands" comprised the colonial world—an area that after the shattering impact of the Second World War had seen or would see the rise of indigenous movements for self-determination. A document consistently cited by postwar independence movements was the Atlantic Charter issued by Franklin D. Roosevelt and Winston Churchill in late summer 1941. The statement posited the "right of all peoples to choose the form of government under which they will live" and the wish "to see sovereign rights of self-government restored to those who have been forcibly deprived of them."[9] There was nothing ambiguous in this phrasing for those living under colonial administrations in Indochina, Indonesia, the Middle East, and French North Africa—the flash points of anticolonial contention.

The fact that emergent peoples looked to the United States for leadership in the postwar era was partly due to the Atlantic Charter as well as to the well-known antiimperial attitudes of Roosevelt, as evidenced in his conversation with King ibn-Saud at Great Bitter Lake in February 1945. At that meeting, Roosevelt expressed support for Syrian and Lebanese independence as well as an end to closed economic spheres in the Middle East. He previously had opposed French restoration in

---

[8] U.S., Department of State, *Foreign Relations of the United States 1947* (Washington, DC, 1971), 5:566 (hereafter cited as *FRUS*, followed by appropriate year).
    [9] Franklin D. Roosevelt, *The Public Papers and Addresses of Franklin D. Roosevelt 1941*, comp. Samuel I. Rosenman (New York: Harper and Brothers Publishers, 1950), p. 315.

Indochina, as expressed via memos to the State Department and in discussions with Stalin at Yalta. There was also a widespread sentiment among American policymakers and consular officials that the United States was traditionally sympathetic to nationalist aspirations; that there was deeply ensconced in American policy motives an anticolonial paradigm awaiting release. In addition, there was the Charter of the newly formed United Nations, which John Foster Dulles declared "opens the door, such as the world has never before seen, to a liberation ultimately of the colonial dependent peoples of the world."[10]

However the hopes of colonial populations for an American-sponsored policy of effective opposition to imperial restoration were not realized. Although nationalist leaders sought contact with U.S. consular officials, they were often not received as was the case in Algeria until 1949. The final conversation between American diplomat Abbot Low Moffat and Indochinese leader Ho Chi Minh took place on 14 December 1946. In Indonesia, even after the Linggadjati Agreement of March 1947 recognized the de facto authority of republican insurgents over Java and Sumatra, the Netherlands administration restricted outside contacts with Indonesian leaders. The hopes for an actively benign U.S. role were so strong that even leftist guerrillas appealed to the U.S. government for assistance. Ho Chi Minh wrote to Secretary of State Edward R. Stettinius, Jr., in October 1945, asserting that the Atlantic Charter implied the "eradication of imperialism and all forms of colonial oppression." In a letter of 16 February 1946 to President Truman, he wrote: "What we ask has been graciously granted to the Philippines. Like the Philippines our goal is full independence and full cooperation with the UNITED STATES."[11] Ho Chi Minh repeated this reference to the Philippines in a *New York Times* interview of April 1947.

In great expectations, however, there was the potential for great disappointment. If the United States chose to respect the sovereignty of the colonial powers throughout dependent areas, nationalist anger and resentment would focus strongly on its policies. An early suggestion of this possibility can be seen in a note from S. Pinkney Tuck, the American minister in Egypt, following a discussion with Azzam Bey, secretary general of the Arab League, an organization then in its fourth month of existence. Bey described the "moral responsibility" of the United States toward the Arab population of French North Africa. "This responsibility which all Arabs know," he said, "emanates from the fact that it was the

---

[10]U.S., Congress, Senate, Committee on Foreign Relations, *The Charter of the United Nations, Hearings before the Committee on Foreign Relations,* 79th Cong., 1st sess., 1945, p. 643.

[11]For text of October 1945 letter, see U.S., Department of Defense, *United States–Vietnam Relations 1945–1967* (1971), vol. 1, p. C, p. 80; for text of February 1946 letter, see ibid., pp. 96–97.

United States Forces that saved France's possessions of North Africa and reestablished complete French domination over these Arab lands."[12] Similar arguments were made by anti-Dutch Indonesian leaders regarding the restoration of the Netherlands control over the East Indies as well as by Indochinese nationalists opposing French domination of Indochina. Americans, reported OSS officer Herbert J. Bleuchel from Saigon, were not perceived as Europeans. He had been observing firsthand the open antipathy between the French and the nationalist Vietminh in Indochina. Captain Bleuchel wrote: "Americans are considered to be a separate people, and the Viet Minh leaders expressed the hope the Americans would view favorably their bid for independence, since we ourselves fought for and gained our independence under a situation considered similar to that as exists in Indo China to-day."[13]

It was true nonetheless that the United States moved quickly after the end of the war to recognize continued French, British, and Netherlands sovereignty over their colonial territories. The U.S. formula for postwar trusteeships, which became part of the UN Charter, was publicly outlined by Stettinius several weeks before the San Francisco conference. The voluntary nature of the system, designed to accommodate plans by the U.S. military for an extensive defense perimeter in the Pacific and also to defer to the interests of the Western European allies, meant that none of the critical colonial areas would come under international supervision. This supervision became especially unthinkable after the inauguration of the Cold War, when international trusteeship was seen as a possible Russian "foot in the door."

There was no timetable for self-determination, by implication or otherwise, in the UN Charter, or among statements by representatives of the Truman administration. U.S. sympathy for the ideal was not unconditional. American policymakers, despite the liberal statements of such figures as Franklin Roosevelt, Sumner Welles, Philip Jessup, or John Vincent, favored only moderate expressions of anticolonial sentiments on the part of dependent peoples, and only within what became an increasingly restrictive policy framework structured by intensified U.S.-Soviet confrontation.

In examining only selective aspects of American foreign policy in the early Cold War years, it might seem that there was no overall program for colonial areas. American leaders often admitted to a lack of specific

---

[12]S. Pinkney Tuck to secretary of state, 21 June 1945, 851R.00/6-2145, Department of State, Decimal File, Record Group 59, National Archives and Records Services, Washington, DC (hereafter cited as NARS, followed by file number).
[13]Bleuchel to commanding officer, OSS Detachment 404, Headquarters SEAC, 30 September 1945, printed in U.S., Congress, Senate, Committee on Foreign Relations, *Causes, Origins, and Lessons of the Vietnam War, Hearings before the Committee on Foreign Relations*, 92d Cong., 2d sess , 1973, p. 284.

proposals, and there was no systematic assistance effort until Point Four legislation. The United States, however, consistently offered as a solution to colonial problems a general program conforming to its postwar perceptions and goals.

The U.S. government first tried to appeal to nationalist movements in a minimal way while working with the western European metropolitan powers in long-range, substantive, common programs necessitating close cooperation. Hence, American leadership continued to support the principle of self-determination in public remarks and began quietly pressing its European allies to adopt a process of evolutionary development toward self-government in colonial areas. In return for implementing such a gradualist approach, the United States offered to use its influence, where feasible and appropriate, to moderate the demands of nationalist groups so that they also might accept a slow mode of decolonization.[14] This policy led to an American program of economic stabilization, restoration of international trade, and forward military installations.

The close concomitant of gradual evolution for dependent areas was the Open Door, a policy expressed publicly and privately on many occasions by Presidents Roosevelt and Truman, State Department officials, and consular personnel. Just as the United Nations ideally would be a vehicle for the solution of colonial conflicts, so would the Open Door Policy, by promoting the end of imperial spheres, lead to a quiet and advantageous dissolution of empire, guaranteeing friendly markets and easy access to strategic materials. This program allowed expression and fulfillment of important policy goals and was apparently in tune with the anticolonial paradigm that was so much a part of the American self-image. Slow decolonization met U.S. desires for short-term maintenance of colonial empires so that overseas territories could contribute to European economic recovery. Strategic bases, communication facilities, and other military rights could be maintained without troublesome negotiations with new and inexperienced governments. It was hoped that the evolutionary process, if implemented, would preclude radical challenges to European sovereignty and control in dependent areas, thus preventing revolutionary elements from seizing power.

A major factor in U.S. postwar policy was the desire for order and stability. The United States supported no immoderate solutions to the problems of imperialism. Peace was indivisible, or as Louis Johnson would later say, "security is multiple."[15] From the perspective of this

<hr>

[14]See, for instance, undated memorandum prepared in Department of State, *FRUS 1947*, 5:535; secretary of state to the embassy in Paris, 10 June 1947, *FRUS 1947*, 5:687–88; memorandum by Policy Planning Staff, 22 March 1948, *FRUS 1948*, 3:688.

[15]U.S., Congress, Senate, Committee on Foreign Relations, *Reviews of the World Situation: 1949–1950, Hearings Held in Executive Session before the Committee on Foreign Relations*, 81st Cong., 1st and 2d sess., 1974, p. 233.

nascent globalism, political upheaval was perceived as a threat to U.S. national security. Inspired by a fledging domino theory, this was clearly the rationale of the Truman Doctrine. Economic chaos, political frustration, and uncertainty were believed to be the sine qua non of Communist advance. In a variation of the "percolator theory," economic recovery and stability in the European focal point of the Cold War would result in the transfer of health and vigor to outlying dependencies, areas that had remained stable long enough to receive this infusion through the machinery of imperial control. Western Europe would be the center or "reservoir" of power, gradually uplifting the middle lands through the ties of empire. Newly formed nationalist governments would be untested, disorganized, and hopelessly vulnerable to the Communist conspiracy. The concept of "benevolent tutelage" remained very current.

The program that the United States recommended to France and the Netherlands was first a commitment to colonial self-government; second, the training of indigenous cadres and encouraging their participation in the transitional process; and third, the establishment of a definite though flexible timetable for independence. Autonomy within an empire system was acceptable.[16] Although George Marshall might object to U.S. "thorn-pulling operations on the British lion" with regard to planned troop withdrawals from certain areas such as Greece,[17] it was the British Commonwealth structure that American policymakers wanted the French and Dutch to emulate. The British never had adopted the highly centralized, "assimilationist" colonial policies of France, nor did they appear to follow the systematic obstructionist tactics of both parties. The independence of India and Pakistan in 1947 was seen as a great precedent for orderly decolonization.

The United States, with regard to empires, was sensitive on two interrelated issues: (1) avoidance of the creation of a hostile, perhaps leftist oriented, bloc of developing nations; and (2) avoidance of close identification with the reactionary colonial policies of its European allies, especially those practices that corresponded with purposes and goals widely attributed to the Soviets. The use of diplomatic talks and negotiated agreements as a cover for colonial restoration, for instance, was not at all dissimilar to the perceived unprincipled tactics of the Soviet Union. American policymakers felt that it was very difficult for nationalist leaders to note the insidious character and comprehend the sophistic complexities of Communist doctrine. Why then should they be confronted with situations in which national aspirations were routinely denied and

---

[16]See, for example, Caffery to secretary of state [recommendations in report of North African conference at Paris], 20 June 1947, *FRUS 1947*, 5:692–97; Caffery to secretary of state [agreed findings and recommendations], 31 May 1948, *FRUS 1948*, 3:697–701; Bruce to secretary of state, 1 August 1949, NARS, 851R.00/8-149.

[17]Secretary of state to acting secretary, 25 August 1947, *FRUS 1947*, 5:313.

negotiations openly abrogated by representatives of the "free world"? In addition, although there was no cohesive international movement genuinely representing or organized by dependent peoples, they nonetheless possessed a general awareness of the status of various anticolonial struggles being fought in different parts of the world. Hence, European intransigence, whether localized or not, threatened the alienation of indigenous populations in widely scattered areas. Charlton Ogburn of the Division of Southeast Asian Affairs was not the only one to notice the "uncanny parallels" between different colonial conflicts. Henry Villard, deputy director of the Office of Near Eastern Affairs, feared that U.S. "indifference or opposition" to the Indonesian nationalist movement, with its Muslim membership, "could do immense damage to American prestige in the Near, Middle and Far East."[18]

However, the overriding importance of the European heartland in American strategic planning delineated clear postwar priorities. Western Europe was the best investment to serve the purposes of the Marshall Plan. It had the greatest potential infrastructural solidarity; it was in itself America's largest foreign market and through the percolator effect could influence a broad area; and it was a vital military theater. The United States would not seek to implement anticolonial policies that might undermine or interfere with economic and military resurgence in Europe, nor would it place its imprimatur on any nationalist struggle that sought by violent action to challenge the leadership of the Western community and thus "play into the hands" of extremists.

Not all nationalist movements, however, were directly analogous. A special example was Indochina, where the Vietnamese struggle against the French clearly was led by leftist cadres. Under the rubric of "monolithic communism," it was assumed by the U.S. government that there was a direct link between Moscow and the Vietminh. It was thought that the Soviet purpose was to draw French troops from Europe, retard French economic recovery through heavy military expenditures in Indochina, and create the requisite civil disorder for Communist advance, with a subsidiary effect of impairing regional economic growth and trade pattern restoration in Southeast Asia.[19] The State Department also realized that France in the foreseeable future could not bring about a favorable military solution. Turmoil in the colonial areas was a source of continuing weakness to the heartland. Leftist revolutionary success might well mean a restriction of American strategic supplies and military rights as well as a closed door to U.S. enterprise. On a broader scale, it could activate the falling dominoes.

In the latter part of 1948 the State Department asserted that Communists in colonial areas, focusing on Southeast Asia, were false

---

[18]Livengood [from Ogburn] to secretary of state, 17 November 1947, *FRUS 1947,* 6:1072; Villard to Bohlen, ibid., 6:995.

[19]Secretary of state to the embassy in China, 2 July 1948, *FRUS 1948,* 6:28.

nationalists. "Organized exploitation of political unrest by Communism," said Walton Butterworth, director of the Office of Far Eastern Affairs, "is the greatest single menace in the Asiatic situation."[20] This idealized dichotomy between communism and nationalism had been expressed previously. In fact, there had been a genuine hope that the internationalist ambitions of communism would prove unattractive to nascent movements for self-determination, similar to the manner in which the Communist attacks on religion and religious institutions were unpopular with Muslim communities. A note of 11 July 1946, sent by the State Department to U.S. consular offices in Algiers, Tunis, Casablanca, and Rabat, had ordered fortnightly reports on Communist activities. It specified that "special attention should be made of attempts, successful or otherwise, to recruit Moslems into the Communist or Communist-inspired parties or groups."[21] American representatives made every effort to convince the French administration in North Africa that Communists were a greater danger than nationalist parties. In Indonesia, American pressure on the Dutch was directed specifically at maintaining the separation of republican and Communist elements. It was assumed that a full-scale colonial war would only push the two groups into an alliance where veteran Communist forces might seize control.

THE NORTH ATLANTIC TREATY

In early 1949, ECA Director Paul Hoffman reported that Western Europe had passed through the first phase of economic recovery. Exploratory talks regarding the establishment of a military alliance comprising the nations of the Atlantic Community had begun in July 1948, following Senate passage of the Vandenberg resolution in June. Although it was generally believed that a Russian military thrust against Western Europe was, as expressed in SANACC 360/11, "improbable," or to use Paul Nitze's phrase, a "tertiary risk," there were still forces dampening the European Recovery Program (ERP) efforts. "Western Europe," recalled Theodore Achilles, "badly needed confidence and energy."[22] The State Department reported that this situation was created by insecurity over the threat of Soviet attack. There was one major reason that civilization teetered on the edge of the abyss. "It was because one nation

---

[20]W. Walton Butterworth, "Asia Today," in Department of State *Bulletin* 19 (17 October 1948): 492.

[21]Secretary of state to American consular officer in charge, Algiers, Algeria, 11 July 1946, NARS, 851R.00/7-1146.

[22]Remarks at a luncheon address, 16 April 1980, "NATO After Thirty Years" conference, Kent State University, Kent, OH.

and its satellites," remarked General Omar Bradley, "saw fit to keep the world stirred up and in a period of turmoil."[23] Just as the Truman Doctrine and the Marshall Plan had been complementary, the European recovery and the Atlantic Alliance also would be compatible and homologous.

The scope of the alliance was defined in two ways: geographical and national security interests. As Dean Acheson outlined it in a memorandum to President Truman, NATO "should be participated in by as many countries as are in a position to further the democratic principles upon which the treaty is based and to contribute to the security of the North Atlantic area. . . ."[24] Geographical proximity was negotiable. The primacy of "democratic principles" was also flexible, as evidenced by Achilles's defense of the Portuguese regime, describing it as "authoritarian" rather than "totalitarian." Senator Tom Connally then noted that "it is a dictatorship by the will of the people."[25]

The initial impetus of the new security arrangement was directed more toward internal than external threats to political stability, especially the so-called "fifth column" Communist parties in France and Italy. State Department and ECA spokesmen previously had emphasized the positive role of the Marshall Plan in restricting Communist influence. Secretary of State Acheson, speaking before the U.S. Chamber of Commerce in May 1949, stated: "Since the beginning of the European Recovery Program, totalitarianism in Western Europe has made no advance."[26] The North Atlantic Pact therefore would broaden and deepen European strength; it would "wage peace."

Questioned about the application of the "armed attack" provision of the treaty to internal problems, Acheson responded by saying that it would not apply to a "purely ideological offensive." This was on 8 March 1949 as he spoke before an executive session of the Senate Foreign Relations Committee. "If you would have a combination of the use of force with an internal fifth column," he said, "of course it would [apply]." Later he commented: "Whether you would reach the same conclusion if the thing were entirely generated from inside, with external political stimulation, is another question."[27] In a press conference of 18 March, Acheson stated

---

[23]U.S., Congress, Senate, Committee on Armed Services and Committee on Foreign Relations, *Military Situation in the Far East, Hearings before the Committee on Armed Services and the Committee on Foreign Relations,* 82d Cong., 1st sess., 1951, pt. 2, p. 885.
    [24]Memorandum for the president, 7 April 1949, NARS, 840.20/4-749.
    [25]U.S., Congress, Senate, Committee on Foreign Relations, *The Vandenberg Resolution and the North Atlantic Treaty, Hearings Held in Executive Session before the Committee on Foreign Relations,* 80th Cong., 2d sess. and 81st Cong., 1st sess., 1973, pp. 297-98.
    [26]*New York Times,* 4 May 1949.
    [27]*Vandenberg Resolution and the North Atlantic Treaty, Hearings Held in Executive Session,* pp. 155-56.

that revolutionary activity supported by an outside power would come under the terms of the "armed attack" provision.[28]

This was a critical point for two reasons: (1) leftist revolutionary activity always was seen as having been stimulated by Moscow; and (2) such activity was most likely to arise (and was in fact ongoing) in the overseas territories of pact signatories. Potential problems certainly would be amplified if projected Russian opposition to the pact involved, as one State Department memorandum outlined, "diversionary troubles throughout the whole colonial world."[29]

The Atlantic Alliance was what Hoffman termed part of a "chain reaction" to the Marshall Plan.[30] As ERP assistance had been centered in Western Europe, to then trickle down to other areas, so a core of military strength in Europe also would enhance security in other and noncontiguous areas. This broad commitment was illustrated by the Title III provisions of the Military Assistance Program (MAP) of October 1949. It was assumed that colonial territories would benefit directly from this reservoir of power in Europe.

The imperial sensitivities and aspirations of the two keystone European countries of NATO, France and Great Britain, were well known in the State Department. At French initiative during treaty negotiations, the "Algerian departments of France" were included in the zone of collective security outlined by article 6 of the pact. Although Charles Bohlen had advised a January 1949 meeting of the International Working Group that such a provision would make congressional approval of the treaty "extremely difficult," the actual Senate debate did not focus on colonial issues.

The public hearings on the North Atlantic Treaty saw only occasional and predictable criticism of ostensible pact insensitivity to nationalist movements: such speakers as Farrell Dobbs of the Socialist Workers party, Norman Thomas of the Socialist party, and in a written statement submitted by Eugene Dennis, general secretary of the Communist party of the United States. Though he favored pact ratification, Thomas feared that the treaty would align the United States too rigidly with European interests in Indonesia and Indochina. "These wars," he said, "create a situation made to order for racist and Communist exploitation against the United States." James Warburg, a nonleftist and often friendly critic of the proposed pact, made many points in his congressional

---

[28]*New York Times,* 19 March 1949.

[29]Reinhardt to Ackerson, 15 February 1949, NARS, 840.20/2-1549. George Reinhardt was chief of the Division of Eastern European Affairs.

[30]U.S., Congress, House, Committee on Appropriations, *Foreign Aid Appropriation Bill for 1950, Hearings before the Subcommittee of the Committee on Appropriations,* 81st Cong., 1st sess., 1949, p. 20.

testimony that he previously had expressed in correspondence with the State Department and Senator Vandenberg, charging that there was a misperception of the Soviet threat and an unclear and dangerous American military commitment. As part of his remarks on clothing the treaty in "moral garments," Warburg asserted that there was an inconsistency in the preamble's adherence to democratic principles amidst the reality of the denial of civil liberties to colonial populations. Only W. H. Hunton of the Council on African Affairs dealt extensively with the colonial issue, claiming that the North Atlantic Treaty would create an unstable "two-world system." He attacked the colonial policies of Belgium, France, Great Britain, the Netherlands, and Portugal, and referred to the United States as the "most powerful colonial power of all time."[31] However, major points of criticism raised during the hearings clustered around such issues as the role of the United Nations and the possibilities for international disarmament.

Meeting in executive session, members of the Senate Foreign Relations Committee had an opportunity to discuss problems they frequently did not want to see debated on the Senate floor. Acheson, appearing on 18 February 1949, noted that the inclusion of Algeria was necessitated by French domestic politics. Looking at it pragmatically, he said: "It is a matter of no importance one way or the other, except from the point of view of French politics, because it is impossible that there would be an attack on Algeria if there were not an attack on France." In this and later committee meetings, the possibility of indigenous uprisings triggering pact provisions, a concern of U.S. military planners, was not conclusively examined.

Committee concerns were more political than strategic, although Senator Claude Pepper voiced a question regarding the possible centrifugal dispersal of European strength to overseas territories. Again, it was Senator Henry Cabot Lodge, Jr., a strong treaty proponent, who identified the central ambivalence: "This is one of the fundamental contradictions in terms of this whole thing; because we need . . . these [European] countries to be strong, and they cannot be strong without their colonies and yet we do not like their colonies, and that is a contradiction in terms."[32] Acheson would make a similar point with reference to U.S. support for the French in Indochina when he appeared before the committee some months later.[33]

Although Algeria was included under the terms of article 6 with, as

    [31]U.S., Congress, Senate, Committee on Foreign Relations, *North Atlantic Treaty, Hearings before the Committee on Foreign Relations,* 81st Cong., 1st sess., 1949, pt. 2, pp. 672–74 [Warburg], p. 732 [Thomas]; ibid., pt. 3, p. 964 [Hunton]. See also Warburg to Vandenberg, 1 February 1949, NARS, 840.20/2-449.
    [32]*Vandenberg Resolution and the North Atlantic Treaty, Hearings Held in Executive Session,* p. 117 [Acheson], p. 256 [Lodge].
    [33]*Reviews of the World Situation, Hearings Held in Executive Session,* p. 357.

John Hickerson has said, "great reluctance," it was nonetheless a good indication of American priorities. The desensitization, militarism, mechanistic perceptions, and political expediency of the Cold War held little room for awareness of and support for the aspirations of emergent societies. There was ample evidence that Algerian nationalist groups opposed the treaty terms, and their criticism was clearly separate from routine Communist party opposition to the Atlantic Pact as a whole.

U.S. deference to the French on the Algerian question was a concession made for the purpose of further consolidating the Western sphere in Europe: an anti-Soviet bloc directed largely by the American postwar drive for order, stability, economic restoration, and the Open Door Policy. As Acheson said to members of Congress in September 1950, "the beginning and the center of everything that we do is really the building up of the strength of the North Atlantic forces. . . . If we get strong forces in Western Europe it will affect the peace in other areas of the world very profoundly indeed."[34]

CONCLUSIONS

Excessive focus on the Algerian issue might lead to the conclusion that it represented an aberrational action—a desperate concession made by the United States to secure vital agreement on other matters. The inclusion of the Algerian departments, however, was in fact part of the evolutionary nature of American anticolonialism. The move was consistent with a European first priority and with a perception of international politics that tied American financial growth and stability as well as military security into a "common heritage," where the anticolonialist paradigm of "traditional sympathy" and "gradual but sure evolution" was inoperative. Colonial areas were zones of potential destabilizing influences and were perceived as certain prey for Soviet-directed revolutionaries if self-government were won without a further period of Western tutelage. The concept of a benevolent United States using Third World nationalism as a weapon against perceived Soviet/Communist expansionism had shown little appreciation for either the spontaneous or planned anti-imperialist eruptions among dependent peoples. American policymakers showed little understanding of the fundamental ramifications of the system of colonial underdevelopment that was imposed on the indigenous societies of the Third World.

U.S. support for the UN Security Council intervention in the Indonesian dispute was based on the fact that: (1) the moderate republican

[34]Ibid., p. 340.

leadership, in defeating a Communist attempt to seize power in 1948, exemplified U.S. hopes for nationalist movements in the postwar era; and (2) Dutch subterfuge and heavy-handed military actions were too reminiscent of activities undertaken by totalitarian forces and threatened to encourage the formation of an anti-Western Asiatic group. In addition, the Netherlands was not the keystone country that France had become for the ERP and NATO structures. However, the U.S. role in the Security Council debate was to moderate much of the harsher and more radical measures suggested by other members. And although ECA assistance to the Netherlands for use in Indonesia was discontinued, aid to Holland was not interrupted.

The incorporation of Algeria into the Atlantic Pact may have been, as Acheson described it, a "troublesome problem," or as Senator Vandenberg remarked, a "pretty lousy inclusion," but it was nonetheless an acceptable turn of events. Senators Lodge and Connally both viewed Algeria as an integral part of France, as much so, remarked Lodge, "as 14th Street and Pennsylvania Avenue is a part of Washington."[35] In a broader sense, the negotiation and ratification of the North Atlantic Treaty buttressed and enhanced the growing pragmatism in American foreign policy. Secretary Acheson's characterization of the Cold War as "playing for keeps" ruled out softness in approaching the implacable enemy. Colonial liberation struggles increasingly were relegated to a policy periphery inhabited by peoples of enigmatic and immature purpose with questionable, perhaps hostile, aims. The Atlantic Alliance capped a two-year process of energetic foreign policy proposals and diplomacy; it also solidified State Department priorities that placed colonial affairs in a tertiary sphere awaiting percolative gains. Third World nationalism, as it subsequently became more militant and leftist in tone, completed the process of alienation.

As the United States passed through the immediate postwar years and looked toward what Vannevar Bush called the "middle future,"[36] the substructure of containment became firmly emplaced, especially with the congressional approval of MAP. A certain degree of ambivalence remained concerning the Euro-American relationship, a wariness and defensiveness on the part of some congressmen who successively had supported the Marshall Plan, NATO, and MAP—the three pillars of U.S. foreign policy according to Acheson. Representative John Davis Lodge remarked during an executive session of the House Foreign Affairs Committee that there was no certainty that the nations of Western Europe

---

[35]*Vandenberg Resolution and the North Atlantic Treaty, Hearings Held in Executive Session,* p. 117.

[36]Vannevar Bush, *Modern Arms and Free Men: A Discussion of the Role of Science in Preserving Democracy* (New York: Simon and Schuster, 1949), p. 122.

would be willing to cooperate as fully or completely as desired. Lodge commented that "they have gotten into some bad habits over a period of 2,000 years or so."[37]

There were definite strains in the relationship. Francis Wilcox, former chief of staff for the Senate Foreign Relations Committee, has noted the divisive role that decolonization played within the Atlantic Community.[38] Under the principle of indivisible peace, there were no unimportant geopolitical areas, but there was a ranked order with Europe first as long as it was perceived as the "vortex" of struggle. And although Acheson asserted that the ideas of the Atlantic Charter "were not cynical slogans,"[39] U.S. policies toward colonial territories in the years after 1949 were rigidly aloof. Leftist agitation was perceived to be of one pattern: the global battle being fought via "satellite" armies. Acheson observed that the conflict in Korea (after June 1950) and the warfare in Indochina fit "very closely."[40] The situation in Indochina, stated Dean Rusk, was "a civil war which has been in effect captured by the [Soviet] Politburo. . . ."[41] Norman Thomas and Acheson agreed on the thesis of an "imperialist" Russia, exercising a "new colonialism" in the underdeveloped world.

Although the public statements of American officials in support for self-determination and nationalist movements did not appreciably dwindle in the period after the signing of the Atlantic Pact, the substance of policy had taken a different turn. The periodic hostility of Third World movements and regimes toward the United States in the past three decades has appeared genuinely perplexing and somewhat incomprehensible to both the American public and many government officials, except within the context of Cold War conspiracy. The alienation is at least partly rooted in the character and implementation of U.S. policies in the early postwar, culminating with the North Atlantic Treaty. Through the 1950s and into the 1960s, the nationalism of emergent peoples clearly became an issue that was not peripheral but rather, as Franz Fanon has written, "at the middle of the whirlpool."[42] It was this development in international relations that the United States was unprepared to accept and to which it

---

[37]U.S., Congress, House, Committee on International Relations, *Selected Executive Session Hearings of the Committee, 1943–50*, vol. 5, pt. 1, p. 279.

[38]Francis O. Wilcox, "The Atlantic Community and the United Nations," in *The Atlantic Community: Progress and Prospects*, ed. Francis O. Wilcox and H. Field Haviland, Jr. (New York: Frederick A. Praeger, 1963), p. 171.

[39]*Military Situation in the Far East, Hearings*, pt. 3, p. 1715.

[40]U.S., Congress, Senate, Committee on Foreign Relations, *Executive Sessions of the Senate Foreign Relations Committee*, 82d Cong., 1st sess., 1976, vol. 3, pt. 1, p. 17.

[41]Ibid., 81st Cong., 1st and 2d sess., 1976, vol. 2, p. 455. Dean Rusk was assistant secretary of state for Far Eastern Affairs.

[42]Franz Fanon, *The Wretched of the Earth*, trans. Constance Farrington (New York: Grove Press, 1968), p. 76.

could not adjust. American leaders had chosen, or felt forced by circumstances, during a critical period to refrain from exercising U.S. power
that would seriously challenge the "implacable dependence" of metropole
and colony.[43] John Carter Vincent, speaking several weeks after the
Japanese surrender in 1945, had noted: "We can be sentimental as well as
practical—as long as we *are* practical."[44]

---

[43]The phrase is from Albert Memmi, *The Colonizer and the Colonized,* trans.
Howard Greenfeld (New York: Orion Press, 1965), p. ix.

[44]John Carter Vincent, "The Post-War Period in the Far East," in Department of
State *Bulletin* 13 (21 October 1945): 648. Emphasis in original.

NATO and the European Community

WALTER LIPGENS

A central question surrounding the Atlantic Alliance is whether it would be more desirable in the age of predominantly "global issues"— military balance, energy, monetary systems, Third World development— for Europe and America to strengthen or to weaken further efforts toward West European unification.

In order to examine this question, it is useful first to look briefly at the history of U.S.-West European interdependence. This includes the elements of continuity in the relationship since the signing of the North Atlantic Treaty in 1949, notably "the broad range of common interests acknowledged," which continues to characterize the Atlantic Alliance.[1] Second, the necessity for European unity as a prerequisite for an effective alliance requires examination. A consensus on this question has been shared on both sides of the Atlantic in the first fifteen years of NATO's history. The allies recognized in this period that the disparity in power between the United States and the nation-states of Western Europe could best be overcome by the building of a European economic and political community. Third, the obstacles to the emergence of a European entity, which became more visible in the second fifteen years of NATO, will be considered. These include division among West Europeans and distrust of the European Economic Community (EEC) by Americans, exacerbated since the era of de Gaulle. Finally, the speculation on questions concerning the future of Western European unification within the framework of NATO will be discussed.

CONTINUITY IN INTERDEPENDENCE

Many aspects have changed since NATO was founded in 1949 but not the following central facts, which provided and still provide the basis of the U.S.-West European association since the beginning of the Cold War, despite all strains and difficulties.

[1]Stanley Hoffmann, "Uneven Allies: An Overview," in David S. Landes, ed., *Western Europe: The Trials of Partnership* (Lexington, MA: D. C. Heath, 1977), p. 56.

165

The West European mid-sized and smaller democracies have had and continue to have no possibility of self-defense vis-à-vis the Soviet Union. With its totalitarian hold spreading over the Eastern half of Europe, it is one of the modern world's superpowers—a territory several times larger than that of all Western Europe. In the early postwar years, as at present, Soviet military strength was recognized as unquestionably superior to that of Western Europe. Remembering that in the late thirties Britain and France were too weak without the United States to prevent Hitler from going to war, West Europeans still realize that in a potential position of isolation vis-à-vis the Soviet Union, the latter would have the overwhelming power to enforce its political will upon Western Europe.

Even an amalgamation of Western Europe's conventional and nuclear forces would be miniscule in size and potential compared to that of the Soviet Union which can be contained only by the forces of the United States.[2] The defense and military security of Europe depends entirely upon the safeguard provided by the United States. The Atlantic Alliance is cohesive essentially because of U.S. nuclear power, which alone provides the vital security to all other member states. The continuing U.S. nuclear guarantee is the central and elemental interest of Western Europe, and there is still no alternative.[3]

The physical security of Western Europe was and remains a strategic priority for the United States, in counterbalance to the Soviet Union. In the contest between America and Russia, Western Europe has indeed been from the beginning a decisive stake in the balance of power. As Senator J. William Fulbright expressed it in 1947: "This country cannot tolerate the expansion of Russia to the point where she controls, directly or indirectly, all the resources and man-power of Europe." Advisers within the Truman administration have stated correctly that "if they gave priority to Western Europe, it was because they felt that this area, next to the U.S. itself, contributed most to the power of the West and that its loss would be an irretrievable disaster."[4] Behind this thought there

---

[2]Andrew J. Pierre, *Nuclear Politics: The British Experience with an Independent Strategic Force 1939–1970* (London: Oxford University Press, 1972); Karl Kaiser, *Europe and the United States: The Future of the Relationship* (Washington, DC: Columbia Books, 1973), chap. 4; Raymond Aron, "La force française de dissuasion et l'Alliance Atlantique," *Défense nationale* 33 (1977): 31–46; U.S., Congress, Senate, Committee on Armed Services, *NATO and the New Soviet Threat,* report of Senators Sam Nunn and Dewey F. Bartlett, 95th Cong., 1st sess., 1977.

[3]Robert E. Osgood, *NATO: The Entangling Alliance* (Chicago: University of Chicago Press, 1962); Stanley Hoffmann, "Weighing the Balance of Power," *Foreign Affairs,* 50 (1972): 618–43; Alfred Grosser, *Das Bündnis die west-europäischen Länder und die USA seit dem Krieg* (München: Hanser, 1978), pp. 30, 442; International Institute for Strategic Studies, *The Military Balance 1979–1980* (London, 1979).

[4]Karl E. Meyer, *Fulbright of Arkansas* (Washington, DC: R. Luce, 1963), p. 159; William G. Carleton, *The Revolution in American Foreign Policy: Its Global Range* (New York: Random House, 1965), p. 126.

was also the vivid historical experience that twice in the first half of this century the United States became embroiled in a world war because she failed to become involved with Europe at critical times. A high price was paid for isolation. This time U.S. decision makers were determined to stabilize Europe and maintain its support in the contest with Moscow. In this compelling sense, one principal interest of the United States remains the well-being of a Western Europe "that is both safe from military attack or nibbling from the East, and sufficiently confident in its capacity to deter such encroachment and not to be tempted to glide into 'Finlandization,' *i.e.* into a policy of accommodation to Soviet demands (for instance, a veto of any extension of EEC activities in diplomacy or defense, always opposed by Moscow)."[5] Consequently, Washington has given its nuclear guarantee to Western Europe and has decided to maintain U.S. troops and tactical nuclear weapons in Europe in order to serve as security for the guarantee. The additional costs of this guarantee are not large. The United States would require almost the same number of missiles, nuclear weapons, polaris submarines, etc., whether Europe needed defending or not.[6] But the necessity to secure Western Europe in the balance of world power is indeed an essential interest of the United States.

In addition to security, economic prosperity remains a central tenet among the common interests of the Atlantic system. Western Europe's prosperity has been a prime objective of U.S. policy since the Marshall Plan, partly because economic weakness would have been a breeding ground for communism in Western Europe, partly because Europe's revival would facilitate the reintegration of West Germany into a productive partnership. America's original interest in Western Europe's recovery eventually turned into a permanent interest in her prosperity as part of the "open" international economy. Previous experience with the devastating effects of the interwar stagnation has resulted in a determined European espousal of the open market, elimination of protectionism, free trade of raw materials, and free export possibilities as elementary conditions for sustained prosperity. This historic lesson from the interwar world crisis coincided with U.S. adoption of a liberal trade policy. The Organization for European Economic Cooperation (OEEC), the EEC, and the Kennedy Round et al., created enormous advantages for both sides of the Atlantic Community, and a wealth of trading links and

---

[5]Hoffmann, "Uneven Allies: An Overview," pp. 56, 78; Walter F. Hahn, "The US-European Strategic Linkage," in W. F. Hahn and R. L. Pfaltzgraff, eds., *Atlantic Community in Crisis* (New York: Pergamon Press, 1979), pp. 73–90.

[6]Harold van B. Cleveland, *The Atlantic Idea and Its European Rivals,* Council on Foreign Relations (New York: McGraw-Hill, 1966), pp. 19–20. "The American nuclear forces needed to back up the guarantee are very nearly the same forces the United States needs for its own protection." The annual overall costs for U.S. troops stationed in Europe (including the Mediterranean) are around $3 billion, subsidized in large part by West Germany's preferential purchasing of U.S. armaments, *Strategic Survey 1971* (London, 1972), pp. 21–23. See International Institute for Strategic Studies.

financial involvement "that make the North Atlantic . . . a co-prosperity sphere."[7] In short, there is a reciprocal interest both for the United States and Western Europe in maintaining the free trade and capital flow policies and the reciprocal exports of goods and services that are the basis of this coprosperity.

The question of alternatives to this Atlantic system of close interdependency has previously arisen, but none of the alternatives discussed has led to a substantial change. First, in the 1950s there was the idea of a U.S. "roll-back" policy with regard to Eastern Europe's occupation by the Soviet Union, which would have led to the elimination of the Soviet threat and to the possibility of the unification of the whole of Europe. However, since direct warfare was excluded as a policy option, this alternative came to nothing; the Soviet Union remained a menace and in resolute control of the Eastern European regimes. The ensuing Gaullist policy of an autonomous, polycentric foreign and defense policy also failed. The old-fashioned idea of a single independent nation-state able to defend itself only with its own resources indeed has been regarded by most European governments as suicidal and parasitic depending in the final event, as is also the case for the neutral states, upon U.S. nuclear guarantee. Finally, a superpower détente policy has been unable to bring about fundamentally new conditions; it reached a certain normalization of the status quo, a certain improvement in the international climate and a reduction of tension, but it has brought about no fundamental "East-West reconciliation." The Helsinki accord and the negotiation over Mutual Balanced Force Reductions (MBFR) produced the paradoxical effect of actually strengthening the blocs.[8] Despite all dissent, the basic interdependence and the military-economic advantages derived from the Atlantic system remain intact as the only viable system for the foreseeable future.

Containment of communism, along with free trade and prosperity, are the two accomplishments that both sides of the alliance equally need in addition to their binding cultural links and common liberal-democratic heritage. In global issues—energy, monetary systems, the Third World—both sides of the Atlantic have equal interest and a reciprocal diplomatic need of each other.

---

[7]Hoffmann, "Uneven Allies: An Overview," p. 78; Cleveland, *Atlantic Idea,* pp. 96–123; William Diebold, Jr., "Economics and Politics: The Western Alliance in the 1970's," in *The United States and Western Europe: Political, Economic and Strategic Perspectives,* ed. Wolfram F. Hanrieder (Cambridge, MA: Winthrop, 1974), pp. 134–63; Elliot R. Goodman, *The Fate of the Atlantic Community* (New York: Praeger, 1975), pp. 449–502; Lawrence Bell, "Trade and the Atlantic Community," *The Atlantic Community in Crisis,* pp. 315–48.

[8]Hans-Peter Schwarz, "Das Atlantische Sicherheitssystem in einer Äre ohne grosse Alternativen," in Karl Kaiser and Hans-Peter Schwarz, eds., *Amerika und Westeuropa. Gegenwarts und Zukunfts Probleme* (Stuttgart: Belser, 1977), pp. 165–203; Walter F. Hahn, "Toward a New NATO Consensus," *The Atlantic Community in Crisis,* pp. 55–72.

The alliance has not developed into a community in the full sense of the word. It has no common law, no common budget, no common directly elected parliament, no common courts, as has the EEC; it is a community of interdependence, reciprocal interests, and mutual cooperation.[9] Under article 13 any member could withdraw from the alliance after 1969, but no state has done so. The alliance seems likely to persist as long as these complementary conditions continue.

FIFTEEN YEARS OF CONSENSUS IN WESTERN EUROPEAN UNIFICATION

From the 1950s to the first half of the 1960s there was indeed a widely held belief on both sides of the Atlantic that Western Europeans should extend "beyond the nation-state," and should build a union so as thereafter to become an equal partner who would greatly facilitate the tasks of the alliance.

In Europe itself, especially in reaction to the outbreak of World War II and as a result of thoughts among the resistance groups, there had been a decisive breakthrough of insight into this issue. The League of Nations, as a loose mechanism of conferences resting on the veto of every member state, clearly did not have enough strength of its own to prevent the coming to power of Fascist regimes, or to secure peace. For this purpose a stronger federal authority in Europe with power of its own would have been necessary. The culmination of the catastrophic economic crisis of 1930, followed by the outbreak of war, provided sharp lessons— the scale of modern economic systems and power finally exceeded those of the European nation-states. This was further demonstrated to almost all Europeans by the breakdown of the nation-states during the war and by the long years of total Nazi occupation. In the final event this last attempt by one of Europe's nations to achieve hegemony was thwarted by the intervention of the two world powers on the periphery of Western Europe. In the future it was clear that Europe only could be heard and participate in world affairs if she managed to speak with one voice and not as a troubled balkanised area between the two new superpowers.[10]

After the war these ideas and experiences were the motivating force

---

[9]See the precise definitions in "Bericht ober Lage der Gemeinschaft," 1 March 1962, in Walter Hallstein, *Europäische Reden* (Stuttgart: Belser, 1979), pp. 335–36; Cleveland, *Atlantic Idea,* pp. 150–70; Goodman, *Fate of the Atlantic Community,* pp. 148–70.

[10]See the documentary collection by Walter Lipgens, *Europa—Föderationpläne der Widerstandsbewegungen 1940–1945* (München: Oldenbourg, 1968). An enlarged English edition is in preparation for the series of the European University Institute, *Documents on the History of European Integration,* vol. 1 (Leyden and Brussels: Sijthoff and Bruylant, 1978). See Lipgens, "European Federations in the Political Thought of Resistance

behind a remarkable group of young leaders and activists who fought for the idea of the "United States of Europe," which still remains a long-term goal among many Western European political circles. During the winter of 1946–47, European groups sprang up in all major cities to promote this grand concept and soon joined together in the "Union Européenne des Fédéralistes," but they initially were unable to influence the governments struggling with the economic chaos of that winter.[11] However, after it became clear that there was a real Soviet threat holding Eastern Europe under its rule and making reconstruction impossible and that the United States would encourage Western European cooperation and integration, the European Federalists, in the framework of the "European Movement" under the leadership of Duncan Sandys, could ensure large majorities in public opinions and parliaments in behalf of unification. Although British reluctance frustrated attempts in 1948–49 to create a European constituent assembly and produced instead a consultative Council of Europe, the success of the Schuman Plan in six continental countries in 1950 was a breakthrough for the process of supranational integration.

In the United States where John Foster Dulles was the first to recognize in a major speech made in January 1947 that Europe could have a future along federalist lines, there developed in the spring of that year a strong support for the idea. The underlying reason for the U.S. administration's support was above all economic, as stated in George C. Marshall's Harvard speech. As William Clayton expressed it in his memorandum of 27 May: "Europe cannot recover from this war and again become independent if her economy continues to be divided into many small water-tight compartments as it is today."[12] Europeans, therefore, were urged to organize themselves and to use U.S. economic aid to its maximum cooperative effect. Soon there were also attempts to enlarge American support for the European idea in the political field as well. In March 1947 resolutions had been introduced in both Houses stating "that the Congress favours the creation of a United States of Europe."[13]

Movements during World War II," *Central European History* 1 (1968): 5–19. Reprinted in F. Roy Willis, ed., *European Integration* (New York: F. Watts, 1975), pp. 1–18.

[11]Walter Lipgens, *A History of European Integration Vol. I: 1945–1947* (London: Oxford University Press, 1980).

[12]U.S., Department of State, *Foreign Relations of the United States 1947* (Washington, DC: Government Printing Office, 1972): 3:23–232 (hereafter cited as *FRUS,* followed by appropriate year). Speech by John F. Dulles, "Europe must Federate or Perish," *Vital Speeches of the Day* 13 (February 1947): 234–36. Similarly, Acheson said in his Cleveland speech of 8 May 1947: "European recovery cannot be complete until the various parts of Europe's economy are working together in a harmonious whole. And the achievement of a coordinated European economy remains a fundamental objective of our foreign policy." U.S., Department of State *Bulletin*, 16:991.

[13]U.S., Congress, Senate, *Congressional Record,* 80th Cong., 1st sess., vol. 93, pp. 2418, 2425. The resolution was referred to the Foreign Affairs Committee but was not passed due to Marshall's intervention. See fn. 15.

Unfortunately, these resolutions were not acted upon because of the intervention of Secretary of State Marshall. He followed the advice in Charles Kindleberger's memorandum: "To avoid injuring sensitive feelings of nationalism, our appeal should be couched in terms of a European recovery plan which stresses the raising of European production and consumption through the economic and 'functional' unification of Europe."[14] Also in his Harvard speech he cautiously stated: "The role of this country should consist of friendly aid in the drafting of a European program and later support of such a program should be a joint one, agreed to by a number, if not all, of European nations."[15]

Encouraged by the Schuman Plan, the American friends of European integration persisted in their efforts. In 1951 Congress stated that the object of U.S. policy was the "economic unification and political integration of Europe."[16] After the failure, attributed essentially to British reluctance, of West Europe's first attempt to establish a political constituent assembly as part of the Council of Europe project, the so-called Europe of Six was created with the foundation of the Coal and Steel Community and was equipped with an Executive High Authority and other prefederal organs. The United States firmly backed this second supranational initiative. Similarly, strong support also was given to the European Defense Community (EDC) project, which the United States hoped would reduce her burdens and responsibilities in Europe.

In Europe there was a growing conviction among the leading European protagonists that the disproportion in the association between the United States as a superpower and the twelve smaller nation-states of Europe had to be rectified and overcome by genuine West European unification. The American policymakers indeed needed more military cohesion, economic prosperity, and united political support from Europe. Furthermore, there was also the idealistic conviction that what had proved to be so beneficial for the North American continent—federal institutions— would be equally good for Europe. After the breakdown of the EDC project, the United States warmly welcomed the founding of the EEC, with its institutionalized integration, as it did the growing economic

---

[14]Max Beloff, *The United States and the Unity of Europe* (Washington, DC: Brookings Institute, 1963), p. 16; *FRUS, 1947*, 3:204–19.

[15]Ernst H. van der Beugel, *From Marshall Aid to Atlantic Partnership* (Amsterdam: Elsevier, 1966), pp. 52, 103–5. Later Fulbright claimed: "The United States might well have exploited the opportunity provided by the European Recovery Program to push the resistant nations toward political federation as well as economic cooperation, but all proposals to this effect were rejected by the United States Government at the time." See J. W. Fulbright, "For a Concert of Three Nations," *Foreign Affairs*, 40 (October 1961): 13.

[16]Beloff, *United States and the Unity of Europe*, pp. 65, 38. A declaration in the extension of the ECA act was approved on 19 April 1949, stating that it was "the policy of the people of the United States to encourage the unification of Europe." The statement, to Fulbright's regret, did not include the term "political unity."

success of the Common Market itself. A further breakthrough seemed possible in the summer of 1961, with the first applications by Great Britain, Ireland, Denmark, and Norway to become full members of the EEC and with the progress made at the Bonn conference of EEC heads of governments, where a declaration favoring ultimate political unity was passed.[17]

Until the beginning of the 1960s many Europeans and Americans shared the belief that Europe would develop into a supranational political entity, overcome emnities and divisions of the past, and indeed become an equal partner to the United States. The expectation was that a unified Europe greatly would facilitate the larger Atlantic Alliance. As President Kennedy formulated in his famous Philadelphia address of 4 July 1962:

> We do not regard a strong united Europe as a rival but as a partner. To aid its progress has been the basic object of our foreign policy for 17 years. We believe that a united Europe will be capable of playing a greater role in the common defense . . . and developing coordinated policies in all other economic, diplomatic and political areas. We see in such a Europe a partner with whom we can deal on a basis of full equality.[18]

A fundamental vision of the creation of a united European partner, which would then move toward a real Atlantic Community, inspired Kennedy's "design." As he concluded, Atlantic partnership "would serve as a nucleus for the eventual union of all free men."[19]

---

[17]M. Margaret Ball, *NATO and European Union Movement* (London: Stevenson, 1959), p. 486; Beloff, *United States and the Unity of Europe,* pp. 49–103; van der Beugel, *Marshall Aid to Atlantic Partnership,* pp. 227–358; Hoffmann, "Uneven Allies: An Overview," pp. 57–61; Ernst B. Haas, *The Uniting of Europe. Political Social and Economic Forces 1950–1957* (Stanford, CA: Stanford University Press, 1968).

[18]U.S., Department of State *Bulletin* 47 (23 July 1962): 131–33; Joseph Kraft, *The Grand Design* (New York: Harper and Row, 1962); Theodore Sorensen, *Kennedy* (New York: Harper and Row, 1965), p. 569. "There is no 'Europe.' I understand their objection to my speaking for them on nuclear matters, but who's to be my opposite number? I can't share this decision with a whole lot of differently motivated and differently responsible people. What one man is to be shared with—de Gaulle, Adenauer, MacMillan? None of them can speak for Europe." See George M. Taber, *John F. Kennedy and a Uniting Europe* (Bruges: College of Europe, 1969), pp. 97–105, 147–57.

[19]See expremier R. Schuman's statement in *Freedom and Union* (June 1955), p. 14: "I have long been an ardent partisan of a European federation, itself to be integrated in the Atlantic Community"; Jean Monnet at Hanover, NH, 11 June 1961, *Freedom and Union* (June 1955), p. 8: "As Europe is now in the process of uniting, so the West must move towards some kind of union"; J. Robert Schaetzel, "The Necessary Partnership," *Foreign Affairs* 44 (April 1966), p. 431: "There is nothing in the concept of Atlantic partnership that precludes an eventual fusing of a united Europe and the United States"; and Goodman, *Fate of the Atlantic Community,* p. 231: "So long as the United States is under the illusion that it can act alone, or for lack of a European partner, is obliged to act on its own, it will have little incentive to delegate power to a wider political body."

FIFTEEN YEARS OF SETBACKS

There followed instead a fifteen-year period of disappointments, crises, and setbacks for this European concept. The basic assumption held by both Americans and Europeans on the matter was now challenged, especially the idea that a unified Europe would be a second pillar of the Atlantic Alliance.

The starting point of the crisis was unquestionably in Europe. There already had been crises in the European unification process, both with Britain's reluctance to enter into any supranational organization and with the divisions and ultimate failure in France regarding the EDC. It was de Gaulle, however, who effectively slowed down the European union concept associated with the founding of the Common Market by producing a sharp antithesis. After having settled the Algerian question, he provoked in 1962 the collapse of the negotiations among the Europe of Six for a political union going beyond the cooperation of national sovereign states. Because of traditional French centralization, he could not accept the dispersion of decision-making powers to the regional, national, and European levels that would be necessary for a supranational federal organization of Europe.[20] He understood to a certain extent the fact that the European nation-states had become too small to manage their own affairs optimally, but he was prepared to tolerate only a Europe united at a confederal level around Paris, in which the pooling of resources would be under French hegemony with the intention of boosting France's prestige and power. For this reason de Gaulle vetoed Britain's entry into the EEC. At the same famous press conference of 14 January 1963, he claimed a more protectionist role for the Common Market and further stated that the "Atlantic Community under American Leadership . . . [was] not at all what France has wanted."[21]

The two central contradictions in de Gaulle's counterthesis were, first, the fact that he totally rejected European supranationalism in the name of an independent Europe but at the same time prevented the

---

[20]See also Robert Bloes, Le "Plan Fouchet" et le problème de l'Europe politique (Bruges: College of Europe, 1970), p. 538. For background see Philippe Mann, Le Rassemblement du peuple français et les problèmes européens (Paris: PUF, 1966). For the best monograph see Edward A. Kolodzie, French International Policy under de Gaulle and Pompidou: The Politics of Grandeur (Ithaca: Cornell University Press, 1974), p. 618.

[21]France, French Embassy, Press and Information Division, Major Addresses, Statements and Press Conferences of General Charles de Gaulle, May 19, 1958–January 31, 1964 (New York, 1964), pp. 216–20. See also Nora Beloff, The General says No, Britain's Exclusion from Europe (London: Penguin, 1963); Miriam Camps, Britain and the European Community 1955–1963 (London: Oxford University Press, 1964); and E. R. Goodman, "De Gaulle, the Disintegrater," The Fate of the Atlantic Community, pp. 50–134.

organic means for achieving autonomy; and second, that he wished
Europe to become independent of the United States in order to seek
détente and eventual entente with the Soviet Union, while insisting on a
precondition of the U.S. nuclear guarantee.[22]

His reaction to the concepts of the Atlantic Alliance was a consequence of his quasi-religious belief in national sovereignty, especially
that of France. This bias resulted in Britain being rejected from joining the
EEC and France withdrawing from NATO, while the EEC integration
mechanism itself was forced into stagnation for six years. In the final
event, however, the Gaullist policy came to nothing; all European leaders
rejected his attempt to place Europe under French hegemony, while the
Soviet Union failed to profit from France's attempt to achieve a closer
rapport. In de Gaulle's last two years as president, France remained
relatively isolated in diplomatic affairs, while de Gaulle himself made
curious analogies between French and Swiss neutrality, fully neglecting
France's role in Europe's destiny.[23] The EEC managed to complete a
customs union, but the integration process stopped there. Even Spaak
resignedly declared in 1967: "The Europe that we wanted, the Europe
whose position in the world we intended to restore . . . is dead forever."[24]

The U.S. reaction was at first to try to ride through the storm and
ignore de Gaulle's position. As Undersecretary of State George Ball
expressed it: "It seems clear enough, however, that this action has not
changed the underlying facts that have dictated the need for greater
European unity and effective Atlantic co-operation." Similarly, Kennedy
still offered the prospect of partnership in his Frankfurt speech of 1963,
declaring in addition that "the choice of paths to the unity of Europe is a
choice which Europe must make."[25]

Statements such as these, however, became more and more inoperative. There was a well-intentioned offer of "multilateral nuclear
sharing," but this was unacceptable; nuclear weapons would remain under

---

[22]"The notion of a European Europe, in opposition to an Atlantic Europe, makes no
sense. French Doctrine is for the moment French and not European"; and France did not
want to risk "to lose the advantage of the American guarantee, which both General de
Gaulle and Georges Pompidou saw as the foundation of France's independent diplomacy."
Raymond Aron, "Europe and the United States," in Landes, *Western Europe*, p. 45.

[23]As a last resort, de Gaulle was opting for a neutrality similar to Switzerland's,
except that "there is a difference between Swiss neutrality and the French version of
neutrality. Switzerland does not intervene, by word or deed, in any of the world conflicts. . . .
Gaullist France intervenes at least with words." Raymond Aron, "From Independence to
Neutrality," *Atlantic Community Quarterly* 6 (Summer 1968): 269.

[24]Paul-Henri Spaak, "Europe, Defend Yourself," *Spectator* (18 April 1967): 482.
See also Miriam Camps, *European Unification in the Sixties from the Veto to the Crisis*
(London: Oxford University Press, 1967).

[25]U.S., Department of State *Bulletin* 48 (18 March 1963): 412–15; and *Bulletin* 49
(22 July 1963): 118–23. See also van der Beugel, *Marshall Aid to Atlantic Partnership*,
pp. 380–85.

the control of the United States.[26] The U.S. administrators, moreover, were increasingly shocked at all levels with the tricky diplomatic methods of Gaullist diplomacy. At the same time military involvement in Vietnam deflected U.S. attention from Europe and drained her economy to the extent that American leaders became highly sensitive regarding the growth and economic success of the EEC. Subsequently, Europe came to be viewed almost as a rival rather than as a neighborly, united, political partner. U.S. sympathetic interest in European blueprints for political union turned instead to a reluctant need to become accustomed "to the fact that conflict is normal in relations between states."[27]

Meanwhile, in Europe the advocates of unification also had to learn that de Gaulle was not the only troublemaker; Britain remained similarly unprepared to surrender sovereignty in favor of supranational institutions and in all countries a persistent "separatism" of the national bureaucracies remained. As Stanley Hoffmann stated: "Two different logics were at work among the nations of West Europe—the logic of integration and the logic of diversity."[28] On the one hand, the old nation-states were "obstinate or obsolete" and needed a supranational tonic for management of their common interests through the integrating machinery of the EEC; on the other hand, different historical traditions, widely divergent internal structures, and traditional political customs had not been erased. The modern nation-states in Europe were becoming more similar on industrial and class levels, but the political and social infrastructure and internal divisions still were leading to internal government crises and discussions of "democratization" at a parochial rather than supranational level. The Western European nations continued to be faced with a whole series of anachronistic problems and conceptions.[29]

---

[26]The MLF project as a wrong answer to a false problem was rightly criticized by Henry Kissinger, *The Troubled Partnership. A Reappraisal of the Atlantic Alliance* (New York: McGraw-Hill, 1965), pp. 119–59. See also George W. Ball, *The Discipline of Power* (Boston: Little, Brown and Company, 1968), p. 94: "Kennedy never fully convinced himself that it might prevent the building up of conflicts and feelings of inequality and irresponsibility that flow from impotence among the Europeans." See van der Beugel, *Marshall Aid to Atlantic Partnership*, pp. 385–93; Cleveland, *Atlantic Idea*, pp. 54–64; and Goodman, *Fate of the Atlantic Community*, pp. 408–24.

[27]Charles M. Spofford's foreword, p. xiv in Cleveland, *Atlantic Idea.* See also Cleveland's concluding remarks, pp. 161–70.

[28]Stanley Hoffmann, "Toward a Common European Foreign Policy," in *The United States and Western Europe: Political, Economic and Strategic Perspectives,* ed. Wolfram F. Hanrieder, pp. 79–105. For what follows in the text see his excellent articles "Europe's Identity Crisis," *Daedalus* 93, no. 4 (Fall 1944): 1244–99; and "Obstinate and Obsolete: The Fate of the Nation-State and the Case of Western Europe," *Daedalus* 95 (Summer 1966): 862–915.

[29]Stanley Hoffmann, "No Trumps, No Luck, No Will," in *Atlantic Lost,* ed. James Chase and Earl Ravenal (New York: New York University Press, 1976); Werner J. Feld and John K. Wildgen, *Domestic Political Realities and European Unification* (Boulder, CO: Westview, 1976); Stanley Hoffmann, "Fragments Floating the Here and Now,"

A fresh start on the logic of European integration has been achieved since de Gaulle's departure, and the Hague Summit of 1969 reaffirmed once more that political union was the ultimate goal of the European Community. The decision leading to the entrance of Great Britain, Ireland, and Denmark into the EEC also appeared to add more impetus to the European idea. Since 1971 there has been a Common European Budget for the EEC that is collected directly by tariffs and a 1 percent Value Added Tax (VAT). In addition, a monetary union has been started, while in reaction to Nixon's direct bilateral foreign policy with the Soviet Union, Europe also has moved toward *Ostpolitik* coordination.[30]

However, the vague promise of "Union by 1980," made at the Paris Summit of 1972, quickly ended in the breakdown of the EEC decision-making process after the Copenhagen Summit of 1973. Attempts to achieve such goals as a full monetary union, a more sensible agricultural policy, and a common strategy for both energy and space programs have all failed. The oil crisis, furthermore, provoked a strict national policy of "every man for himself."[31]

During this time a U.S. policy of blatant national interest also became the mode under the Nixon-Kissinger team. In sharp contrast to the State Department's former open methods of Western World diplomacy and international negotiation, an exclusive and secretive style was introduced by Kissinger that mixed subtle threats with confrontation methods and hard-line pressures with secret diplomacy based upon a combination of neo-Bismarckian realpolitik and neo-Gaullist nationalism. The American public, moreover, turned increasingly inward after the Vietnam debacle, leaving Nixon and Kissinger free to pursue their global acrobatics.[32]

Daedalus 108 (Winter 1979): 1–26; Suzanne Berger, "Politics and Anti-politics in Western Europe in the Seventies," *Daedalus* 108 (Winter 1979): 27–49.

[30]Hoffmann, "Uneven Allies: An Overview," pp. 80–85; Uwe Kitzinger, *Diplomacy and Persuasion* (London: Thames and Hudson, 1973); Brian Griffiths, "Monetary Policies in the Atlantic Community," *Atlantic Community in Crisis*, pp. 283–97. At another level for the logics of integration, see John E. Farquaharson and Stephen C. Holt, *Europe from below: An Assessment of Franco-German Popular Contacts* (London: Allen and Unwin, 1975).

[31]Martin J. Hillenbrand, "Die USA und die EG: Spannungen und Möglichkeite," in Kaiser and Schwarz, *Amerika und Westeuropa*, pp. 288–300; *Les politiques extérieures européennes dans la crise*, ed. Alfred Grosser (Paris: Fondation Nationale des Sciences Politiques, 1976); Robert J. Lieber, *Oil and the Middle East War: Europe in the Energy Crisis* (Cambridge: Harvard University Press, 1976); Christian Lutz, "Das unmündige Europa. Bilanz eines Krisenjahres," *Europa Archives* 29 (10 January 1974): 1–8.

[32]Hoffmann, "Uneven Allies: An Overview," pp. 64–68, 73–75; M. J. Hillenbrand, "Die USA und die UG," in Kaiser and Schwarz, *Amerika und Westeuropa*, pp. 289–91; Alastair Buchan, *L'Europe et L'Amèrique, de l'alliance à coalition* (Paris: Institut Atlantique, 1974); Roger P. Morgan, "Europe and America: The Uneven Dumb-Beau," *High Politics, Low Politics Towards a Foreign Policy for Western Europe* (London:

The U.S. policy that ensued can be briefly summarized along three major lines. First, in connection with the withdrawal from Vietnam, the years 1970–73 witnessed a new priority in U.S. foreign policy—the formation of bilateral working arrangements with the two major Communist powers. The "China card" and détente with the Soviet Union were given clear precedence over any relationship with Europe. However, because U.S.-Soviet relations remained largely antagonistic, Kissinger increased pressure on Europe to augment its NATO commitment.

Second, the EEC increasingly was considered as a competitor and rival, whose eventual political union was no longer viewed as being in the immediate U.S. national interest. The customs union itself was regarded as discriminatory against the United States. The subsequent American economic policy decided by Secretary of the Treasury John Connally in 1971 was described by William Diebold as "a simplistic economic nationalism that the world has scarcely heard since 1934." Many of the past "concessions" to Europe were now revoked in the assessment of a series of import surcharges, suspension of convertibility, devaluation (aimed at recreating a trade surplus), negative reaction to the EEC's Common Agricultural Policy, a drive against reserve preferences, and pressure to bring about a zero tariff on industrial goods to Europe. Despite all these defensive measures, however, the United States benefited as a whole in her trading relationship with the EEC.[33]

Finally, the Nixon administration viewed European political unity as either unlikely or unnecessary. At an official level Nixon stated in February 1972 that "the essential harmony of our interests is the durable link between a uniting Europe and the United States." In reality, however, the Nixon-Kissinger team adopted quite a hostile approach to this idea and strictly neglected the beginning of European foreign policy cooperation. Rather than pursue a policy of strengthening the commission and of encouraging further European institutional development, they instead dealt on a distinctive bilateral basis with the national governments in the community. As Kissinger already had alluded in his study, *The Troubled Partnership*, it is easier for an alliance leader to deal with a Europe of

---

Sage Publications, 1973); Maurice Ferro, *Kissinger, diplomate de l'impossible* (Paris: France Empire, 1976); J. Robert Schaetzel, *The Unhinged Alliance: America and the European Community* (New York: Harper and Row, 1975).

[33]William Diebold, Jr., "The Economic System at Stake," *Foreign Affairs* 51, no. 1 (October 1972): 172. The United States always maintained a trade surplus in her agricultural exports to the EEC, while it was only in 1972 that the first U.S. deficit was recorded with regard to exchange of industrial goods, for which in fact the EEC is more liberal than the United States. See, Kaiser, *Europe and the United States*, chapts. 2, 3; *International Economic Relations of Western World 1959–1971*, ed. Andrew S. Honfield (London: Oxford University Press, 1976). See also "Handling of Economy," in E. W. Czempiel and D. A. Rustow, eds., *The Euro-American System* (Frankfurt: Campus, 1976), pp. 31–140.

separate states; he thought that a united Europe would be much more troublesome.

In his "Year of Europe" speech of April 1973, Kissinger paternalistically suggested that America would now have the time to establish a closer relationship with Europe, but only on the basis of Europe creating trade concessions due to the "linkage" between economics and security. The message was clear: if Europe wanted to maintain the U.S. guarantee, she had to pay for it. A withdrawal of the guarantee or a reduction of U.S. conventional forces in Western Europe, however, was resisted by the administration, despite grumblings in Congress, mainly because such action might have stimulated Europeans to develop their own separate defense strategy and autonomous political union.[34]

The results of this relapse into nationalist approaches on both sides of the Atlantic, the accompanying crisis in European integration, and U.S. internationalism, all served as a major warning for the future. At one level a crisis resulted over containment in Europe of the Soviet's overwhelmingly superior conventional forces and nuclear missiles. President Tito gravely declared that such a tilting of military power in favor of the Soviet Union was a danger not only for Europe but also for the world balance of power. On still another level a crisis arose in the Western liberalization of trade terms; the global lessons of the 1930s were partly ignored. Finally, the replacement of America's former concept of U.S-European partnership with one of a strained relationship based upon hard pressure, open threats for unilateral concessions, and a general atmosphere of confrontation politics was a bitter event.[35] Indeed, compared with the first fifteen years of postwar U.S.-West European relationship, the record of the second fifteen years appeared as disastrous, abrasive, and negative.

FUTURE LESSONS

It is impossible after fifteen years of setbacks merely to return to the formulas of the first fifteen years. After all the disappointments of the

---

[34]Henry Kissinger, "Creativity Together or Irrelevance Apart" (Pilgrim address, 12 December 1973), *Atlantic Community Quarterly* 11 (Winter 1973–74); Kenneth N. Waltz, "America's European Policy Viewed in Global Perspective," *The United States and Western Europe: Political, Economic and Strategic Perspectives*, pp. 35–36. See also the literature concerning Kissinger's European policy in fn. 32.

[35]Arnulf Barring, "American Isolationism, Europe and the Future of World Politics," *The United States and Western Europe: Political, Economic and Strategic Perspectives*, pp. 50–53; Kurt Birrenbach, "Partner oder Rivalen?" *Europa Archiv* 28 (February 1973): 77–84; Hoffmann, "Toward a Common European Foreign Policy," pp. 91–103; Benjamin J. Cohen, "The Revolution on Atlantic Economic Relations: A Bargain Comes Unstuck," *The United States and Western Europe: Political, Economic and Strategic Perspectives*, pp. 106–33.

1970s one simply cannot repeat Kennedy's generous vision of Atlantic partnership "on a basis of full equality." This pointed in the right direction but proved to be too vague, particularly after the experiences with de Gaulle. Americans and Atlantic-minded Europeans rightly concluded that any form of European integration was not automatically good in itself; it could not be in the interest of the United States and the Western World as a whole to support the creation of a potentially hostile economic and political rival. Two developments in the 1970s especially helped to formulate the limits and conditions of what is realistically possible and desirable. First, the growing military superiority of the Soviet Union and serious economic setbacks taught the West Europeans that the notion of "full equality" is far from reality. The fact that the United States possessed approximately 97 percent of the nuclear power in NATO, and the comparison between the gross national product and per capita income in the United States and all West European countries taken together preclude "full equality" for the near future.[36] And second, the growing predominance of global issues such as oil, energy, the monetary system, and the Third World exposed to the West Europeans, in addition to their military weakness vis-à-vis the Soviet Union, their increasing dependence on cooperation with the United States and growing interdependence of both parts of the Atlantic World. In comparison to the early 1960s in Europe, unrealistic ambitions have declined considerably, and in each country political forces still clinging to the illusion of an independent Europe definitely have become even smaller minorities. Between the actual competing political forces the range of foreign policy alternatives became very narrow—all acknowledged the definite interdependence of Europe and America. Autonomy yes, independence no. Accordingly, American scholars should stop regarding European integration as an attempt to resist American views, as a revolt against the United States and NATO cohesion, or as an act toward independence.[37] Excluding this illusion we should state the real question as to whether or not it is desirable to strengthen the efforts toward Western European unification within the framework of the Atlantic Alliance—the creation of an Atlantic-minded "United States of Europe."

In brief, a decision of the United States or of leading political forces in Europe to downgrade the EEC, to view the "Monnet mystique" with irony, and to dismiss as an illusion the goal of a European governmental structure sufficiently integrated to conduct a single foreign and military policy eventually could lead to chaos and perhaps to the alternative of direct U.S. hegemony. A U.S. decision to deal with Western Europe in ways that deny its specificity, preferring to deal bilaterally with single governments in a fragmented Europe, would encourage the centrifugal trends that threaten to disrupt the tenuous network woven by the EEC and

---

[36]Van der Beugel, *Marshall Aid to Atlantic Partnership,* pp. 393–412.
[37]Hoffmann, "Uneven Allies: An Overview," pp. 76–79, 83–85.

NATO and would promote an unraveling that could lead to selective neutralism or disastrous "beggar-my-neighbor policies." It would be ideal for perpetuating the resignation to pettiness, the abdication from world influence of the Europeans, as Kissinger suggested, under "the lulling conviction that Uncle Sam will do," while allowing them to voice "laments and whines blaming Washington alternatively for being too soft or too tough,"[38] as during the Iran and Afghanistan crises. Discouraging European integration would be the formula for guaranteeing permanent mutual resentment, perpetuating an attitude of collective impotence, and for being at the mercy of the protector.

Thus, we come to the policy that appears to be the only recommendable one, a policy encouraging Western Europe to unite. The United States should, as Hoffmann stated, devise European institutional policies "on as broad a range of issues as the Europeans themselves are capable of tackling."[39] There can be no doubt that in every field the necessary actions could be much better afforded by a progressively united Europe than by a fragmented one. The urgent need to reform the international system could be much better met if the European Monetary Union, at present a loose grouping around the franc and the deutsche mark, would develop in its second stage a strong European currency based on all European wealth that together with the dollar as a second pillar would bear the structure of a world monetary system. In the economic realm the mutual dependence of the European and American economies is such that a revitalized EEC would have no reason to break it. To assure the coprosperity of both sides of the Atlantic, the "open" international economy undoubtedly would win if the United States dealt with developed authorized European institutions rather than with nine differing governments. A joint approach on these increasingly important global issues, especially energy and Third World, would be much easier and more effective with developed authorized European institutions.[40] Surely, in the military realm in order to overcome the present weakness of the alliance and end the tragedy of non-standardization a real remedy would be either a completely standardized European army or armies whose weapons were interoperable with those of the U.S. Army. In the strict sense, vis-à-vis the possibility of a defeat of the Western World, a European army—also a European government—becomes an elementary interest of the United States.[41] As a result the

---

[38]Ibid., pp. 92–94.

[39]Ibid., p. 95.

[40]Ibid., pp. 76, 96, 103–4; Michael J. Brenner, *The Politics of International Monetary Reform: The Exchange Crisis* (Cambridge: Bollinger, 1976); William Diebold, Jr., "Die Reform des internationalen Wirtschaftssystems als Zukunftsaufgabe," in *Amerika und Westeuropa*, pp. 111–27; Lawrence Bell, "Trade and the Atlantic Community—Some Avenues of Resolution," *The Atlantic Community in Crisis*, pp. 334–48.

[41]General Robert Close, *L'Europe sans défense?* (Brussels: Arts et Voyages, 1976); Pierre Lellouche, "Frankreich und die Amerikanische Sicherheitspolitik gegenüber Europa,"

Western European entity could express more vigorously its own opinions on a given problem. However, pluralism of opinion, the existence of alternative courses, is better than hegemony; competition between ideas should be seen as a positive advantage.

In Europe it is still true that there exists an undecided balance between the logic of integration and the forces of diversity. The community organs, in fact, have continued to survive and have indeed slowly gained ground during the last few years, helped along by both the insecurity of the world economy and by Kissinger's attacks on the community itself. The Common Agricultural Policy has been preserved and will be revised; a stronger regional policy with substantial funds has been developed; an industrial policy has been devised; economic divergency and inflation has to a certain extent been held in check by monetary union; protectionism has been controlled; and liberalization enforced. An international network of cooperation and understanding between the community and the forty-nine developing nations has been set up through the Lomé convention as well as through cooperative measures between the community and the Asean group, both of which are of vital concern to U.S. interests in stabilizing political and trading relations with the Third World. Finally, the community has established a working system of direct elections to the European parliament and has encouraged the supranational potential of the EEC and the federal control of the community's budget.[42]

There is indeed a difficult struggle ahead between the forces of integration and diversity in Europe, one that will take more than a decade or more to solve. As the president of the European Community's commission, Roy Jenkins, has said: "We do have the threats of inertia, parochialism, narrow nationalism, and through misplaced and unimaginative caution, standing still when immobility is a much greater risk than

Europa Archiv 33 (December 1979): pp. 705–18. A starting point could be the strengthening of the Eurogroup in the NATO Council (comprising all European ministers of defense, except for France, Portugal, and Iceland); Hoffmann, "Uneven Allies: An Overview," pp. 101–3; Richard Wayke, *Die NATO in den Siebziger Jahren* (Opliaden: Leske, 1977).

[42]Roy Jenkins, "The United States and a Uniting Europe," *Atlantic Community Quarterly* 15 (Summer 1977): 209–20. For accounts of the progress of liberalization, the new regional fund, reduction of divergency, and European monetary union, see Pierre-Henry Laurant, ed., "The European Community After Twenty Years," *Annals of the American Academy of Political and Social Science* 45 (November 1978); Albert Bress, "The New European Economies," *Daedalus* 118 (Winter 1979): 51–73; Donald J. Puchala and Carl F. Lankowski, "The Politics of Fiscal Harmonization in the European Communities," *Journal of Common Market Studies* 15 (March 1977): 155–79; Norbert Kloten, "Das Europäische Währungssystem," *Europa Archiv* 35 (February 1980): 111–22; Paule Bouvier, *L'Europe et la coopération au développement; un bilan: La convention de Rome* (Bruxelles: de l'université, 1980); David Combes, ed., *The Future of the European Parliament* (London: Policy Institute, 1979).

moving forward. We do have a lack of vision and energy among our present European statesmen."[43]

What remains important and perhaps decisive in this struggle for an integrated Europe is the attitude adopted by the United States. The United States cannot create European unity but it can prevent it. President Carter indicated the correct choice when he stated:

> Europe will be better able to fulfill its role in U.S.-European-Japanese cooperation in the degree that it can speak with one voice and act with one will. The United States has sometimes seemed to encourage European unification with words, while preferring to deal with national governments in practice. I believe that we should deal with Brussels on economic issues to that extent that the Europeans themselves make Brussels the focus of their decisions.[44]

This constitutes one of the most important areas of practical support. History consists of facts and institutions on one side and of possibilities and activists for progress on the other. It is of great importance that the United States should facilitate a European solution by dealing with the common institutions where Europe does in fact speak with one voice, by avoiding bilateralism in issues concerning Western Europe, and by avoiding initiatives that would make the development of a strong West European unity more difficult.

Progress in European integration is indeed an experiment of great significance for the regulation of international problems. Progress in political integration depends not only on the will of Western Europeans to overcome factors of division and inertia but also on the role of the United States. The fate of Western democracy and of free spiritual values depends upon the success of the Western World's progress toward unity, with Western European unification as the necessary first step.

---

[43]Jenkins, "The United States and a Uniting Europe," p. 220; Raymond Aron, *Plaidoyer pour l'Europe décadente* (Paris: Laffont, 1977).

[44]Jenkins, "The United States and a Uniting Europe," p. 216; Hoffmann, "Uneven Allies: An Overview," pp. 95, 98–100.

NATO IN ARMS

Prelude to NATO: Two Examples
of the Integration of Military Forces

ANDRÉ KASPI

The integration of forces is an expression that from a historical point of view requires further explanation. Since 1956, as cited in *Grand Larousse de la langue française,* one of the meanings of "integration" has been "the close union of several States from an economic or a political point of view," an example that refers specifically to the construction of Europe. In other words, the use of integration in reference to the military is a result, not a cause, of the creation of NATO. However, the integration of military forces stemmed from existing practices of the countries that signed the North Atlantic Treaty.

If the term did not exist before 1956 the notion itself was widespread. It was expressed in words such as unification, fusion, or amalgamation. Yet immediately after the Second World War amalgamation evoked the fusion of the French Forces of the Interior and of diverse political hues with the First Army commanded by General Jean de Lattre de Tassigny. As a result, NATO did not mark an absolute beginning for the French or for their partners. Earlier experiments, successful or otherwise, had had an effect on military thinking.

How far back should historical reflection be taken? Any war involving coalitions or any army that is assembled from heterogeneous contingents presents integration problems. In the framework of this inquiry it is not necessarily worthwhile to go further back than the First World War. Two reasons support this chronological limitation. First, the nature of the world conflict that began in 1914. Despite certain phenomenal parallels with previous wars, the nature of the World War I conflict rendered it qualitatively different from all preceding struggles. It was a twentieth-century war, especially after 1917 when the Russian revolutions and the entry of the United States profoundly transformed its nature. And the second reason is the military personnel itself. The generals of 1940 and 1950 were the captains and colonels of 1918. Obviously, their experiences during the Second World War left lasting impressions; memories of their earlier experiences were not eradicated. For this reason the American Expeditionary Force (AEF) and the forces of the 1948

Brussels Treaty can be used as bases for reflecting on the origins of NATO's integrated command.

THE FRANCO-AMERICAN AMALGAMATION DISPUTE

During February-March 1917 the French realized that American entry into the war was imminent. To them this was a most welcome development, but at the same time they were perplexed and uncertain as to exactly what assistance the Americans would provide. American military unpreparedness was scarcely encouraging. Moreover, even if American troops were available, the problem remained of transporting them across the Atlantic without allied troops being sunk by German submarines. An official connected with the minister for armaments wrote at the time: "Military aid from the United States can't be first-rate; nonetheless volunteers will come and die in the trenches; America will raise an army."[1] In short, the French government counted on contingents of volunteers. Additionally, Minister of War Paul Painlevé stated explicitly that "it is desirable, as soon as possible, to send small units of volunteers, companies or battalions, whose aid will be most useful in averting the *manpower crises* from which the Entente, and especially France, is beginning to suffer."[2] After being consulted, General Robert Nivelle, head of the French armies, replied that he needed specialists: "drivers, skilled workers for the automobile service, woodcutters, telegraphists, qualified personnel to handle equipment, etc. . ."[3] Projects became more clear and changes occurred during the month of April.

Major James A. Logan, whose role in Paris was that of American military attaché, contributed to the change in attitudes as did the efforts of the general staff in Washington. Among the French, Marshal Henri-Philippe Pétain was the first to grasp the importance of major military aid from the United States. Pétain felt it was necessary to move quickly, think on a large scale, and respect the autonomy of the American army.

Pétain agreed it was necessary that the United States should send volunteers immediately and provide the allies, especially the French, with much needed relief. These volunteers temporarily would be incorporated

---

[1]Louis Albert to Albert Thomas, France, 12 March 1917, Ministère des affaires étrangères (MAE), 1914–18 war, United States, box 505.

[2]Paul Painlevé to military attaché, France, 24 March 1917, Historical Services of the Army, 16N 203/1 (hereafter cited as SHA, followed by file number).

[3]General Robert Nivelle to Théâtres d'opérations extérieures (TOE), 4 April 1917, SHA, 16N 205/1. A similar note can be found in National Archives and Records Service, Washington, DC, RG 16S, file 100 (hereafter cited as NARS, followed by appropriate file number).

into French units. Thinking in large terms meant training the cadres for at least 100 divisions, an enormous army three or four times greater than the million-man force that President Wilson had in mind. This army would be formed with its artillery, aviation, and support units. Autonomy would be the final stage of the formation of the American army. "This is an issue of moral necessity. The great American people must fight under its own flag, and its cooperation would thus make a greater impression, on the Allies and on the enemy."[4] Until this last stage was reached, however, the United States would have to place more confidence in France than in England; the training of the American troops would be entrusted to France. Before the American units were formed into regiments and divisions they would form, for example, the third or fourth battalion of French regiments. After six months' training the artillery would serve for the next two months on the French front. To lessen the deficiencies in the American divisional staffs, French officers would be detached to the service of American generals. Collaboration between the two armies would extend to the manufacturing of war materials and artillery munitions. This dispersion of the American war effort would be provisional.

The advantage of Pétain's project lay in the fact that it synthesized several contradictory projects. The United States would provide men and materiel, volunteers and divisions, immediate aid to France, and an autonomous army. However, in his project there was a noticeable lack of detail concerning the passage of the American forces from amalgamation to autonomy. What would happen, for instance, if the French and the Americans did not share the same opinion as to when the time was propitious for the passage to autonomy? Nor was the plan satisfactory insofar as American national pride was concerned. Pétain's line of conduct would not be followed by the French government. It officially declared that it was in favor of the presence of an American division in France that would serve as the core of a future army and also of the training of cadres and eventually entire units by the French. The notion of strict amalgamation was rejected. As an expression of the times, the American flag flew over the trenches. This is the position that Marshal Joseph Joffre was to defend during his mission to the United States in April and May 1917, although the minister of war remained rather vague about the course to follow. Nonetheless, it is necessary to make a distinction between what he thought and what he said.

Several examples make this distinction clear. On board the ship that took him to America, Joffre held discussions with his officers, and a working document was prepared. "In our dealing with foreigners, and particularly with the Americans, we must emphasize our present military strength and scrupulously conceal the weakness that our manpower

---

[4]*Les Armées françaises dans la grande guerre* (France), pp. 50–52.

shortage will create for us in the future." The document stated the necessity of putting on a war footing "a great American army," but that that could not be attained in 1917. The best the Americans could do in the near future would be to reinforce the services of the rear armies and above all raise French morale. On the other hand, in 1918 "a regular army capable of playing a role analogous to that of the English army at the side of the French army" would be organized. This would presuppose the recruitment and training of staff and line officers as well as support forces. Part of the training would take place in France, with only basic training done in America. To Joffre and his colleagues the issue was to "strengthen the ties of friendship which must exist between the two armies."[5] The American forces would be autonomous but fight "à la française" alongside the French and provide specialized units. Close cooperation would have to be established between the French army, which was suffering from a severe manpower shortage, and the American army, still lacking experience, would have to be trained and organized along the lines of the French forces and furnish them with needed reserves.

Was Joffre's attitude both friendly and deceptive? Undoubtedly, but it was an attitude held not only by Joffre. André Tardieu, high commissioner to the United States, acted no differently. Since the Americans lacked modern arms in sufficient quantity, France was ready to sell them howitzers, machine guns, shells, bullets, etc., not as a moneymaking venture but to secure American cooperation. Financial and business interests were raised, but they gave way to the political arguments expressed by Tardieu in the following terms: "Our influence on the way the war is pursued will undoubtedly be greater with the army of our new allies than it has been with the English army, since given the fact that the Americans will be using our matériel they will have to turn to our officers for the training of American officers, and this issue was, as you know, extremely delicate."[6] The American Department of War and General John J. Pershing would have to be brought under French influence. This union in combat would pave the way for a postwar alliance, and France would have a powerful ally on which to rely. Furnishing arms to the AEF was part of an overall plan aimed at controlling its combat methods, the training of its officers and men, and ultimately its use at the front. By selling war materials to the United States, France was not seeking dollars and contracts so much as the consolidation of her power. In trying to link her army closely with that of the United States, France was attempting to increase her military might to achieve victory and attain her political objectives following the armistice. Obviously, the aid France gave to her allies on the other side of the Atlantic was not altruistic.

[5]Cf. "Note Rédigée par le commandant, Fabry, à l'état-major du Maréchal Joffre à bord avec le concours des autres officiers, chacun en ce qui concerne sa spécialité," SHA, Fonds Lecomte, box 191.
[6]Telegram, André Tardieu to prime minister, France, 16 July 1917, SHA, 17N3/2.

The French position, however, was not monolithic. It evolved in the course of time and circumstance. It was also multifaceted. At the end of 1917 French authorities underlined the insufficient numbers of men arriving in France and the lack of training among American staff officers. As one French general said: "They don't need to learn, they need to learn everything."[7] To this a training officer added: "Everyone agrees that it would be inopportune to entrust the American high command and staff with offensive operations in 1918, no matter how limited their nature. Their direction on the army corps level should be left to the French command and staff, and this direction should be extended to a divisional level where artillery is involved."[8] General Bordeaux, who commanded the French 18th Infantry Division, pointed out:

> The American army has a great deal to do to attain combat readiness. Its officers realize this fact. Accustomed as they are to deploying their wings in wide open terrain, they now find themselves confronted with the organization of the minutest detail in very close terrain. Their wings are clipped. They are astonished and perplexed. They think that they will need a great deal of time [to become prepared], and they seem to take for granted the fact that, indeed, they will have all the time they need. If this attitude were to become doctrine, it would be most unfortunate, the more so since the Americans, like Orientals, have no notion of time; duration means as little to them as accuracy. Even if they wanted to move more rapidly, they couldn't. They don't know how to work smoothly and rapidly; something that is essential today to staff and line commands. Given their distance from their country, from their home base, it takes them all the longer to put into effect plans they adopt. The extremely rapid expansion of their army causes a continual dispersion of well-trained personnel who are lifted from their unit to be engulfed into a new unit as instructors. Finally, their progress will still be slow for another reason: they have neither acquired the great experience nor been subjected to the accelerating goad of the first three months of war, as have the English.[9]

There are many quotations of this nature, and from them it can be determined that amalgamation was of prime urgency for the French high command. Doubtless, it would not have prevented the Americans from playing the role that was their justice and would have enabled them not "to miss the boat." However, as conceived by the French, amalgamation took no consideration of American feelings of national pride. Moreover, it favored the French who provided the staff at the expense of the Americans who provided the troops. This was not exactly along the lines of pooling resources between equal partners. Moreover, American military leaders, whose views were vigorously expressed by Pershing, wanted to establish

---

[7]Report by General Hirschauer, France, 24 November 1917, SHA, 16N 1923/8.
[8]Report by Captain Bouvard, France, 4 November 1917, ibid.
[9]Report by General Bordeaux, France, 23 November 1917, ibid.

an army that would play a decisive role in the war. They had no intention of accepting the protection of an associate no matter how great its prestige. Why did Pershing reject the notion that the AEF be amalgamated? He felt that the principle was destructive even if its application were limited to the training period. Dispersion would be dangerous for the morale of the troops and the future of the AEF.[10] Furthermore, if the United States were to yield to French pressure, how could it resist the British, who at that moment were proposing to transport 150 American battalions that would be earmarked as reinforcements for the British army? It would be an endless task to attempt to analyze all the different components that enter into a sense of national pride. Pershing, for example, believed that the linguistic barrier between the French and the Americans was insurmountable.[11] However, he was forgetting that he rejected amalgamation just as strongly with the British forces, a rejection based on a long list of reasons: traditional mistrust of a cynical and decadent Europe, the fear of being dragged into military adventures, the desire to weld together the disparate elements of the American people, and a willingness to defend liberty and law and not national interests that are not those of the United States.

The prime motivation behind Pershing's stance was that only the American army could end the war victoriously. It was the army that had to be counted on to "strike the blow which would end the war."[12] The allies were exhausted, so it is not surprising that Pershing recommended that his country make its maximum effort in 1918. "The following year," he wrote on 2 December 1917, "it could be too late. It is doubtful that they [the allies] can hold out until 1919 unless we give them substantial aid this year."[13] Like French and British military leaders Pershing wanted an acceleration in the transportation of American troops, but it is probable that he also had the end of the war in mind: a strong and victorious American army would give the United States considerable influence in world affairs. Pershing favored the concept of a unified command and also thought that the leader of a powerful American army might well, in the near future, accede to the post of commander in chief. The American soldier must show himself worthy of his task; his training must be according to American methods and not those of the British or French.[14]

---

[10]Telegram, Jean-Jules Jusserand to the Foreign Affairs Ministry, France, 19 December 1917; Ragueneau to Philippe Pétain, 6 March 1918, SHA, 17N 1/1; House-Pétain conversation, 6 December 1917; *Les Armées françaises,* pp. 611–22.

[11]An interesting study in 1942 by the office of the chief, military history (OCMH) shows that the language barrier did not play a major role in 1917–18. NARS, 7200-E.

[12]General John J. Pershing to Pétain, France, 6 January 1918; *Les Armées françaises.*

[13]U.S., Department of Defense, Pershing to Agwar, 2 December 1917, in *United States Army in the World War* (Washington, DC: Government Printing Office, 1948), 2:88.

[14]Cf. memorandum of Colonel Fox Conner, 14 November 1917, RG 120, folder 683A, NARS, 1003.

It should be recalled that Pershing had the support of the American government. As Secretary of War Newton D. Baker wrote to President Wilson: "It seems evident to me that if our regiments are integrated into British or French divisions, it will be difficult to get them back when we need them, and that the upshot of such a dispersal will be to spread our troops here and there among the French and British divisions, under British and French command, and all the while weakening in proportion those forces under General Pershing's command which are aimed at."[15] As for President Wilson, he was embarrassed by the Franco-American dispute. Certain statements, despite their impressive terms, clearly revealed his refusal to contradict Baker and Pershing. His trust lay with the commander in chief of the AEF, who was in Europe. In writing to Baker concerning Pershing on 1 February 1918, he stated: "We wish to place our trust in his judgment for everything concerning the training and testing under fire of our officers and men. And so counsel him to permit nothing which might hinder the organization of a large, independent American force, fighting under its own flag and its own officers, unless warranted by a situation of clear-cut urgency."[16]

The American course of action was plain and clear. The president of the United States had no intention of making the slightest modification in the instructions given to Pershing at the beginning of his mission to France. America expected great feats from its expeditionary force. Like Pershing, the United States had the task of ending the war and going to Berlin, because American soldiers had the necessary morale and knew how to fight.[17] It was for these reasons that the AEF units had to be grouped together. "Neither the French, nor the English, nor both together can take Berlin. Berlin shall be taken only by an American army, well-trained, and completely homogeneous, in which the initiative and the independence of its officers and troops shall have been developed to the maximum."[18]

Several observations should be made concerning the failure of amalgamation. The ambiguity of French policy on the issue seems clear. France appealed to America's noblest sentiments, with frequent reference to Lafayette, while at the same time stealthily making every effort, without seeming obvious, to guide the American war effort. She wanted to win the war as well as plan for the postwar period. In both cases she felt that success would be more readily and amply obtained if she had the unreserved support of the United States.

[15]Newton D. Baker to Woodrow Wilson, 3 January 1918, Papers of Newton D. Baker, box 8, Library of Congress, Washington, DC.
[16]Ibid. See also Wilson to Raymond Poincaré, 8 January 1918, Papers of Woodrow Wilson, ser. 4, box 167, Library of Congress.
[17]Memorandum from Colonel Fiske, 4 July 1918, RG 120, folder 695B, NARS, 1003.2.
[18]Ibid.

The United States behaved quite the contrary, making every effort from April 1917 on to conserve its independence. It never had any intention of bowing to the will of one of its allies. There existed a certain degree of cooperation on the economic level and consultations on the diplomatic level, but the military field remained one of separate action. President Wilson clearly indicated that he had no intention whatsoever of delivering the United States, bound hand and foot, over to the moods and wishes of his European partners. He avoided committing himself and continuously pointed out, through words and actions, that association did not mean alliance. This incident demonstrates that if political aims are not stated forthrightly and firmly, military integration remains an impossibility. Refusal of amalgamation is not simply a military posture but is also and above all a political posture. Thus, there is a clear parallel between the policy of association that was recommended and followed by President Wilson and Pershing's stubborn resistance to allied pressure. At the risk of committing the sin of anachronism, Gaullist overtones in Wilson's attitude can be detected to a considerable extent. This is evidenced in the notion that the army is the primary instrument of the national will. To dissolve it into a foreign army, even if only temporarily, amounts to striking a mortal blow at the nation's will, its morale, its foreign policy.

What about the urgency of the situation at the time? By refusing amalgamation Pershing ran an enormous risk. He believed that the allies would hold on until the moment when the American army would be ready to go into action as an independent force. If, however, his calculations had proved erroneous and the French and the English had been defeated by the Germans, how long would it have taken for the Americans to win the second round? In the event of such an outcome Pershing's responsibility would have been enormous. Instead of being hailed as the founder of the modern American army, he would have gone down as one of history's villains.

In spite of his intransigency, real or imaginary, Pershing did know how to compromise. For example, he waited until June 1918 before dismissing the foreign instructors who claimed the role of initiating the doughboys into combat. He never stopped accepting French and British arms, without which the AEF would have been incapable of combat. He was able to maintain a relationship of confidence and friendship with General Pétain, a relationship that continually grew stronger in light of the obstacle that existed for both men—the authority of Marshal Foch. In January 1918 he relented to French demands when he authorized the total amalgamation of two black regiments into French units, although he did call for their return several months later. He bowed to the exigencies of unity in giving unhesitating recognition to Foch's authority. In short, the flexibility of his behavior was more pronounced than his defense of principles. What was manifested the most was that in the victory parade of 14 July 1919 General Pershing clearly appeared as the leader of an independent army and not simply the commander of a handful of volunteers. This is undoubtedly the proof that the amalgamation desired by the French was an unsound policy and that it is always better to deal with a strong friend than a weak one.

INTEGRATION ACCORDING TO THE TREATY OF BRUSSELS

In considering the period following World War II, it is generally admitted that French historians have not undertaken sufficient research in the period in question to have uncovered so-called conclusive results. With the imminent opening of French official archives and the documentation already available, it is hoped that young scholars will pursue research in this period. The end of the 1940s is unique in itself, notably for the subject under consideration. However, there are various differences with the preceding example that should be discussed.

The second time around the organization of a common defense was undertaken in peacetime. Wartime improvisation was no longer a factor, although the international tension in 1947, the coup in Czechoslovakia, and the Berlin blockade in 1948 gave rise to fears of another war. But in contradistinction to 1917 and 1942 hostilities were not yet open. The most obvious result was the feeling that a course of action had to be initiated quickly, but it was not necessary to simultaneously conduct battles and solve the day-to-day problems of wartime. However, a nuance should be added to this first observation: France at that time was involved in a colonial conflict that had not yet reached the proportions of an all-out war and that mobilized a major portion of her military potential.

The Brussels Treaty was signed by Great Britain, France, Belgium, Luxemburg, and the Netherlands on 17 March 1948; it was for a period of fifty years. Essentially, it was aimed against the reemergence of a German threat. Article 4 stipulated: "In the event that one of the High Contracting Parties should be the object of armed aggression in Europe, the others will provide it, in accordance with the dispositions of Article 51 of the United Nations Charter, with aid and assistance of all the means in their power, military or otherwise." Furthermore, to avoid any ambiguity, article 7 advises the signatories "to consult together as to the attitude and the measures to take in the event of the resumption of an aggressive policy on the part of Germany, or of any situation which could constitute a threat to peace no matter where it takes place, or of any situation which endangers economic stability." Economic, social, and cultural cooperation were also added to military cooperation, but there was no concealing the fact that the problems of common defense eclipsed all others. Therefore, it would appear that the Brussels Treaty grouped nations of equal power, at least two of which, France and Great Britain, had approximately equivalent weight in international affairs. In fact, in the spring of 1948 negotiations began concerning the possibility of uniting the signatories of the Brussels Treaty and the United States in the same defense system. The prevailing philosophy on the subject in Western Europe was expressed by French Prime Minister Henri Queuille on 25 February 1948:

> The United States must never let France and Western Europe be invaded by Russia in the same way that they were by Germany. . . . France, insofar as she is the advance sentry of Europe, cannot hold out alone. . . . If, for example, we could count on a force sufficient to prevent the Russian army from crossing the Elbe, then European civilization could breathe [easily] once again . . . even as little as two weeks after the invasion, it would be too late [to send help].[19]

In other words, it was inconceivable that Western Europe could defend itself alone without the support and the presence of American troops. The five European defense ministers who were establishing the institutions for a common defense were aware that they were working in view of the coming months, not the coming years, and that in a very short time American participation in Europe's defense would completely transform the nature of the problem.

The issue was no longer one of troop amalgamation as it was in 1917. This time integration would be restricted to the command level; it was a progression all the more notable since war had not been declared and Franco-British relations were apparently on an equal footing. Integration, however, was difficult to achieve.[20] On 25 August 1948 the chiefs of staff of the five signatories of the Brussels Treaty indicated that for the present time it would not be possible to appoint a supreme commander. Nonetheless, the commanders in chief of the different services should draw up plans with their respective committee chaired by an officer entrusted with the task of coordination.[21] A month later a meeting of the defense ministers took place in Paris. They concluded that it was necessary to establish "a common defense policy which would guide the individual efforts" of each country's command. A permanent organization for this purpose was created under the authority of the defense ministers. It was to include "command elements on land, sea and

---

[19]Quotation cited in Jean-Baptiste Duroselle, *Histoire diplomatique de 1919 à nos jours*, 7th ed. (Paris: Dalloz, 1978), p. 498. A good overall presentation of the problems of Western European defense can be found in Geoffrey Warner, "The Reconstruction and Defence of Western Europe after 1945," in Neville Waites, ed., *Troubled Neighbors* (London: Weidenfeld and Nicolson, 1971).

[20]I wish to express particular thanks to Mme. la Maréchale de Lattre de Tassigny who was kind enough to open her husband's archives to me and who displayed the utmost cordiality. I also wish to thank General Maurice Redon for his guidance.

[21]Papers of Jean de Lattre, M 151 (hereafter cited as de Lattre Papers).

air, with a permanent military president." This president would be
appointed "as a matter of temporary convenience," but the British defense
minister added that he "should be an officer with qualifications sufficient
to permit him to take supreme command in case of emergency."[22]

This stipulation was a detail that complicated the entire matter.
Indeed, on 4 October 1948 a communique was issued with specific names
alongside each post. General Jean de Lattre was named commander in
chief of the ground forces of Western Europe, Marshal Sir James Robb
was to occupy the post of commanding officer of the air forces, Admiral
Robert Jaujard became admiral for Europe and was to be the naval
representative on the committee, and the permanent military president
was to be Field Marshal Bernard Montgomery, Viscount of Alamein. It
was not long before Montgomery and de Lattre clashed, a conflict that was
to last for some time but eventually end with the reconciliation of the two
military leaders.[23]

There were both similarities and profound differences between the
two men. Both were authoritarians and in their lifetimes both were
legendary figures. It is indeed unfortunate that no biography of de Lattre
has been written to date. However, the volume of his personal archives
and the importance of the documents contained therein, which are
remarkably well-filed, offer a marvelous perspective to the future biog-
rapher. Judging from written evidence he was worthy of his myth in
several respects. His final mission to Indochina offered far more pitfalls
than advantages for his reputation and his place in history. He accepted
the mission out of a sense of duty and emerged from it morally and
physically shattered even though he was almost successful. He previously
had been similarly motivated to accept the post of commander in chief of
the ground forces of Western Europe. Starting on 10 March 1947 he was
the inspector general of the land forces; on 5 May 1948 he became
inspector general of the armed forces—a post specially created for him.
Originally, the post of commander of Western Europe's ground forces had
been proposed to Marshal Alphonse-Pierre Juin, who preferred to remain
in Morocco. De Lattre accepted the post. His former "patron," General
Weygand, wrote to him at the time: "You are being given a particularly
difficult and dangerous mission given the current state of the military
strength of the western powers . . . a very heavy responsibility . . . it will
require vigilance at every moment, stubbornness of energy, and enormous
steadfastness of character. It will give you no respite."[24]

---

[22]Ibid.

[23]For proof of this conflict consult the Jean de Lattre archives and Field Marshal,
Viscount Montgomery of Alamein memoirs.

[24]De Lattre Papers, M 115. *France-Dimanche,* on 25 October 1948, transformed
General Weygand's remarks into "Weygand to de Lattre: In Your Shoes, I'd Need Sleeping
Pills!"

Still another dimension existed in the conflict between these two strong personalities. De Lattre had led the First French Army to victory. He wished to restore France to her place in Europe, and the experience of the Second World War had left profound effects on him. Montgomery, on his part, crowned with his victories and reasoning like an Englishman, had no patience with the nationalism of continental Europeans and had little faith in the effectiveness of continental European armies. He wrote in his memoirs:

> When the war ended, they [the continental Europeans] should have made the utmost effort to rebuild their forces from scratch; in many cases their high ranking officers had spent the war either in London or in German prisoner-of-war camps. One could see enormous ignorance concerning the organization needed to create armed forces adapted to modern warfare. Few generals were familiar with modern war.[25]

It appears, however, that there was no conflict over strategy. De Lattre was firmly convinced that "there is no such thing as a battle for France, but for Western Europe."[26] As for Montgomery, on 30 January 1948 he wrote: "We must all agree on one point; in case of attack the nations of Western Europe must resist the attack the furthest possible to the East."[27] In his opinion the military potential of France and the Benelux countries was negligible and they had to be reassured. To this aim Great Britain must maintain its place in Western Europe and assure its leadership, but de Lattre was not entirely convinced by British assurances. He pointed out that while the Battle of the Rhine would be vital for France and Benelux, the British would be able to think in terms of a second battle—that of Great Britain:

> The Continental nations thus need a guarantee that their own defense on the continent will be all out. If an Englishman or even an American is supreme commander they cannot be assured of such a guarantee if sole responsibility [for defense] lies in his hands. It would be quite another matter if the commander-in-chief of ground forces, who is a continental European and whose armies actually cover Western Europe, were entrusted with direct and personal responsibility and whose area of responsibility should [sic] clearly be spelled out.[28]

Under such conditions it was impossible to entrust an important part of the national sovereignties on the continent to a native of the British Isles.[29] On the one hand, the line that extends from the Rhine to the Alps should be defended by a continental commander in chief. On the other hand, the

---

[25]Field Marshal the Viscount Montgomery of Alamein, *The Memoirs of Field Marshal the Viscount Montgomery of Alamein* (London: Collins, 1958), p. 509.

[26]De Lattre Papers, 20 June 1948, M 110.

[27]Montgomery, *The Memoirs of Field Marshal the Viscount Montgomery of Alamein,* p. 500.

[28]De Lattre Papers, 4 April 1949, M 158.

[29]The same notion is expressed in the report of the Fontainebleau meeting, 20 June 1950, de Lattre Papers, M 598.

theater of operations extending from the Scandinavian countries to the Mediterranean and including the British Isles, could be under the command of an Englishman, or even better of an American "given the extent and complexities [of this theater]." De Lattre went even further in his analysis. The organization of the high command was dominated by the British. Montgomery, he added, wanted to move quickly and achieve his purposes before the signing of the Atlantic Pact: "The fact is that this is a maneuver orchestrated by the British [and perhaps the Americans] to assure themselves of the absolute control of the military organization of Western Europe by settling the problem of command before the even more delicate discussions which will take place after the signing of the Atlantic Pact."[30] In taking into consideration all of the above facts, the best principle could be summarized as one in which the commander in chief comes from the army that disposes of the greatest resources. That was the solution adopted during the Second World War; it was also that of 1918.

The last facet of the conflict concerns the technical organization of the high command. The chiefs of staff of the five Brussels Treaty nations formed a committee known as Western Union Chiefs of Staff (WUCOS). What exactly was the relationship between the chairman of the committee of commanders in chief and the commanders in chief themselves? What was the relationship of both with WUCOS? Montgomery, backed by his minister, considered himself as performing the duties of supreme commander; he was, in essence, acting supreme commander. Theoretically, however, the commanders in chief were to report to WUCOS. A decision had to be made; on 27 October 1948 General Lecheres suggested a compromise. Montgomery would be acting supreme commander but would delegate his duties to the commanders in chief. De Lattre agreed, but he realized that Montgomery "wasn't playing the game," and that he placed himself outside the committee; in practice he did not want to delegate in theory what he had delegated in actuality.[31] De Lattre noted that this was understandable since Montgomery was a land-oriented soldier who was naturally inclined toward concentrating on land battles that subsequently encroached on de Lattre's province.

Nonetheless, this was a situation that had to be changed, and in this matter de Lattre had the support of French Defense Minister Paul Ramadier. In Ramadier's opinion any disagreement among the commanders in chief had to be settled within the framework of WUCOS. In the event that WUCOS was incapable of defining a position, the issue would be taken up by the defense ministers.[32] Montgomery, however, sought to create an intermediate body somewhere between WUCOS and the commanders in chief. De Lattre viewed this solution as technically unsound. It was also not the approach taken by Eisenhower in 1944; a four-headed system was worthless. The commander in chief should be

---

[30]Ibid., 4 April 1949, M 158.
[31]Ibid., M 151.
[32]Ibid., 25 February 1949, M 145.

assisted by a commander in chief of the air forces and by a commander in chief of the naval forces; that is, the trilateral system. In addition, there should be commanders in chief of the three subtheaters (Scandinavia, continental Europe, and the Mediterranean) and commanders for the rear zones (British Isles, Iberian Peninsula, and French North Africa). In order for integration to be effective, "since the forces placed under the command of the supreme commander and the various commanders-in-chief will be of diverse nationalities, it is indispensable that the points of view of the different nations involved be represented in the various interallied commands."[33]

Ultimately, tensions cooled rather quickly. In a note dated 14 October 1950, dealing with the organization of the interallied high command in Europe, de Lattre expressed his satisfaction with the situation. He pointed out that in peacetime the operations plans were the responsibility of the committee of the commanders in chief—two out of four of whom were French. In wartime a Frenchman would be in command of the ground forces of Western Europe, but "after more than a year of effort, it was agreed that this command should have sufficient operational independence effectively to wage the *covering battle* of Western Europe, the initial battle on which will hang the fate of our territory."[34] The headquarters at Fontainebleau enabled the staff to become better acquainted and to learn how to cooperate in matters of daily routine. As a result interallied commands were established. There is no doubt that great progress was made even before General Eisenhower took command and finally settled the nature of NATO.

Are the examples of 1917–18 and 1948–50 distinct from each other? Perhaps not. In fact, from the period of the First World War to that just before the elaboration of the military organization of the North Atlantic Treaty both what was possible and impossible came clearly to view. What was impossible was the complete fusion of one army with another, the disappearance of a national identity in favor of a "de-nationalized" entity. What was possible, however, was the awareness that the defense of Western Europe had to be planned in common and that the battle of the Elbe or the Rhine could not be waged in a framework of improvization and national individualism.

What is even more apparent is that without the willingness to create a common policy there can be no integration of military forces, even if integration is restricted to an integrated command and if a solution such as amalgamation is rejected a priori. Such political willingness grows not only from a danger that threatens each member of the community but also from a sense of weakness on the part of each nation in that community. On this point the lesson of the post-World War II period is clear.

---

[33]Ibid., 21 June 1949 and 17 November 1949, M 610.
[34]Ibid., note of 14 October 1950, M 505.

NATO Standardization:
An Organizational Analysis

JAMES R. CARLTON

No historical discussion of the military dimension of NATO would be complete without an examination of the complex issue of "standardization." The search for that seeming panacea for all the alliance's problems has produced some very determined efforts during the last three decades, yet they have yielded only the most marginal success. There are still many who believe that standardization would eliminate most of NATO's economic, military, and perhaps political troubles.[1] To others, standardization is a desirable outcome in principle but must be qualified to meet particular national situations.[2] There are also those who have not been so impressed. Starting with the most basic issue, the authors of *NATO Standardization, Interoperability and Readiness,* a 1977 report prepared by a special subcommittee of the U.S. House Committee on Armed Services, state that:

> The Department of Defense is unable to define clearly many of the terms it uses to explain standardization and interoperability concepts.

---

[1] This line of thought has been championed mostly on the American side of the Atlantic. Its exponents range from the present administration, e.g. see Jimmy Carter's speech to the "NATO Heads of State London 1977," *New York Times,* 11 May 1977, to members of Congress, e.g. Nunn-Bartlett report, Committee on Armed Services, *NATO and the New Soviet Threat,* 95th Cong., 1st sess., 1977, to Public Laws of the United States, e.g. PL 93–365, and finally to informed parties, e.g. Thomas Callaghan, Jr., *US/European Economic Cooperation in Military and Civil Technology* (Center for Strategic and International Studies: Georgetown University Press, 1974).

The Europeans are a little more reserved in their expectation of the benefits of alliance-wide standardization; they seek standardization because of the economic rewards, the Americans because of the military benefits. See R. W. Dean, "The Future of Collaborative Weapons Acquisition," in *European Security: Prospects for the 1980's,* ed. Derek Leebaert (Lexington, MA: D. C. Heath and Company, 1979), pp. 79–101.

[2] This has been the French position as stated at the Western European Union meeting in Paris, March 1977, Committee on Defense and Armaments, *A European Armaments Policy Symposium* (Paris: Office of the Clerk of the Assembly of the Western European Union, 1977), pp. 22–23.

Standardization and interoperability are ambiguous definitions. These definitions have produced confusing and often conflicting guidance for translating policy into action.[3]

Translating policy into action—sometimes even its very formation—has proved to be agonizingly difficult. Standardization is a multidimensioned and highly complex concept that has been loaded with economic and political issues related to full employment, maintenance of national industrial bases, transfer of technology, arms exports, varied production techniques, high research and development costs, equity of overall contributions to NATO's defense, and finally the balance of payments. The military problems resulting from different perceptions and doctrines, particularly as they affect logistics, communications, reinforcement, and readiness, has added another dimension to the difficulties facing NATO policymakers.

Today there is a general consensus within the alliance that improvements must be made in NATO's conventional capabilities. The Soviet buildup in Europe, as well as the achievement of nuclear parity between the Soviet Union and the United States, has had a sobering effect upon the alliance. When President Jimmy Carter issued PRM-10 in 1977, many in Western Europe saw it as still another official indication that the United States might not use its nuclear arsenal in the defense of NATO. Part of the result was a reemphasis on the conventional deterrent. That shift has prompted the European members to address economic issues related to improving their conventional posture; subsequently, shrinking political and economic resources have spurred them into exploring new avenues of cooperation. The increasing costs of research and development for new weapons so far have constrained most European members from entering upon numerous individual ventures. Although most nations in the alliance perceive their defense industries as a source of political and economic wealth, the economic conditions of the 1970s induced them to reassess their positions and needs. Would standardization provide an effective solution? The history of earlier NATO programs may help to place current efforts in useful perspective.

NATO has tried a series of different avenues and approaches in an attempt to achieve greater armament cooperation and eventually standardization. Four distinct periods of NATO efforts can be identified: the "institutional" phase (1949–57), a "consortium" or "extramural" period (1957–68), the "European initiative" phase (1968–74), and the "two-way street" period (1974–80).[4]

---

[3]U.S., Congress, House, Committee on Armed Services, *NATO Standardization, Interoperability and Readiness,* 95th Cong., 2d sess., 1978, H.R. 11607 and H.R. 12837.
[4]This is not intended to include all the NATO standardization efforts but to emphasize those projects and approaches that best represent each particular phase.

INSTITUTIONAL PHASE (1949–57)

During NATO's incipient or "institutional" phase, the alliance came as close to comprehensive standardization as at any time in its entire history. American arms and equipment, to a significant extent, had carried the Western European allies to victory in the Second World War. Coupled with an initially prostrate continental defense industry, the American Military Assistance Program in its special Offshore Procurement phase had the overall effect of creating de facto standardization. American efforts were designed to help the continental allies both economically and militarily while at the same time providing a vehicle for U.S. foreign policy.[5] Along with credits and material aid, the United States offered Western Europe the licenses necessary to produce certain weapons and equipment. The possible economic consequences of such a program seemed obvious; new jobs, new industry, and new hope would do a great deal for a population that had been devastated by the horrors of six years of recent warfare and two major wars in a single generation, and everyone would benefit militarily through access to standardized modern arms and equipment.

In April 1949, when the major nations of Western Europe and America joined together for the purpose of mutual defense, NATO created two agencies to address the standardization question. It was the opinion of many of NATO's early leaders that standardization would result in real military, economic, and political advantages for the alliance. Interoperability of fuels, ammunition, and parts would allow the combined NATO forces to operate more efficiently and standard equipment would lead to a common doctrine resulting in a more precise definition of their mission. Negative experience during the Second World War proved to be an important influence in the formation of these opinions. Through standardization NATO could reap the benefits of economies of scale as well as specialization, with each producing substantial savings for the allies. From a political standpoint such cooperation would be a sign of solidarity within the alliance, especially important because it would help NATO demonstrate appropriate cohesiveness and singleness of purpose in the light of increasing Soviet pressure.

Many of the alliance members approached the problem with optimism, if the variety of programs tried is any indicator.[6] The early years were marked by a series of institutional efforts. Many hoped that the

---

[5]Brigadier General E. Vandervater, Jr., *Coordinated Weapons Production in NATO: A Study of Alliance Process,* RM-4169-PR (Santa Monica: Rand Corporation, 1967), pp. 17–19.

[6]NATO always has been optimistic about the future of coordinated arms production, NATO Information Service, *Defense Production and Infrastructure* (Paris: Aspects of NATO, 1963).

impetus and momentum of any effort could be generated through NATO's central organization. NATO's leaders visualized a system of international administration within the NATO framework whose task would be to amalgamate the many different national requirements and orders, while simultaneously monitoring any research and development programs within the alliance. The agency would select the appropriate designs as needed and the final steps would be the standardization of the systems. During the alliance's first decade, in an attempt to find the key to coordinated organizational control, several experiments were undertaken. The initial organization, known as the Military Production and Supply Board, sought to survey the production capabilities of the allies. At the time NATO also created the Defense Financial and Economic Committee and charged it with the development of overall economic and financial guidelines for defense programs. The operations of both agencies exemplify the centralized control approach.[7]

In 1951 NATO created two new agencies to help in its search for the right organizational scheme. The Defense Production Board replaced the Military Production and Supply Board; NATO was hoping that the new agency would be better able to coordinate armament production on an alliance-wide basis. In addition, in an attempt to find the most efficient and effective modes of cooperation between the alliance armed forces, the Military Committee of NATO established the Military Agency for Standardization (MAS).[8] To aid the process, MAS instituted what became known as "Stanags" (standardization agreements). Through the Stanags, MAS and NATO were confident that a consensus on procedural and material issues eventually would lead to greater cooperation in other areas. The operationalism of the Stanags agreement was a highly complex procedure requiring consensus at every level. It is little wonder that only one major operational system—the Breguet Br1150 *Atlantique* ASW aircraft—has resulted from a standardization agreement.

In 1952 the Production and Logistic Division of the newly created International Staff assumed the responsibilities of the Defense Production Board. The new agency was served primarily by a "group of experts" whose concerns were more technical than political. The fact that it still survives today, twice altered, is perhaps witness to its utility, although it failed to provide the "key" in 1952.[9]

The Defense Production Committee (DPC), established in 1954, represented the final NATO standardization effort during the original

---

[7]Lord Ismay, secretary general of NATO, *NATO: The First Five Years* (Netherlands: Bosch-Utrecht, 1955), pp. 25–27.

[8]Ismay, *NATO: The First Five Years*, pp. 41–48.

[9]The Defense Production Board was replaced by the Armaments Committee, which in turn was replaced by the Special Armament Groups under the Conference of National Armaments Directors.

phase. Its purpose was to coordinate work on standardization and to handle the exchange of technical information and know-how. Comprised of top-level policy spokesmen from each nation, the DPC tried to exercise control over standardization questions but did very little toward actual implementation of any system.[10]

By the mid-1950s NATO appeared to have exhausted most of the institutional avenues to greater standardization. The alliance had presided over an organizational progression from the loosely structured Military Production and Supply Board to the "group of experts"; the final change was the creation of a subministerial level of the DPC. However, in the process each successive attempt at a more centralized approach met with increased resistance. The nations that signed the treaty in 1949 were not the same in nature or number in 1950 let alone 1957, and centralized control proved to be almost impossible given the NATO composition of fifteen sovereign and rapidly evolving nations. During the economic recovery it was inevitable that emphasis would be placed on the development of each individual nation, not on multilateral arms production or cooperation. As long as America's nuclear umbrella provided protection, the other NATO allies were free to pursue single-minded recovery strategies.

CONSORTIUM OR EXTRAMURAL APPROACH (1957–68)

Following the first successful *Sputnik* in 1957, NATO moved out of the institutional phase into a period distinguished by a "consortium" or "extramural" approach. President Dwight D. Eisenhower, reacting to the Soviet achievement, proposed a new attempt at alliance-wide equipment cooperation. Eisenhower's purpose was to close the technology gap through increased cooperation within the alliance, and there was constant pressure in the United States for Europe, who sufficiently had recovered from the Second World War, to assume its fair share of the defense budget. The balance of payments question was an extremely sensitive issue for American policymakers, and many believed that increased standardization in NATO could in part ease the financial problem.

NATO actually standardized on five major U.S. systems during that period. The M-44 torpedo, the F-104F fighter, as well as the Hawk, Sidewinder, and Bullpup missiles were placed successfully in operation in the majority of NATO's armed forces. The achievement was due primarily to American hard sell and horse trading; private corporations and motives provided the incentives. Only after the initial agreements had

---

[10]Ismay, *NATO: The First Five Years*, p. 129.

been reached between the nations involved and the vendors did NATO take an interest, and then only in a perfunctory role. American technology and financial aid were still dominant. There was little reciprocal buying, or joint production, and this was to put great strains on the alliance, dimming the long-term prospect of significant standardization. As one observer noted: "For most Europeans the American definition of standardization meant buy American."[11] The American hard sell was so effective that the British navy came close to standardizing on the McDonnell Douglas F-4 Phantom. It had the effect of retarding the development of a modern European armament industry.[12]

NATO tried still another institutional approach during this period. In 1959 the alliance adopted the NATO Basic Military Requirement procedure (NBMR). Instead of production and financial control, the NBMR was to aid in the development of common military requirements in order to serve as a basis for all future alliance efforts in the search for greater standardization. The procedure proved to be unworkable. Although NATO appeared to be moving into a very promising area, the differently perceived military needs of separate nations were just too much to overcome. In recognition of its failure the NBMR procedure was abolished in 1966.[13]

In 1966 the Conference of National Armaments Directors (CNAD) by the North Atlantic Council was established. It was to be under the authority of the council with regard to defense equipment and related problems. Particular attention would be paid to the economic, political, and technical difficulties associated with any standardization efforts. It was NATO's hope that the CNAD would be more flexible than the procedurally rigid NBMR. The CNAD assumed a supervisory role over three armament groups: the naval, air force, and army, plus a new research defense group. Each of the military groupings was responsible for promoting cooperation in developing and producing equipment, handling both operational requirements, and the initiation of cooperative projects for each of their respective services. The challenge of the research group was to promote alliance-wide research and development cooperation that possibly could lead to future military equipment or relevant technological advances. Any efforts initiated through these organs would be carried out only if all those involved perceived the effort as being in their best interest. Each nation was free to act on a case-by-case basis. If any of NATO's members agreed to join together in a undertaking they would receive the support of the alliance, while at the same time their efforts would not be regulated by the organization. NATO would have no say in whether a

---

[11]Robert Rhodes James, *Standardization and Common Production of Weapons in NATO* (London: International Institute for Strategic Studies, 1967), p. 3.

[12]Vandervater, *Coordinated Weapons Production in NATO*, p. 22.

[13]James, *Standardization and Common Production of Weapons in NATO*, p. 11.

project would be undertaken or not. That decision would be determined by those nations considering it.[14]

The best explanation of the role and purpose of the CNAD probably comes from its present director of Planning and Support, John C. Stone:

> While achievement of cooperative projects was set as the main goal of the CNAD and its new groups, *it was recognized from the start* that exchanges of information on operational concepts, national equipment programs and technical and logistic matters would be extremely valuable in encouraging cooperation in general terms. *Even if there was no prospect of such exchanges leading to definite projects.*[15] [Emphasis added]

The CNAD indeed has contributed significantly to improved arms cooperation and eventually should have an impact on standardization. Yet, because of its "flexible system" it still has not proved to be very effective on an alliance-wide basis. What had started as a period of high expectations ended with NATO once again searching for the proper "key."

EUROPEAN INITIATIVE PHASE (1968–74)

Faced with the prospect of problems from two sides, Soviet and American, the European members of the alliance formed the Eurogroup; the extramural phase had ended and the "European initiative" phase had begun. In 1968 the West Europeans were spurred into action for several reasons, especially fear of unilateral American withdrawal as signaled by the proposed "Mansfield Amendment," and by the growing U.S. commitment in Southeast Asia. The European NATO nations were forced into reassessing their continental security needs.[16] French military withdrawal from NATO seemed to increase the need for greater European cooperation. The Czech invasion and the subsequent Soviet military buildup in Europe had an additionally sobering effect.[17] Thus, faced with increasing pressure to take a more active role in NATO defense, the European members responded with far greater inter-European cooperation.[18] The Eurogroup, established in 1968, was created to increase

---

[14]John C. Stone, "CNAD and NAIG: The Conference of National Armaments Directors: Its Intergovernmental Groups and the NATO Industrial Advisory Group," *NATO's Fifteen Nations* 24, no. 6 (December 79–January 80): 28–35.

[15]Stone, *NATO's Fifteen Nations*, p. 30.

[16]William C. Cromwell, *The Eurogroup and NATO* (Philadelphia: Foreign Policy Research Institute, 1974), pp. 9–18.

[17]*The Eurogroup*, aspects of NATO series (Brussels: NATO Information Service, 1975), p. 10.

[18]Cromwell, *Eurogroup and NATO*, pp. 9–18.

European defense procurement cooperation: "The basic aim of the Eurogroup can be simply stated: it is to help to ensure a stronger and more cohesive European contribution to the common defense and thus to strengthen the Alliance and the security in which its people live."[19] The new agency was to proceed in two ways. First, it would ". . . enhance the effectiveness of their contributions to overall Alliance security by coordinating their defense efforts by making best use of the resources available for defense." That effort surely would help further alliance-wide standardization. Second, the Eurogroup would provide ". . . a forum for the harmonization of European views on important political and strategic questions."[20] Therefore, many saw the new unit as the only available means to influence the United States to maintain forces at acceptable levels, a critical point if U.S. troops were to continue to provide the link between NATO and America's nuclear arsenal. The debate over the "flexible response" strategy provided the impetus.[21]

The first two years of Eurogroup operations were relatively quiet while they concentrated mainly on organizational matters; no concrete action was undertaken until 1970. Consequently, with the initiative provided by the NATO sponsored AD-70 the Eurogroup initiated the European Defense Improvement Program. It was designed to improve the NATO infrastructure, particularly communications and aircraft survival capabilities. A direct result was the hardening of all aircraft and communication sites.[22] Funded by a $1 billion budget derived from special national defense contributions, the Eurogroup entered the 1970s with renewed resolve and enthusiasm that carried over into the establishment of a number of subgroups. Euronad, Eurocom, Eurolog, Eurolongterm, Euromed, Eurostructure, and Eurotraining addressed problems of communications, logistics, medicine, infrastructure, and training. They so far appear to have proved successful.[23] In 1972 the Eurogroup adopted the

---

[19]*The Eurogroup*, pp. 9–10.

[20]Ibid., pp. 9–10.

[21]Cromwell, *Eurogroup and NATO*, p. 27.

[22]Federal Republic of Germany, Ministry of Defense, *Bulletin der Bundesregierung,* 30 June 1972. Cited in *Survival* 14 (November–December 1972), p. 271.

[23]Euronad, est. 1972; comprised of the European members of the Conference of National Armaments Directors whose goal is to establish principles to govern equipment collaboration with an aim toward reducing any duplication and improving any possibilities of standardization and interoperability. Eurocom, est. 1970; its purpose is to achieve better coordination and interoperability in tactical communications systems between allied armies in the battlefield area. Eurolog, est. 1970; to improve greater logistical support among the member nations. Eurolongterm, est. 1972; this organ is essentially concerned with planning and studying the concepts and doctrines that will be used by NATO because of standardization and interoperability. Euromed, est. 1970; addresses the problem of cooperation in the military medical field. Eurostructure, est. 1974; its task is to compile information on the structure of Eurogroup armed forces and to exchange information on matters of common interest. Eurotraining, est. 1970; designed to improve and expand existing cooperative training programs and to initiate new bilateral and multilateral training arrangements. See *The Eurogroup*, pp. 28–35.

Principles of Equipment Collaboration. The members had agreed to: (1) lower any potential defense production barriers between them; (2) exchange information regarding future needs; (3) review any possible avenues of joint cooperation; (4) draw up plans for such an operation or operations; (5) cooperate in logistic support; (6) increase awareness of cost control and management decisions; and (7) maximize standardization within the group.[24] It was certainly a revolutionary document. Given NATO's past record, the signatures of all ten Eurogroup members marked one of the few times a consensus on standardization has been reached, subordination of national interests for the greater good not having been one of NATO's strong points.[25]

The Eurogroup has been successful in a number of weapons projects including the FH-70 and SP-70 Howitzers, as well as two types of multiple role combat aircraft (MRCA) that were conceived, developed, and produced by Eurogroup members. Besides demonstrating its ability to work within its own organizational confines, the Eurogroup also has proved to be effective in coordinating the purchase of American equipment. In 1973 the Federal Republic of Germany, Belgium, Italy, Holland, and Great Britain purchased the U.S. Lance battlefield missile system. Later in 1975 the American F-16 fighter was standardized with the forces of Belgium, Norway, Holland, Denmark, and the United States.[26] During the years 1968–74, the Eurogroup was the most successful ever to address the standardization issue; the momentum continues to this day.

TWO-WAY STREET PERIOD (1974–80)

With the winding down of the Vietnam War, the United States again turned its attention toward Europe and NATO. The U.S. relative neglect of its forces in Europe for almost a decade was reflected in their readiness and capabilities. Yet, residual antiwar sentiment was running high in America as witnessed by continuing pressure for force reduction. Responding to the public mood while attempting to increase America's sagging military commitment to NATO in 1974, the 93d Congress of the United States passed Public Law 93-365. As a compromise, it reduced authorized U.S. European forces by 18,000, while simultaneously making a definite commitment to improving those forces through greater standardization of weapons systems within the alliance.[27] It was the enactment

---

[24]At the present time there are existing "Principles of Cooperation" for training and logistics. Both have contributed to increased standardization within the Eurogroup.

[25]Cromwell, *Eurogroup and NATO*, pp. 18–22.

[26]*The Eurogroup*, p. 13.

[27]U.S., Congress, Department of Defense, Appropriation and Authorization Act of 1975, Pub. L. 93-365, 93d Cong., 1974, H.R. 14592, p. 1.

of this law that signaled the opening of the fourth phase of NATO standardization efforts. "The United States began an initiative to make standardization in research and development—as well as procurement and support—an integral part of the NATO planning process."[28] Public Law 93-365 instructed the U.S. secretary of defense to:

> Undertake a specific assessment of the costs and possible loss of nonnuclear combat effectiveness of the military forces of the North Atlantic Treaty Organization members, including the United States, to *standardize weapons systems, ammunition, fuel and other military impedimentation* for land, air and naval forces. The Secretary of Defense shall also *develop a list of standardization actions* that could improve the overall North Atlantic Treaty Organization nonnuclear defense capabilities or save resources for the alliance as a whole.[29] [Emphasis added]

The development of a "list of standardization" actions has resulted in the United States once again taking the lead in NATO-wide efforts.

Eurogroup continues to coordinate continental efforts; in February 1976 the ten NATO members of the Eurogroup plus France formed the Independent European Program Group. Its purpose was to stimulate European defense cooperation outside NATO.[30]

In June and July 1976 the U.S. Congress passed two important laws, PL-94-329 and PL-94-361. The former, titled the International Security Assistance and Arms Export Control Act of 1976, waived a number of import/export trade restrictions to facilitate U.S. participation in NATO standardization efforts. The latter, the Department of Defense Appropriation Authorization Act of 1977, instructed the secretary to waive the "Buy American Act" when there was an acceptable European system available; thus, it recognized the Eurogroup's success and the need for even greater cooperation. PL-94-361 states:

> That standardization of weapons and equipment within the Alliance on the basis of the 'two-way street' concept of cooperation in defense procurement between Europe and North America could only work in a realistic sense if the European nations operate on a united and collective basis. Accordingly the Congress encourages the governments of Europe to accelerate their present efforts to achieve European armaments collaboration among all European members of the Alliance.[31]

---

[28]*NATO Standardization, Interoperability and Readiness*, p. 1500.
[29]Appropriation and Authorization Act of 1975, Pub. L. 93–365.
[30]The Assembly of the Western European Union, through its Committee on Defense Questions and Armaments, also offered a forum from which to discuss greater arms cooperation and standardization among its members.
[31]U.S., Congress, Department of Defense, Appropriation and Authorization Act of 1977, Pub. L. 94–361, 94th Cong., 1976, H.R. 12438, p. 2.

The "Buy American Act," which instructed the Department of Defense to select American systems whenever possible, was probably the greatest stumbling block on the road to standardization. Any change would signal a genuine U.S. desire for greater cooperation. European systems in theory would be able to compete for sale to the American armed forces. The 1977 act was a congressional attempt to establish a two-way street for procurement and licensing in any NATO effort. The United States pledged actively to seek to offset any American armament sales to any European nation by its own selection of specified equipment in return. This policy would address the balance of payments problem based upon the pattern of a World War II American-Canadian agreement. The objective of that policy had been to balance the military purchases between the two countries and it worked.[32]

President Carter reaffirmed the two-way street policy at the London NATO summit in May 1977: "We should also improve cooperation in development, production and procurement of Alliance defense equipment. The Alliance should not be weakened militarily by waste and overlapping, nor should it be weakened politically by disputes over where to buy defense equipment."[33] In addition, Carter pledged, along with the other members, to increase the American contribution to the alliance defense budget by 3 percent. Both actions indicated that the United States was once again very concerned with conditions in Europe and within NATO.

Two additional "lists of standardization" actions occurred during 1977. First, at the NATO ministerial meeting in Brussels President Carter and Secretary of Defense Harold Brown began promoting the idea of a NATO Long-Term Defense Program (LTDP), thus emphasizing U.S. recognition of the need for long-range planning if there were to be effective standardization. Second, the Appropriations Act of 1977 (PL-94-419) also provided that restrictions on the "procurement of specialty metals produced outside the United States would not apply when it is necessary to further standardization . . . requirements in NATO," thus opening another avenue to alliance-wide cooperation.[34] A year later in Washington the LTDP, in a modified version, was endorsed by the NATO heads of states who saw it as the basis for long-range defense planning to improve military capabilities within their limited resources.[35]

In January 1979 the United States took still another standardization action. A report prepared by the Defense Science Board examined the problem of achieving improved NATO effectiveness through armaments

---

[32]Testimony by Thomas A. Callaghan, Jr., in *NATO Standardization, Interoperability and Readiness*, pp. 55–57.

[33]*New York Times*, 11 May 1977.

[34]U.S., Congress, Department of Defense, Appropriation Act of 1977, Pub. L. 94–419, 94th Cong., 1976.

[35]*NATO Standardization, Interoperability and Readiness*, p. 1502.

collaboration. The study focused on three means to overall improvement. Two of the avenues—Dual Procurement Memoranda of Understanding (MOUs) and dual protection—are modified versions of avenues already available to NATO. The "family of weapons" concept is new and represents the most advanced form of present Department of Defense armament collaboration.[36]

During the last six years the United States has spent a great deal of time and effort convincing its allies that greater standardization is desirable and attainable. The United States, however, has a rather unimpressive record of implementation. Although there have been some successful two-way street deals—the F-16 and the MG-58—the controversy, for example, over U.S. Army trials of the West German *Leopard* II and the recent debate over the British Rapier missile illustrate a continuing inconsistency. The double standard that appears to have continued to characterize American actions over the last few years has caused Edgar O'Ballance to comment:

> For a long time the United States has been glibly and blandly saying that weapon procurement is a two-way street, indicating that it is open for the United States to buy arms from Europe, just as much as it is for NATO to buy arms from the United States. The Americans insist they are perfectly prepared to purchase European equipment if it meets United States' requirements, which somehow it never seems to do. On the other hand the United States is always urging the NATO allies to buy U.S. arms, and uses high pressure salesmanship to sell them, but never seems to buy from Europe in return. The United States Congress is swayed by powerful pressure lobbies that tend to emphasize national parochial or ethnic interest, often to the detriment of those in NATO. The United States government must open up the present commercial one-way street and make it a two-way defensive one.[37]

In a summer 1978 article in *Foreign Policy,* Elliot Cohen argued that domestic concerns and interests are so strong that America will accept new systems from its European allies only when there is no comparable system offered by U.S. defense industries.[38] The truth is that "Buy American" is almost as strong a guiding principle as it ever has been.

---

[36]U.S., Department of Defense, Defense Science Board, *Achieving Improved NATO Effectiveness Through Armament Collaboration,* 1978 Summer Study (December 1978), pp. 21–39.
    [37]Edgar O'Ballance, "From the West," *Armies and Weapons* 5 (November/December 1978), p. 7.
    [38]Elliot Cohen, "NATO Standardization: The Perils of Common Sense," *Foreign Policy* 31 (Summer 1978): 72–90.

CONCLUSIONS

In the last thirty-one years NATO has experienced many setbacks and a few successes in its struggle toward greater standardization. Its success rate has been greatly influenced by the various approaches used and by the constantly changing needs of each alliance member. During the original phase NATO tried to achieve standardization through a number of centrally oriented boards and staffs, but this approach met with little success for a number of reasons.[39] The biggest impediment stemmed from the need for unanimity at each individual decision level; centralized control proved to be impossible because the fifteen sovereign nations jealously guarded their independence. The extramural phase started out well but ended poorly. The consortia met with only partial success because the favorable initial conditions for cooperation quickly faded. The nature of modern weapons production soon began to restrict cooperation; new proprietary technology and its transfer caused most nations to scrutinize each situation most carefully. Finally, slow production schedules and the high cost of production runs dealt the final blow to the approach.[40]

The Eurogroup effort proved to be innovative and adaptable. It approached the standardization issue with a uniquely European style. Heeding the lessons to be learned from the first two phases, the Eurogroup has sought to achieve standardization, combining the need for a specific centralized direction with agencies that address each different standardization need as a unique problem. The approach has resulted in a maturing of Eurogroup defense industries. The newly found strength has had a positive effect on many facets of NATO operations.

The American drive toward standardization during the most recent phase has sought to return the United States to the historical position of alliance leader and weapons vendor. Recognizing the potential of the newfound industrial muscle of its European allies, the United States has revived a once successful bilateral approach to defense production cooperation, claiming that any cooperation between each side of the Atlantic must be conducted along the two-way street. The United States has proposed several methods to improve NATO efforts at collaboration

---

[39]The Vandervater report mentions the deficiencies caused by the need for unanimity of committee agreement at several stages: the formation of the military, characteristics of technical specifications, and design and financing. Vandervater, *Coordinated Weapons Production in NATO*, pp. 20–24.

[40]Comptroller general of the United States, *Standardization in NATO: Improving the Effectiveness and Economy of Mutual Defense Efforts*, report to Congress, GA 1.13, PSAD 78–2.

in research and development and its coordination by LTDP. Past experience has shown that if a serious effort is to be made toward standardization, the cooperative elements of major systems replacement schedules and future perceived military needs, as well as closer technological cooperation, must be worked out in advance. Through the LTDP, NATO might possibly reach an agreement on how to proceed with effective coproduction and "family of weapons" programs.

After more than thirty years many of the deterrents to real standardization within the alliance remain the same. The varying NATO members' individualistic perceptions of their military needs and equipment requirements continue to be a source of friction. Probably NATO's severest handicap has been the most obvious: the continual display of national self-interest when addressing political and economic problems. All alliance members believe that they must maintain control over inflation, unemployment, the balance of payments, and safeguard their own industrial capabilities. When it may be directly affected by standardization efforts no amount of group pressure can influence a NATO state to act against what it sees as its national interests. Throughout the years there has never been a NATO organization that could plan and direct standardization efforts that were acceptable to all members. Another persistent area of concern has been the differences in cost effectiveness and competitiveness among the member nations; cost overruns and hard selling provide examples. Finally, NATO has experienced virtually no cooperation in equipment replacement schedules.[41] Even though both the Eurogroup and American LTDP efforts address these problems, cooperation, especially between the two sides of the Atlantic, has yet to prove lasting.

Today, the alliance may be standing at the crossroads of standardization. Although all member nations recognize the need for greater arms cooperation and increased standardization, any long-term success is contingent upon a much stronger political commitment to general cooperation by the membership as a whole. At the present time it is generally recognized within the alliance that "complete standardization of military equipment . . . is an ideal that is neither practicable nor desirable." In the future NATO will concentrate on those "cooperative equipment programs" that are economically and militarily efficient, particularly in the reduction or elimination of duplicate programs and production procurement waste.[42]

The alliance undoubtedly will continue to seek both the short- and long-term advantages that undeniably accompany any successful standardization effort. For the short-term the alliance probably will strive for

[41] Ibid.

[42] John B. Walsh, "Armaments Co-operation in NATO," *NATO's Fifteen Nations* 24, no. 6 (December 1979–January 1980): 8–14.

greater interoperability of equipment, fuel, and doctrines. These under-takings will produce modest increases in NATO military readiness and capabilities without the economic, political, and military concessions that are required by standardization programs. For the future the alliance very likely will continue also to rely on its LTDP; this cooperation eventually could mean real standardization. Another potentially successful avenue would be the establishment of an effective organizational structure within NATO. Although that approach has failed in the past, the present sense of urgency may be sufficient to promote an effective alliance-wide consensus.

NATO and Arms Control*

LUC CROLLEN

From earliest times mankind has sought to mitigate the horrors of war through measures for the reduction and limitation of armaments as well as through a wide variety of written and unwritten rules to soften the violent character of armed conflict. The increasing destructiveness of weapons and the enveloping nature of modern warfare have only lent urgency to this quest.

In the late nineteenth century disarmament was a frequent theme of political discourse. After World War I it became a primary goal of the League of Nations and played an important role in the foreign policies of some major and lesser European powers. However, little substantial progress was made until, as a consequence of World War II and the emergence of nuclear and thermonuclear weapons and intercontinental delivery systems, it was realized that it was finally time to give some concrete content, if not to the universal idea of a disarmed and perpetually peaceful world, at least to the idea that efforts at stabilizing the arms race and at building confidence between those who are deeply suspicious of each other's intentions should be joined together with efforts for maintaining equilibrium and deterrence.

The Atlantic Alliance is a coalition of nations determined to safeguard the freedom, common heritage, and civilization of their peoples, founded on the principles of democracy, individual liberty, and the rule of law. It is an alliance for the preservation of security; it is an alliance for peace; and it is an alliance of democratic nations. In other words, nations in which governments are not responsive to the inner wishes of their peoples do not survive. Consequently, the Atlantic Alliance, if not from its inception in the midst of the Cold War then at least from the first signs of relaxed tensions between East and West, has paid careful attention to the desires of its citizens for peace and their wishes to maintain security through détente as well as through defense, arms control, and deterrence.

Few people are aware that NATO, or some of its major members such as the United States, have been the initiators of a great majority of nonarmament and arms control negotiations. Such negotiations range from the Antarctic, Outer Space, and Non-Proliferation Treaties, as well

---

*Portions of this chapter have appeared under the same title in *NATO Review* 28 (October 1980): 20–24; and ibid. 28 (December 1980): 24–30.

as to the Mutual Balanced Force Reductions (MBFR), the Strategic Arms Limitation Talks (SALT), and the "confidence-building" talks in Europe. On French initiative, these have included a disarmament conference in Europe aimed initially at securing more transparency and predictability in the military posture, movements, and maneuvers of each side.

The origin of NATO's involvement in arms control as well as the evolution of the alliance's arms control consultation practice will be presented in this article. There is no attempt here to deal with the substance of each of these arms control negotiations but rather with the question of how and to what extent the alliance managed to preserve its cohesion and solidarity, while confronted with a wide gamut of extremely complex negotiations that all bear either directly or indirectly on the security of the alliance as a whole and on each of its individual members.

THE RISE OF POLITICAL CONSULTATION IN NATO: REPORT OF THE THREE WISE MEN

NATO's interest in disarmament and arms control issues can be traced back as far as to the mid-1950s. The final communiqué of the Council of Ministers meeting in December 1955 mentions the USSR's unwillingness to accept any effective system of verification, including the "Open Skies" plan proposed by President Dwight D. Eisenhower. At that time, just as today, Soviet attitudes toward transparency and openness, verification, and the exchange of military data constituted an extremely serious roadblock on the way to concrete results, due to their frequently expressed fear of "espionage" and their desire to maintain internal social control and ideological purity.

In the meantime, many bilateral and multilateral arms control treaties relying mainly on so-called "national technical means of verification"—intelligence—have been signed and implemented, while NATO's involvement in those matters has increased. Over the years the smaller powers recognized that arms control negotiations conducted by the superpowers, but bearing on the security of their friends, could lead to nervousness among allies and threaten alliance cohesiveness if allies thought that their vital interests were being bargained away. Although such fears could affect Warsaw Pact as well as NATO countries in Europe, the dangers that mistrust could lead to disruption are more serious in alliances among democratic nations than in alliances of totalitarian regimes. In the former, disalignment remains not only a theoretical option but also a practical political choice.

In an age where the concept of a "go it alone" national defense has become obsolete and where the security of the West is based on an integrated multinational military organization, there can be no question of

pursuing separate national arms control policies without a clear understanding of the needs of alliance as a whole. In fact, the more arms control
tends to shift away from declaratory policies and rhetoric toward substantive security issues the greater the necessity of an alliance-wide
integrated arms control concept and strategy.

The need for more thorough arms control consultations was part of
a broader need for expanded cooperation and consultation in the political
field, as recommended in the May 1956 report of the Committee on Non-
Military Cooperation. This committee, frequently referred to as the
committee of "Three Wise Men," was instructed to "advise the Council
on ways and means to improve and extend NATO co-operation in nonmilitary fields and to develop unity within the Atlantic Community."[1] The
role of the council as the privileged forum for political consultations, either
at the level of the foreign ministers or at the level of the permanent
representatives, was thereby enhanced. As a followup, a political committee, originally the Committee of Political Advisers (POLADS), was
established in 1957; their role in the arms control field also would grow
over time.

The principle of arms control consultations was and still is vague;
indeed, it could have various connotations. Did it include informing the
allies about past, present, or future considerations? Did it mean asking for
the advice of the allies and providing a wide exchange of views, with or
without the intention to take these views into account? Did it imply an
unspectacular but relentless quest for the harmonization of the policies of
the allies, or was it aimed at establishing collective decisions and/or
binding guidance?

Until 1962 arms control consultations were still very informative in
nature and more or less on an *ad hoc* basis mainly at the council level.
This was the case with the Eastern and Western schemes for a general and
complete disarmament, as well as with the regional arms control and
disengagement schemes of those proposed in 1957 by Polish Minister
of Foreign Affairs Adam Rapacki and in 1960 by Polish Prime Minister
Wladyslaw Gomulka.[2] Both suggested, although to different degrees, a
denuclearization of Central Europe that would include both Germanies,
Poland, and Czechoslovakia.[3]

---

[1]See *International Organization* 10 (August 1956): 504. See also *NATO Letter* 4
(6 June 1956): 3–4.

[2]In those days there was much talk about far-reaching reductions in the stocks of
existing weapons at the disposal of nations eventually leading toward their quasi elimination
under plans for general and complete disarmament except for forces needed. James E.
Dougherty, "For National and International Police and Peace Keeping Purposes," *How to
Think About Arms Control and Disarmament* (New York: Russak and Company, 1973),
p. 22.

[3]On 7 September 1959 in a meeting in Geneva, the Ministers of Foreign Affairs of the
United States, the Soviet Union, the United Kingdom, and France decided to create a
Disarmament Committee consisting of the four major powers plus Bulgaria, Canada, Italy,

IMPACT OF ENDC'S CREATION

With the creation of the Eighteen Nation Disarmament Committee (ENDC) in Geneva in 1962, consultations at NATO's council level were held on a regular basis.[4] After each ENDC session one of the four Western powers present in Geneva would brief the council; written reports were presented by the four. However, Arms Control Consultations remained essentially informative in character.

As early as the mid-1950s, U.S. efforts toward establishing a "first-step philosophy" and partial arms control measures rather than a general and complete disarmament approach led to the signing in Moscow on 5 August 1963 of the Treaty Banning Nuclear Weapon Tests in the Atmosphere, in Outer Space and Under Water (the Limited Test Ban Treaty).[5] Still later efforts resulted in the signature on 27 January 1967 of the Treaty on Principles Governing the Activities of States in the Exploration and Use of Outer Space, Including the Moon and Other Celestial Bodies (the Outer Space Treaty),[6] as well as the Treaty on the Non-Proliferation of Nuclear Weapons (the Non-Proliferation Treaty) on 1 July 1968. The latter stated that nuclear countries would agree not to transfer such weapons to states not already possessing them and the other signatories would commit themselves to refrain from acquiring them.[7]

Poland, Romania, and Czechoslovakia. This committee called the Committee of Ten was later endorsed by the UN Disarmament Committee to which it reported. In 1961–62 it was decided to expand its membership to include eight neutral and nonaligned states: Brazil, Burma, India, Mexico, Nigeria, Sweden, the United Arab Republic, and Ethiopia. This eighteen-nation Disarmament Committee was replaced in 1969 by the Conference of the Committee on Disarmament (CCD), and its membership was expanded to twenty-six by adding Argentina, Hungary, Japan, Mongolia, Morocco, the Netherlands, Pakistan, and Yugoslavia. It was the arms control negotiating organ of the international community where smaller nations could vent their frustrations with the superpowers' arms policies. They were less eager to advocate a form of universal disarmament applicable to them. See Dougherty, *How to Think About Arms Control,* p. 9.

[4]In 1974 five new members were added: the German Democratic Republic, the Federal Republic of Germany, Iran, Peru, and Zaire. In fall 1978 the CCD was restructured and renamed the Committee on Disarmament and was enlarged to forty members. In addition to the thirty-one members, it now contains: Algeria, Australia, Belgium, China, Cuba, Kenya, Indonesia, Sri Lanka, and Venezuela.

[5]In contrast to disarmament, which entails the elimination or reduction of armaments, arms control presupposes the continued existence of national military establishments and usually aims at "some kind of restraint or regulation in the qualitative design, quantitative production, deployment, protection, control, transfer and planned, threatened, or actual use of arms for political strategic purposes." Dougherty, *How to Think About Arms Control,* pp. 29–30.

[6]This treaty prohibits the emplacement of weapons of mass destruction in orbit around the earth, moon, or other celestial bodies.

[7]This series was preceded by the Antarctic Treaty of 1 December 1959, which demilitarized the region and prevented nuclear weapons tests in this area.

Both the Limited Test Ban Treaty and the negotiations leading to the Non-Proliferation Treaty were greeted with mixed feelings by many European governments. On the one hand, Europeans generally welcomed the attempts of the superpowers to tone down their hostility, back away from confrontation, and enter the era of détente. On the other hand, there was "fear that the two nuclear giants, in their quest for mutual interest agreements, might strike bargains over the heads and at the expense of the Europeans in between."[8] In addition, there was widespread concern among the smaller nations within the alliance about their perceptions regarding their insufficient technical and scientific knowledge concerning arms control. As a result of this concern, on 24 November 1965 a joint German-Danish initiative within the NATO Council sought to establish a pattern of regularity in their meetings with experts, which by this time already took place on an *ad hoc* basis within the framework of POLADS. It was officially decided that meetings of the Committee of Political Advisers, along with disarmament experts, would be held at regular intervals—spring and fall.[9] It was agreed in March 1966 that the responsibility of the committee chairman would be to make oral reports to the council, which later were made in written form.[10]

These consultations, in general, strengthened the position of those NATO nations that played a leading role in arms control negotiations, particularly that of the United States. They also introduced a new dimension in arms control consultation practices, as views were to be exchanged prior to rather than after national decision making. In addition, it became customary for the allies privately to discuss Western tactics and allied behavior in the United Nations; sometimes those tactics were even coordinated. Moreover, these consultations helped to proliferate knowledge of arms control matters within the alliance. They also created a series of unwritten basic principles consistently opposing arms control proposals that were aimed at the following:

1) placing an absolute ban on the use of weapons prior to the creation of an effective control system;[11]

---

[8]Dougherty, *How to Think About Arms Control*, p. 61.

[9]In addition to the semiannual meetings with disarmament experts, the Committee of Political Advisers holds other meetings with experts to discuss specific matters such as humanitarian law in armed conflicts (prohibitions or restrictions of the use of certain conventional weapons, additional protocols to the Geneva Convention).

[10]The council took note of the first written report in October 1968.

[11]The Convention on the Prohibition of the Development, Production and Stockpiling of Bacteriological (Biological) and Toxin Weapons and on Their Destruction signed on 10 April 1972 is the notable exception. The United States and the United Kingdom were convinced that anyone who launched germ warfare attacks might in fact infect his own side as well as the enemy. They believed that this class of weapons posed no real military threat and could, without too many risks, be banned without verification of the destruction of

2) weakening the North Atlantic Alliance vis-à-vis the Warsaw Pact; for example, proposals tending to drive a wedge between the United States and the European allies;
3) creating an impression of progress while in reality there is none;
4) reducing arms without verification and if necessary on-site inspection; and
5) declaring pledges such as no first use of nuclear weapons or non-aggression pact proposals.

THE HARMEL EXERCISE: QUALITATIVE BREAKTHROUGH IN NATO'S ARMS CONTROL CONSULTATION PROCESS

The real breakthrough in the quality of NATO's arms control negotiations was the emergence of détente diplomacy as an important pillar of NATO's security strategy. Détente, reality or illusion, divisible or indivisible, was the magic word of the latter sixties and early seventies. Some believed that the era of conflict and confrontation was on the verge of being replaced by an era of cooperation. Convergence theories were fashionable. Students all over Europe predicted the end of both capitalism and totalitarian communism. Hence, in both East and West a new society was about to be born: socialism with a human face.

Whatever judgment can be made concerning the validity of the above contention, it was undeniable that forces had been at work contributing to the erosion of bipolarity in the international system, the loosening of the blocs, and the search for a new pattern in intersuperpower relations—from all-out antagonism to peaceful competition.[12] The loosening of NATO was reflected in 1966 with France's withdrawal from all integrated NATO commands and from the expulsion of all NATO military headquarters, equipment, and personnel from French soil. Moreover, President Charles de Gaulle claimed that the time was ripe to reject American predominance in the alliance, and for European nations to seize

---

stockpiles. France, however, continued to claim that adequate international controls were a necessity. Nevertheless, she enacted domestic legislation prohibiting biological weapons in June 1973.

[12]Those forces were: 1) the nuclear balance of terror or stalemate symbolized by the Cuban missile crisis; 2) the liberalization within the Soviet regime that followed the death of Stalin in 1953; 3) the emergence of polycentric tendencies behind the Iron Curtain, Poland, Hungary, Romania, and Czechoslovakia; 4) the disruption of the Sino-Soviet axis beginning with an ideological struggle within the world Communist movement and culminating in the armed clashes on the Amur and Ussuri rivers in 1969; 5) the resurgence of Western Europe as a prosperous, dynamic, and self-confident group of nations: and 6) the acquisition of independence by the colonial societies throughout the Asian, Arab, and African worlds after World War II.

the opportunity to determine their own fate, presumably under French leadership.

Although de Gaulle's move met with little enthusiasm among his NATO partners and although eventually none of them withdrew from the Atlantic Alliance after the initial twenty-year period established by the treaty, it stimulated prolonged debates in many of the smaller members (Norway, Denmark, Belgium, the Netherlands, and Luxemburg) over the advantages and disadvantages of continued membership in the Atlantic Alliance.[13] Consequently, they all demanded a more active role for the alliance in the pursuit of détente and in the creation of a platform for joint political action to that end.

In a major effort aimed at reassessing the alliance's future tasks, the NATO Council in a 1966 winter session asked Belgian Foreign Minister Pierre Harmel to undertake a broad analysis of the international developments since the signing of the North Atlantic Treaty in 1949 in order to ascertain their influence on international relations and on the alliance itself. One year later the council unanimously approved the Harmel Report, which called for further improvement in the political consultation process within NATO and defined the main political task of the alliance as the pursuit of the "search for progress towards a more stable relationship in which the underlying political issues can be solved." In particular, it defined the role of the allies and their consultations as one promoting an improvement in relations with the Soviet Union and the countries of Eastern Europe, while emphasizing that this improvement only could be accomplished if the alliance maintains adequate military strength and political solidarity to deter aggression. "Military security and a policy of détente are not contradictory but complementary. Collective defense . . . is the necessary condition for effective policies towards a greater relaxation of tensions." It explicitly mentioned intensification of alliance studies on disarmament and practical arms control measures, including the possibility of balanced force reductions as reflecting the will of the allies to work for an effective détente with the East.[14]

In the aftermath and as a consequence of the Harmel exercise, the NATO arms control machinery was further strengthened. The Senior Political Committee (SPC), i.e. the Political Committee meeting at the level of deputy permanent representatives, was created in January 1968. During the same year a new section was established at NATO's international secretariat whose purpose was to deal with disarmament and arms control matters.

The alliance, having adopted the collective improvement of East-West relations as one of its main political aims and having strengthened its

---

[13]Cf. O. De Raeymaeker et al., *Small Powers in Alignment* (Leuven: Leuven University Press, 1974), p. 424.

[14]Harmel Report in *NATO Letter* 16 (March 1968): 10–13.

consultative mechanisms, was well equipped to enter a period of intensive and fruitful East-West dialogue. NATO and the Warsaw Pact each made a number of proposals and counterproposals concerning the holding of a conference on European security. While the main concerns of Warsaw Pact policy initially remained the question of holding a European security conference that would be aimed first and foremost at multilateral recognition of the status quo and the Soviet position in Eastern Europe, the NATO members sought as their major policy goal to negotiate on balanced mutual force reductions. The ministers of all the NATO nations, except France, issued a clear call for talks on MBFR at Reykjavik in June 1968 and reiterated it at every ministerial council meeting until mid-1972.[15] Together with sufficient progress in Germany's *Ostpolitik* and the inner-German dialogue, SALT, and the talks in Berlin with the four major powers, a certain linkage between the Conference on Security and Cooperation in Europe (CSCE) and force reductions talks became a condition sine qua non for the NATO members to participate in the CSCE.[16]

After the former three preconditions had been fulfilled, NATO's attitude toward the holding of a CSCE became more complaisant. In May 1972 when President Nixon extracted an agreement from the Soviet leadership regarding the parallel running of the CSCE and MBFR, the heart of the problem seemed to have been resolved. On the occasion of an additional visit of Henry Kissinger to Moscow, it was decided that preliminary talks on the CSCE could begin on 22 November 1972 in Helsinki and on force reductions on 30 January 1973 in Vienna. However, while the CSCE eventually resulted in the signature of a final document, the Final Act on 1 August 1975, the negotiations in Vienna are still far away from a successful conclusion.[17]

MBFR: BEYOND TRADITIONAL CONSULTATION

By the time Leonid Brezhnev made his speech at Tbilisi in 1971, indicating Soviet interest in NATO's offer of talks on MBFR, the alliance already had accomplished a significant amount of work on the subject. Almost three years had passed since NATO's call for action at Reykjavik.[18]

---

[15]See NATO Ministerial Council communiqué, Reykjavik, 24–25 June 1968, in *Atlantic Community Quarterly* 6 (Fall 1968): 443–44.

[16]Cf. Michael Palmer, *The Prospects for a European Security Conference* (London: Chatham House, 1971), p. 15.

[17]Final Act, CSCE, in *Atlantic Community Quarterly* 13 (Fall 1975): 364–94.

[18]Brezhnev's Tbilisi speech, 20 May 1971, in *Current Digest of the Soviet Press* no. 20, p. 5.

Many symmetrical or asymmetrical reduction models and different packages had been studied thoroughly and much time had been devoted to finding the best way to promote discussion with the Soviet Union and other Eastern European countries.

After the Tbilisi signal, MBFR became a key focus of alliance interest that was dealt with at considerable length in the final communiqué of the Council of Ministers meeting held in Lisbon in June 1971. It was announced at this meeting that a representative would be appointed at the appropriate time who would be responsible to the North Atlantic Council for conducting exploratory talks with the Soviet government and other interested governments. Somewhat later this exploratory function was offered to and accepted by Manlio Brosio, former secretary general of NATO.[19] Although the Soviet Union never responded to this NATO initiative and Brosio never went to Moscow to hold exploratory talks, the episode is noteworthy. It clearly shows how anxious the allies were to emphasize the need for the Western nations to speak with a single voice on such an important matter bearing on the security of the entire alliance.

The same anxiety to protect the cohesion and solidarity of the allies led them to create an unprecedented structure for intraalliance consultation and for the development of a common allied position vis-à-vis the East, even if the nations participating in the Vienna negotiations did so as sovereign states. Allied unity was considered essential not only to the security of every ally but also to the success of the negotiations themselves. All efforts on the part of the other side to divide the alliance, to play one ally off against the other, and particularly to create a split between the United States and the European members of the alliance have been so far successfully resisted.

The NATO negotiating machinery for MBFR is based on a triangular structure: the council and its subsidiary bodies that develop the general strategy; the Ad Hoc Group (AHG) in Vienna that discusses Western tactics and carries out the day-to-day negotiations, and the national governments in capitals that reflect on both strategy and tactics and give the necessary instructions to their representatives in Brussels and Vienna.

It is the task of the NATO Council in Brussels to deal with all questions of objectives and policy. On instructions from their governments, ministers (or permanent representatives) determine general alliance goals and strategy in the form of binding guidance. The council must ensure that the conduct of the negotiations is consistent with this guidance, which is the expression of the common will of all concerned allies. It is assisted by the Political Committee, which helps coordinate policy and draft guidance,

---

[19]Final communiqué, Lisbon, North Atlantic Council of Ministers, in *Atlantic Community Quarterly* 9 (Fall 1971): 390–93. For Brosio's appointment see *New York Times*, 6, 7 October 1971.

and by the MBFR Working Group that supplies the indispensable military/technical analyses. The alliance's Military Committee provides advice on military matters. In principle, no ally is excluded from MBFR deliberations of the council, SPC, or Working Group. France is usually present at the council or SPC level, but as a rule her representatives do not intervene in discussions unless they feel France's interests are directly or indirectly threatened. All decisions, whether at council or any other level, are arrived at on the basis of consensus in a spirit of allied solidarity.

Alliance action in Vienna is coordinated by the AHG, which is comprised of the delegations from all alliance members concerned; for example, the fifteen countries minus France and Iceland, which has no armed forces, plus the representatives of the secretary general of the International Military Staff and of the Supreme Allied Commander Europe (SACEUR). On the basis of instructions of the respective governments and of council guidance, the AHG has the responsibility for determining allied tactics and for conducting the day-to-day negotiations with the East.

The AHG, like the council, works on the basis of the consensus principle. Since in practice AHG decision making is often subject to time constraints, there is less room for dissent or discussions, but the expression of different viewpoints is in no way precluded.[20] Contacts with the Warsaw Pact delegations are made during "informal" or "plenary" negotiating sessions,[21] or during a wide variety of bilateral or multilateral informal meetings and gatherings.[22] The AHG frequently submits written reports to the council, and once every three weeks a reporting team from the AHG pays a visit to Brussels and delivers oral reports that are sometimes followed by frank exchanges of views or lively debates.

It is not necessary to elaborate on the third element of the triangular structure—the national governmental authorities in the capitals. With their physical and emotional remoteness, both from the place where the negotiations are carried out daily and from the forum where allied viewpoints regarding the basic strategic options confronted each other, the decision makers in the capitals can reflect all of this in peace, striking the

---

[20]The chairmanship of the AHG is rotated on a weekly basis among all the participants. The influence of the various allies on the decision making is not only a function of their relative weight within the alliance and of their status of being a direct or indirect participant but also of the quantity and quality of their representations.

[21]Informal sessions are conducted at least once a week between the East and the West. Each side is represented by three of the direct participants; the Soviet Union and the United States are always present. As a rule the extended and more innovative discussions occur at the "informals." The plenary sessions are attended by all participants. They are conducted on a weekly basis and consist generally of a prepared statement delivered by a representative of one or both sides.

[22]Bilateral discussions held at luncheons, receptions, and other gatherings provide the opportunity for further exchange of views, problems, and to sound out new approaches prior to raising them in the AHG.

proper balance between deterrence and détente, tactics and strategy, alliance solidarity and national goals, and foreign and domestic policy. They are also free to consult one or several other allied governments in order to coordinate their approach to a tactical question or to problems of grand strategy.

Important roles are played by both the SPC and the MBFR Working Group and deserve further attention. The SPC deals specifically with the political aspects of MBFR by interpreting NATO Council policy and drafting guidelines that the council may then decide to forward to the AHG. The SPC also recommends areas for further examination by the MBFR Working Group; it receives technical studies and inputs from the national capitals and from the MBFR Working Group.

The MBFR Working Group is an open-ended joint civilian/military unit created by the council in December 1969 in order to respond rapidly and substantively to council requests for military/technical advice or assessments on MBFR options and possibilities. This very special politico-military institution has in the past rendered immense services to the alliance, providing it with an integrated, alliance-wide, politico-military view in military/technical questions. It has distinguished itself through proficiency, efficiency, and speed, although speed is a function of a nation's desire to move ahead with the study of a specific question or to restrain progress on certain issues. In short, if the MBFR Working Group did not exist it would have to be invented.

The smaller NATO members and the NATO military authorities, whether the Military Committee or the SACEUR, both have a stake in maintaining the existing institutional MBFR negotiating framework. Since the NATO institutions work on the basis of consensus, a smaller NATO member under certain circumstances (generally in concert with one or several other countries) may withhold its consensus if it thinks that the alliance is not heading the right way in terms of its negotiating strategy or if it believes that its vital interests are threatened.[23] Conversely, delegations of smaller nations often are able to contribute usefully and to influence the course of events in a positive fashion.

Indeed, it may be that the delegations of the smaller NATO partners are more free to play a creative role than representatives of the major countries concerned, if only because they do not represent the common denominator of a variety of often quarrelsome or divided bureaucracies.[24] In some instances the smaller partners operate as go-betweens or compromise initiators. In other cases they insist on the necessity to respect the

---

[23]Turkey, particularly sensitive about questions of circumvention, at times has played a very active role in allied attempts to design a proper noncircumvention formula.

[24]For example, the Netherlands' preoccupation with the nuclear aspects in the alliance's strategy and deterrence posture induced it to call for the introduction of nuclear elements into the negotiations.

NATO DECISION-MAKING STRUCTURE FOR MBFR

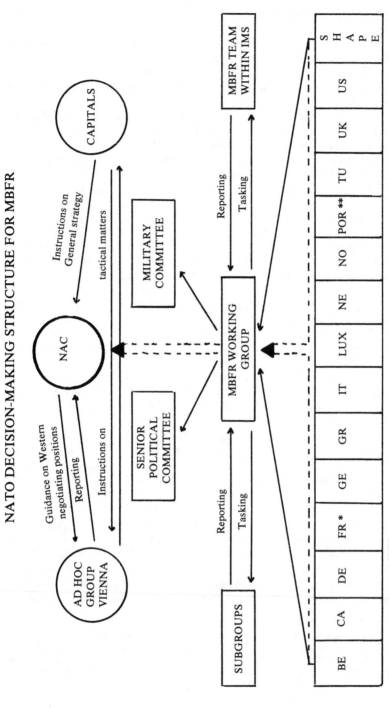

*Does not participate in MBFR.
**Has observer in AHG, Vienna.

basic principles upon which the exercise is predicated; they endeavor to protect the procedural and institutional arrangements that the alliance so carefully designed but which at times has been threatened in the name of expediency and for the purpose of achieving rapid progress in the negotiations.[25]

Contrary to the practices in other arms control forums, whether the Conference of the Committee of Disarmament in Geneva or the CSCE, the MBFR negotiations are the only ones where the alliance has managed to associate institutionally both the Military Committee and the Supreme Headquarters Allied Powers Europe (SHAPE) to its work on the spot, especially in the cities where the negotiations with nonalliance members are effectively taking place.

The triangular structure of the alliance's decision-making process in MBFR, the symbiosis of the political and military/technical aspects of analyses and viewpoints as a result of the creation of the MBFR Working Group, and the excellent relations existing between the SPC and the Working Group make the following possible for the alliance:

1) to safeguard its political and military cohesion and solidarity throughout the negotiations;
2) to ensure that its MBFR negotiating positions are in harmony with the alliance's deterrence and defense posture and more specifically with its strategy of "Flexible Response" and "Forward Defense"; and
3) to see that the MBFR negotiations will not in any way result in diminished security for the alliance as a whole, or for any member individually.

Some have argued that the alliance's MBFR decision-making mechanism and procedures are responsible for the slow pace of the negotiations themselves or even for the lack of success. This contention is not substantiated by the facts. There are a great many reasons for the absence of progress in Vienna, ranging from the East's unwillingness to table the data essential to arrive at an agreement to the extreme complexities of the issues involved, such as the geographical and other asymmetries that make it so difficult to find compromise formulae to satisfy both the East's and the West's quest for security.

---

[25]Belgium contributed substantially when the basic alliance negotiating position was laid down by presenting the so-called "Fourth Option," an amalgam of elements contained in former U.S. papers. The Belgian representative intervened more than once to protect the triangular structure and was very consistent in its insistence that overt verification measures should be included in a package known as "associated measures." Thus, Belgium managed to create an image for itself of being a very active MBFR participant.

CONFIDENCE-BUILDING MEASURES: HARMONIZATION AND COORDINATION OF THE WESTERN VIEWPOINT

Discussions of measures to avoid surprise attack and miscalculation as well as the creation of a certain transparency of military activities, establishments, and structures of both sides are reminiscent of the days of the "Spirit of Geneva" and President Eisenhower's "Open Skies" proposal of 1955 and of the Geneva conference in November-December 1957 on surprise attacks. Neither the Eisenhower initiative nor the Geneva talks produced concrete results.

Throughout the sixties and seventies many in the West remained convinced that the existence of two rival alliances in Europe, which had not found a way to resolve their political and ideological differences but which for a variety of reasons were compelled to avoid nuclear war, would have to enhance the safety of the international military environment and to dampen the rate of arms competition. This imposed upon both of these alliances a common search for a series of measures in the field of confidence building. The question is how to reduce the dangers of armed conflict and of misunderstanding or miscalculation as a result of military activities that could give rise to apprehension and a feeling of insecurity or threat. Such fears particularly might arise when one side lacks precise information about the nature of military activities of the other side. In other words, it was believed that a stabilized, predictable pattern of military activities should be established under normal peacetime conditions against which it would be simpler to identify conditions and investigate any abnormal activity that could be interpreted as provocative or could give cause for alarm.

These fears appeared to be a sine qua non before the West could conclude an MBFR agreement. Indeed, without enhancement of NATO's warning reaction time (the time between receiving clear warning that a Soviet bloc attack against NATO is being launched and the implementation of countermeasures on NATO's side), reductions of ground forces, even if carried out on a truly asymmetrical basis, might place the alliance in a less favorable security position than before. Furthermore, in the beginning of the seventies no one foresaw if and when the MBFR negotiations would begin, let alone result in an agreement. It was precisely for this reason that it was felt that military security should be included in the CSCE context, a nucleus of measures perhaps stressing the political impact rather than military effectiveness, while still safeguarding the idea that in the long run détente could not survive without improving the security situation in Europe.

During 1972–73, NATO worked on concrete suggestions as to confidence-building measures (CBMs) that might be proposed at the CSCE, specifically the prior notification of major military maneuvers and the exchange of observers. However, the CBM documents that were approved by the NATO Council were never considered as binding instructions or loose guidances for the negotiators of alliance members in Helsinki or Geneva. They were instead useful instruments that gave inspiration to allied governments and their negotiators as well as a basis for a further exchange of ideas on the premises, both among the members of the Atlantic Alliance and among the members of the European Community.

In fact, the four CBMs eventually incorporated in the Final Act of the CSCE were of NATO origin. Although Brezhnev claimed fatherhood of the idea in later years, the CBMs were effective because of the support of the neutral and nonaligned countries. On 11 November 1977 at Belgrade, the major Western proposals on CBMs were first circulated by four NATO members: Canada, the United Kingdom, Norway, and the Netherlands. Later on 21 February 1978 they were submitted by all the NATO allies except France but including neutral Ireland.[26] The purpose was to develop and enlarge the CBMs provided by the Final Act.

France introduced a new element into the CBM debate in 1978 by proposing a Conference on Disarmament in Europe (CDE).[27] France proposed a set of measures aiming at greater transparency, the reinforcement of warning time, and the prevention of surprise attacks that were none other than reinforced CBMs or MBFR-style stabilizing and verification measures projected on a larger, entirely European scale. In France's opinion neither MBFR nor Helsinki CBMs are capable of solving by themselves the West's desire for security through transparency. Indeed, they believe that a MBFR agreement would lead to a zone with a special status in which certain allies, notably the Federal Republic, would accept discriminatory treatment leading to a situation of greater insecurity for the West,[28] while Helsinki CBMs do not solve the territorial question

---

[26]The ideas circulating among the four NATO members were: 1) prior notification of small-scale maneuvers (fewer than 25,000 but more than 10,000 troops); 2) more frequent invitations of observers to a greater number of MBFR participants and in better observation conditions; and 3) compulsory prior notification of major military movements of more than 25,000 troops.

[27]During the UN Special Session on Disarmament in summer 1978, France united the thirty-five CSCE nations and Albania to express views on a French memorandum that eventually lead to the establishment of the CDE, which would be held in two phases. The first phase would be a confidence-building phase; the second phase would deal with reductions and limitations of major conventional weapons and equipment in Europe—tanks, guns, APCs. France stresses the fact that in the actual climate there is a lack of information about the military capabilities or military intentions of the other side. Such a climate tends to create suspicion whereby the capacity of the potential adversaries is overestimated and their intentions always interpreted with the greatest mistrust. Hence, the arms race and the necessity for more transparency.

[28]The Federal Republic of Germany falls within the MBFR reduction zone, while the Soviet Union lies outside it.

satisfactorily, have only a minor military security content, and are not juridically binding.[29]

The French CDE initiative has been countered by an Eastern European call made at Budapest and in East Berlin in 1979 for a conference on military détente and disarmament, which has been put in concrete form by the Polish government's offer, endorsed by Sweden on 3–4 March 1980, to host such a conference. The French and Eastern European, along with neutral and nonaligned initiatives in this field, are being thoroughly studied among both the Nine and NATO.[30] These initiatives may lead to discussions in Madrid in November 1980 that would involve a mandate to be given by the CSCE for establishing a first-phase CDE aimed at a series of new CBMs that might be militarily significant, verifiable, or implemented in the whole of the European continent—from the Atlantic to the Urals.

The CBM consultations that were begun inside NATO prior to the preparatory multilateral Helsinki negotiations have since become a permanent feature of NATO life. After the signing of the Final Act, the Political Committee coordinated the implementation by the allies of the dispositions of the Final Act concerning CBMs. Allied intentions regarding notification were discussed, and comparisons were made between national views on the question as to whether more or less stringent parameters were to be applied. Steps were made in the direction of the harmonization of standards for the treatment of observers. A calendar of maneuvers and military activities that possibly might fall under the dispositions of CBMs has been established and updated regularly. As a result of the alliance's efforts there are comprehensive tables as well as a data pool on the implementation by each of the allies of the CBM provision of the Final Act.

The Political Committee also made assessments regarding the implementation record of the other parties to the Final Act, particularly the Soviet Union and her allies. This is extremely useful; if it were not for the intelligence and sharing process within NATO there would be no way for smaller countries to determine whether and to what extent the Soviet Union and Eastern European countries are complying with their pledges in order to provide notification of certain military activities.

To answer the question of how the alliance coordinated their viewpoints during the CSCE, it is necessary to remember that the Helsinki

---

[29]Insofar as the prior notification of major military maneuvers is concerned, the Final Act stipulates: "In the case of a participating state whose territory extends beyond Europe, prior notification need be given only of maneuvers which take place in an area within 250 kilometers from its frontier facing and shared with any other European participating state." This means that only a small stretch of Soviet territory is involved.

[30]In various Warsaw Pact communiqués, as well as in Brezhnev speeches of 2 May and 6 October 1979, the East has made equally numerous proposals to enlarge the CBMs.

procedural rules contained in the so-called "Blue Book" provide that "all States participating in the Conference shall do so as sovereign and independent States and in conditions of full equality." The "Blue Book" also states that "the Conference shall take place outside military alliances."[31] In spite of these restraints during the September 1973–July 1975 negotiating phase of the CSCE that took place in Geneva as well as during the Belgrade meeting, it still was possible to organize a caucus of the fifteen alliance members in parallel with a European Community caucus. The alliance caucus was chaired by alliance members on a rotating basis.

NATO papers were available for use by national delegations and provided the necessary data and intelligence background as well as broader analyses of the impact of certain concrete proposals on the defense posture and strategy of the alliance. Although neither the secretary general and members of NATO's International Staff nor the chairman of the Military Committee or his representative could be present in Geneva or Belgrade, the Political Committee at NATO headquarters was kept informed. Where necessary additional military advice, such as on Eastern counterproposals, could be requested through the committee.

Nevertheless, it is apparent that the CSCE procedural principles and rules, notably the one on the sovereignty and independence of the participating states, by no means preclude consultations among NATO allies, either before, during, or after CSCE meetings, or the organization by those allies of a cohesive alliance approach toward these issues. It is also evident that the CBM discussions have strengthened arms control consultation practices within the alliance to the degree that they come close to a harmonization of views and even to a coordination of policies.

SALT: THE PRAGMATIC WAY

The alliance's ability to adapt to new challenges and to find the proper consultation procedures and mechanisms suitable to the issues it confronts was once more proven in the case of strategic and theater nuclear arms control.

During the first strategic arms limitation negotiations—from 17 November 1969 to 20 May 1972—and in the early phases of SALT II, the allies certainly were informed by the United States, specifically at the council level, as to how the negotiations were proceeding. Still, it is fair to say that they were for the most part only bystanders.[32] As the United

---

[31]Final recommendations of the Helsinki consultations of 8 June 1973.

[32]The negotiations often were followed by a question and answer session at the expert level.

States continued to enjoy important strategic advantages and the Atlantic Alliance was believed to possess superiority in the field of tactical nuclear weapons, the allies confined themselves to ensuring that U.S. forward based systems (FBS)—systems deployed in the European area in support of alliance commitments—would not be included in the limitations. Neither did they accept the fact that non-U.S. allied nuclear systems, the British and French nuclear deterrent forces, be taken into account in the American totals.[33].

The Soviet thesis was, and still remains, that it is entitled to define "strategic"—negotiable in SALT—as any U.S. or Soviet nuclear weapons system capable of reaching the territory of the other side.[34] This would include FBS but exclude, for example, the Soviet intermediate range missiles aimed at Western Europe. Throughout SALT I and SALT II the U.S. view was exactly the opposite. It consistently held that the only weapons to be considered in SALT should be intercontinental systems, since the acceptance of the Soviet approach seriously would have prejudiced U.S. alliance commitments.

Over time, however, as the SALT negotiations addressed more and more issues bearing directly on the security of the alliance in Europe, the United States was confronted with a particularly difficult challenge: "How to conduct a sensitive bilateral negotiation on a matter as grave as the strategic balance, while at the same time taking into account the security interests of a number of countries."[35] While in principle the United States alone did indeed bear the responsibility for developing positions, conducting negotiations, and agreeing on resolutions of issues, it nevertheless acted on behalf of the interests of the entire alliance.

After the adoption in May 1977 of a three-tiered negotiating framework—a treaty lasting until 1985, a short-term protocol ending December 1981, and a statement of principles for SALT III—the SALT consultations intensified.[36] As a partial result of the three-tiered agreement, which included a protocol limiting ground- and sea-launched cruise missiles capable of a range in excess of 600 km, alliance political interest in the negotiations was focused more sharply than in the early phases of SALT II. Indeed, the codification by the SALT II agreement of "essential equivalence" in the central strategic systems of the two superpowers, as well as the Soviet deployments of modern long-range theater systems such

---

[33]Chiefly, short- or medium-range bombers on aircraft carriers are based in Europe.

[34]These nuclear weapons included the SS-4, SS-5, and SS-20 missiles as well as the Badger, Blinder, and Backfire aircraft.

[35]U.S., Congress, Senate, Committee on Foreign Relations, *SALT II Treaty*, 96th Cong., 1st sess., no. 96-14, p. 239.

[36]The U.S. ambassador to the Geneva negotiations, Ralph Earle, enumerated over twenty meetings with the North Atlantic Council in the last two and a half years of negotiations as well as numerous multilateral and bilateral sessions.

as the SS-20 and Backfire, greatly increased NATO's and particularly certain European nations' interest in the possibility of deploying cruise missiles as part of a modernized long-range theater nuclear force (LRTNF). Consequently, allied concerns existed over whether the protocol limitations on GLCM[37] and SLCM[38] would jeopardize potential LRTNF modernization and weaken U.S. leverage in possible future negotiations to limit Soviet theater nuclear forces. However, the NATO Council recognized the validity of the U.S. administration's arguments that the protocol limits on U.S. theater cruise missiles would expire on 31 December 1981, and therefore no U.S. theater nuclear program of relevance to NATO's long-range TNF requirements would be affected.

In at least three instances consultation extended beyond informational briefings, permitting the consideration of the views of allied governments on key issues of concern to them before U.S. proposals were made or actions were taken in the negotiations. Specifically, this was to be the case with the noncircumvention provision, the interpretative statement, and the status of theater systems in SALT III.

Article 12 of the SALT II treaty deals with noncircumvention.[39] The present formulation of this provision was proposed by the United States in order to avoid an all-out "nontransfer" provision like the one included in the Anti-Ballistic Missile Treaty that forbids transfers of systems and technology by the United States to its allies.[40] Certain allies feared that this formulation might provide the basis for Soviet challenges to U.S. allied defense cooperation, particularly in the area of cruise missile technology. Those concerns were held strongly, and at least two European governments were very outspoken in the council.

In the end the United States persuaded its allies by promising to make a formal statement of the U.S. interpretation of the provision in the North Atlantic Council—an interpretation that the noncircumvention provision did not in any way have the de facto effect of a nontransfer clause sought for so long by the Soviets. The United States managed to reassure its allies that the noncircumvention clause would not interfere with existing patterns of collaboration and cooperation or preclude assistance in modernization.

---

[37] Ground-Launched Cruise Missiles.

[38] Sea-Launched Cruise Missiles.

[39] "In order to ensure the viability and effectiveness of this treaty, each party undertakes not to circumvent the provisions of this treaty, through any other state or states or in any other manner." See "SALT II Agreement," Vienna, 18 June 1979, U.S., Department of State, *Selected Documents,* no. 12A.

[40] Article 9 of the Anti-Ballistic Missile Treaty states: "To assure the viability and effectiveness of this Treaty, each Party undertakes not to transfer to other States, and not to deploy outside its national territory, ABM systems or their components limited by this Treaty."

Finally, to make it clear to the allies that SALT II did not foreclose future options regarding either arms control or modernization of theater nuclear weapons, the United States stated in the North Atlantic Council on 29 June 1979 that "any future limitations on U.S. systems principally designed for theater missions should be accompanied by appropriate limitations on Soviet theater systems." Indeed, the issue of the theater nuclear balance and its possible arms control implications enhanced the quality of the SALT consultation process. It also led to institutional innovations based on pragmatism and efficiency. Consequently, two study groups were created by the allies concerned (except France)—the High Level Group (HLG)[41] and the Special Group (SG). The essential characteristics of these two groups were that:

1) they both worked within the general framework of the alliance, but under the chairmanship of the United States and not under the secretary general (however the International Staff and NATO's military authorities were always present);
2) their national delegations generally were headed by and composed of high-level foreign affairs and defense experts from respective NATO capitals;
3) their experts, who often represented their governments' viewpoints, in no way committed these governments; and
4) in both groups the influence of the United States was paramount. As the leader of the alliance, particularly in nuclear matters, it was perfectly natural for the United States to provide the majority of all studies, analyses, reports, and intelligence information.

On the basis of the work accomplished by the HLG and SG, officially submitted to the Ministers of Foreign Affairs and Defense by their permanent representatives on the NATO Council, the ministers on 12 December 1979 decided in a special meeting on a double approach—modernization and arms control. On the one hand, NATO's long-range TNF would be modernized.[42] On the other hand, ministers decided to support fully "the decision taken by the U.S., following consultations within the Alliance, to negotiate arms limitations in LRTNF and to propose to the USSR to begin negotiations as soon as possible based on a set of agreed principles."

---

[41]The HLG was created in fall 1977 at the Ministerial Nuclear Planning Group meeting in Bari, Italy. Their purpose was to study to what extent the alliance should modernize its theater nuclear forces. The conclusions reached by this group formed the basis of the alliance's TNF modernization decision of 12 December 1979. See Special Meeting of Foreign and Defense Ministers, communiqué, 12 December 1979, *NATO Review* 28 (February 1980): 25.

[42]Ibid. The deployment in Europe of U.S. ground-launched systems, comprised of 108 Pershing II launchers, would replace existing U.S. Pershing 1A launchers and 464 ground-launched cruise missiles—all of which were wide, single warheads.

The ministers also decided that given the special importance of these negotiations for the overall security of the alliance, special consultative arrangements would have to be constituted within the alliance in order to support U.S. negotiations on a continuous basis and to report to the foreign and defense ministers. Consequently, to carry out this ministerial guidance, to meet the wishes of the Europeans (expressed by some as early as December 1977), to be more closely and institutionally associated with the SALT negotiations involving theater nuclear systems, and to draw on the Special Group experience, the NATO Council provides a mandate for the Special Consultative Group on Arms Control involving LRTNF. This group, chaired by the director of the Bureau of Politico-Military Affairs of the U.S. Department of State, started its activities on 25 January 1980.

The establishment of such a group had become a necessity, since the Western LRTNF that will be included in the SALT III negotiations will be stationed on European soil. Certainly, these systems remain the appanage of the United States who produces them, provides the necessary funds, and operates them. Nevertheless, the deployment of alliance systems in the United Kingdom, the Federal Republic of Germany, Italy, and possibly the Netherlands and Belgium, justifies a new approach to the SALT consultations involving theater nuclear systems.

Since the arms control negotiations involving LRTNF are theoretically a step-by-step process, the first focuses on the most immediate threat—land-based LRTNF. Subsequent steps could result in the expansion of the scope of systems to be covered; for instance, to include provisions on medium nuclear systems (between 100 km and 1000 km). The influence of the Europeans is bound to grow; medium-range TNFs are not only deployed in Europe but also owned, manned, and operated, insofar as the launchers and carriers are concerned, by Western European nations under dual-key arrangements. Therefore, the question remains whether in such a stage, which is admittedly in the distant future, the alliance will not need an institutional framework extending beyond the present one by giving the Europeans some additional weight not only in the formulation of the alliance's negotiating positions but also at the negotiating table itself.

CONCLUSIONS

NATO's interest in disarmament and arms control issues can be traced back to the first thaw in East-West relations. At that time consultations on these issues were still fairly sporadic and unstructured; they meant "informing the allies about something one had done" rather than asking them for advice before reaching one's own decision. However, over time these consultations evolved from a purely informative stage, in the fifties and early sixties, to exchanges of views prior to national decision making (for instance, in meetings of the SPC with disarmament experts), to harmonization of policies (CBMs), and even to collective decision making and binding guidance in the case of MBFR.

The consultation machinery and procedures that NATO created were timely and adapted to the problems faced by the alliance. The MBFR negotiations definitely have a direct impact not only on the strategy of the alliance and the security of all its members but also on the size and structure of the Western defense organization in Central Europe as a whole and on the defense policies of each of the direct participants. Therefore, a tighter and more collective institutional framework is needed than previously required by the SALT negotiations in their early days. Indeed, during SALT I and the first years of SALT II these primarily bilateral—U.S.-USSR—negotiations were felt to impinge less directly on the question of theater nuclear equilibrium in Europe.

It is hoped that the alliance will be able to display the same flexibility if and when it is faced with the concrete implementation of new far-reaching disarmament and/or arms control schemes. Thus, if the allies ever were to decide to pursue an even more ambitious arms control negotiation, they only could do this without risking the disruption of its politico-military cohesion by creating an institutional framework very similar, if not identical, to the one existing in MBFR. By the same token an expansion of TNF negotiations to medium- or short-range systems should be accompanied by a further strengthening of the European presence in these negotiations.

NATO clearly has demonstrated that it is an alliance for peace. It has endeavored to maintain military equilibrium in Europe through deterrence and collective defense efforts. And since the Harmel Report it also has taken important initiatives in the field of hard-core arms control in an effort to contribute fully to détente.

The Military Role of NATO

THOMAS H. ETZOLD*

The only point upon which Machiavelli can be faulted is that with a
certain indecency he called things by their right name.

— Carl von Clausewitz

NATO is a military alliance with no military history, a fact that
creates difficulties for serious analyses of its military roles. Instead of a
military history, NATO possesses a chronicle of political-military concerns, strategic concepts, and preparatory activities. Like a prizefighter
without a win-loss record, NATO has been training and exercising for a
contest that has never materialized. Its actual physical condition, its game
plan, and its skills remain untested and therefore unverified. Consequently,
in military affairs NATO has an image but not a reputation. Images flow
readily from publicity and posturing, but reputations derive from actions
that over time constitute a record. From the outset any useful discussion
concerning NATO's military roles must be wary of dealing too much with
NATO's self-promotions rather than with actualities.

In assessing NATO's military roles there is also a formidable
problem of logic: the rules of reasoning do not readily permit proof of a
negative hypothesis. It is regrettably common, in Western throes of self-
congratulation, to assert—not demonstrate—that the absence of Soviet
military initiative in Western Europe confirms NATO's efficacy. Furthermore, the incomplete logic of self-approbation advanced in some quarters
of the alliance has been more than counterbalanced by alarms elsewhere
in NATO over perennial shortcomings in force structure, doctrine,
readiness, and other operational factors—all more worrisome in the
context of Soviet military programs of the last decade. Therefore, to write
about NATO's military roles involves a topic that is strewn with political
hazards and intellectual traps; the margin between safety and disaster
must be measured with a fine gauge. Finally, success consists only in

---

*The views expressed herein are those of the author. They should not be taken to
represent those of the Naval War College, the U.S. Navy, or the Department of Defense.

modest forward movement, and the dangers remain to threaten any attempted return to earlier havens.

STRATEGIC VERSUS POLITICAL REQUIREMENTS—PART I

NATO's military dimensions have been shaped by the continuing need to reconcile the strategic requirements imposed by NATO's circumstances with the political limitations imposed by its framework. It is an axiom of classical military theory, prominent in the work of Carl von Clausewitz, that war and politics inextricably run together and that there can be no such thing as a purely military matter until one arrives at the lowliest details of routine operations.[1] If that proposition is true in the affairs of individual nations, it is even more so in those of NATO. As Dean Acheson once expressed it, NATO at its birth was like a "body—or more accurately twelve bodies—without a head."[2] This characteristic of the alliance has continued to grow more pronounced over time.

Although treatments of NATO's strategic developments and military roles should remain sensitive to domestic political currents of individual alliance members, it may be surprisingly difficult to accomplish. In recent years American academicians, at least, have demonstrated an alarming tendency to become fascinated by military technology. This unfortunate tendency toward glorification of gadgetry has encouraged discussion of military and strategic problems in terms that soon exceed the competence of most academic commentators. It may indeed be the main reason why so many discussions involving NATO problems appear to result in two universal, but essentially unhelpful, prescriptions: (1) buy more of everything—the prescription most favored by military professionals; and (2) do everything right—the formula preferred by critics of the first remedy.

In one of its least invidious forms the academic instinct for the capillaries has been shown in a "particularizing" approach to NATO's strategic concerns and military problems. Literature exists by the score on such topics as defense versus deterrence, theater nuclear deployments, burden sharing, command and control, reserves, the flanks versus the center, maritime versus land requirements, U.S. global obligations versus NATO concerns, out-of-area operations and interests, interoperability, standardization, the short war, and strategic and tactical warning. And in

---

[1]Michael Howard and Peter Paret, eds. and trans., *Carl von Clausewitz: On War* (Princeton, NJ: Princeton University Press, 1976), pp. 605–8.

[2]Dean Acheson, *Present at the Creation: My Years in the State Department* (New York: W. W. Norton, 1969), p. 397.

individual cases a particularist approach has led to useful analyses. However, as a chief characteristic of a varied literature, intellectual particularism permits, if it does not actually encourage, a certain confusion between ends and means. In dealing with NATO's shifts of doctrine, its technical issues, and its logistic problems, it has been easy to blur the outlines of the overall strategic requirements dominating NATO's military situation for all of its thirty-one years of endeavor.

Three such strategic requirements form the framework within which NATO's military roles have their significance: the requirement to deter Soviet military initiative against Western Europe; the requirement to retain usable military positions on the continent of Europe even during large-scale war; and the requirement to guarantee the integrity of lines of communication between North America and Western Europe. Rooted in the consequences and lessons of the twentieth century's great wars, these requirements have varied over time and with circumstances in regard to their relative priority, urgency, and difficulty. NATO's attempts to adjust to such variations have accounted for or produced the major shifts in strategic concepts and doctrine in the alliance. Efforts to meet these requirements have varied over time and with circumstances in regard principle of unanimity in decision making have in turn produced the classic political-military issues usually associated with NATO strategy.

THE FIRST DECADE:
STRATEGY OF FLEXIBLE RESPONSE

NATO's first decade was marked by reliance on a strategy of deterrence; it still has not faced an immediate challenge to its other two strategic requirements. NATO took shape during a time not only of low confidence among Western Europe's governments but also of minimal threat in any realistic military terms. As many memoirs and published government documents now reveal, in the late 1940s Western governments were facing the possibility of internal collapse for economic and psychological reasons rather than the probability of armed incursions by Soviet troops.

The principle of deterrence became NATO's first strategic touchstone. The great powers of Europe simply had learned once again the lesson of the wars of Napoleon and of the First World War; namely, that they could not afford the costs and strains of large-scale engagement in the near future. They had to hope that with some combination of technology, politics, and posturing to hold renewed war at a distance. In addition, however, there was an almost overnight infusion of deterrence theory into NATO defense thinking and terminology. This was largely a result of an offshoot of strategic air power doctrine—much exaggerated in its early promise—and especially of the mystique surrounding air-delivered atomic weapons. It was impossible to separate from that constellation of ideas the fact that the United States possessed a monopoly on atomic weapons and expected to do so for an indeterminate length of time.

NATO's early deterrent strategy came to be a virtual mirror image of American "massive retaliation" doctrine. Despite Soviet acquisition of atomic and hydrogen weapons in NATO's earliest years, the United States and the NATO allies retained high confidence in doctrines and weapons of air power as epitomized in the strategic bomber force which, together with naval forces, was according to early agreements to constitute the principal American material contribution to NATO's military needs.[3]

In retrospect, NATO's first few years can be described only as leisurely in terms of the approach of its members to their supposed defense requirements. The existence of a military alliance apparently sufficed to allay the concerns of most governments and leaders, both concerning the American commitment to Europe's future and the putative Soviet threat. There was no sustained effort to calculate the forces and capabilities necessary for European defense until almost three years after the alliance was formed; that is, until the 1952 meeting in Lisbon. Indeed, the Korean War brought notable results, and not only at Lisbon; NATO made real progress toward developing needed command arrangements and toward a general military buildup. However, since 1952 there has been no real commitment on the part of alliance members to fulfill the force goals established at Lisbon, although Soviet capabilities have multiplied many times in the intervening years. The considerable and continuing disparity between alliance exertions and the scale of the supposed threat suggests the central significance of symbols in NATO's military affairs, as well as healthy amounts of optimism and residual confidence in the deterrability of war despite the discrediting of classical air power theory and changing correlations of forces.

NATO enjoyed a "Golden Era" during the fifties. Western Europe's economies recovered and prospered. In many NATO countries political parties and governments achieved a certain stability, a reliable competence not immediately threatened by the extreme Left. The alliance took in new members in the Mediterranean and accepted a rearming West Germany as a partner—most important for both NATO and for the course of the Cold War. These developments induced a growing confidence, perhaps an overconfidence. Lawrence S. Kaplan reflected the mood of a more confident and perhaps simpler time when he wrote in 1954:

---

[3]Thomas H. Etzold and John L. Gaddis, eds., *Containment: Documents on American Policy and Strategy, 1949–50* (New York: Columbia University Press, 1977). See chaps. 3 and 6, especially "Strategic Concept for the Defense of the North Atlantic Area," pp. 335–38. This particular document also appears, without analysis or commentary, in U.S., Department of State, *Foreign Relations of the United States, 1949*, 4:352–56 (hereafter cited as *FRUS*, followed by the appropriate year).

"NATO's response to the [military] challenge . . . has constituted its greatest achievement. While there were alliances in the past, there is no precedent for the range of political, economic and military cooperation which NATO has planned since 1949."[4] He went on to quote one of the first important British studies of NATO's initial work, similarly enthusiastic in tone: "The work done to find out what each nation can fairly be asked to do for common defense is one of NATO's major achievements; should it prove successful it will be one of the great planning achievements of this century."[5]

This era of confidence and deterrence, via a strategy of massive retaliation, ended as the 1950s came to a close. Soviet acquisition of the ability to deliver nuclear weapons against the United States ended the brief postwar interval of American invulnerability to attack; it struck heavily at the basis of massive retaliation strategy. In Europe, to the surprise and certainly to the dismay of military and intelligence experts (who had believed Soviet supplies of weapons-grade fissile materials to be severely restricted), the Soviets deployed their own tactical nuclear weapons. This deployment created political and military conditions in Europe that would give rise to some of the most difficult issues in subsequent NATO strategy.

As a legacy, NATO's first strategic era left the alliance with an unwarranted confidence in nuclear weapons. This legacy had long and serious effects, some of which will be discussed further. George F. Kennan blamed NATO's initial reliance on nuclear weapons on "highly inflated estimates of Russian conventional military strength that had already become ingrained . . . in the official assessment of NATO defense needs, and with the resulting belief on our part that we could never meet the Russians successfully on non-nuclear ground."[6] Inside the government, as important decisions in the late 1940s led to the development of the hydrogen "super bomb," Kennan held out his conviction that the United States, and by extension NATO, would be better off to avoid formulating strategies that offered no chance of success without resort to nuclear weapons. One eloquent passage from Kennan's paper on "International Control of Atomic Energy" still deserves wide attention: "I fear that the atomic weapon, with its vague and highly dangerous promise of 'decisive' results, of people 'signing on dotted lines,' of easy solutions to profound human problems, will impede understanding of the things that are

---

[4]Lawrence S. Kaplan, "NATO and Its Commentators: The First Five Years," *International Organization* 8 (Fall 1954): 450.

[5]Ibid., p. 448. The study quoted was prepared by the Royal Institute of International Affairs, *Atlantic Alliance: NATO's Role in the Free World* (London: Royal Institute of International Affairs, 1952).

[6]George F. Kennan, *Memoirs 1925–1950* (Boston: Little, Brown and Company, 1967), p. 475.

important to a clean, clear policy and will carry us toward the misuse and dissipation of our national strength."[7]

Rear Admiral Henry Eccles, arguing from different premises, reached similar conclusions:

> NATO political leaders . . . assumed that United States atomic power was such a safeguard that no real effort to build NATO forces up to the 1952 Lisbon Conference levels was necessary. They went on to assume that the use of tactical atomic weapons would fill the resultant defense gap. Then in 1958–1959 without there being an explicit statement, they gradually came to the conclusion that the use of tactical atomic weapons in Western Europe was not acceptable. But in the meanwhile, the people had been convinced that large conventional forces were not needed.[8]

Because of either overestimation of the Soviet threat or overestimation of the usability of nuclear weapons, NATO strategy in its beginnings took on a nuclear imprint that it would carry beyond the era of massive retaliation and on into NATO's next strategic epoch, that of flexible response.

THE SECOND DECADE:
STRATEGY OF FLEXIBLE RESPONSE

From the early 1960s through the mid–1970s, NATO's principal strategic discussions employed the terminology of the flexible response strategy. Soviet ability to inflict nuclear damage on the United States and to answer in kind tactical nuclear weapons in Europe facilitated NATO's adoption of a strategy that again mirrored in some respects, including that of official language, the strategic evolution of the American defense establishment. In the United States flexible response strategy had dimensions unrelated to NATO Europe, for in the 1960s the United States set out to deal energetically and directly with the national revolutions and Communist provocations so troubling in the 1950s. The American flexible response doctrine also had an important nuclear dimension; this aspect became most significant in the NATO context.

NATO's version of flexible response was adopted to revitalize a deterrent strategy then in question and to respond to an increasing Soviet challenge to NATO's second important strategic requirement—the need to hold usable military position on the continent in war. As Morton Kaplan has noted, the Soviet Union emerged from World War II "as a

---

[7]Memorandum by Counselor Kennan, 20 January 1950, *FRUS, 1950,* 1:38.

[8]Rear Admiral Henry Eccles, *Military Concepts and Philosophy* (New Brunswick, NJ: Rutgers University Press, 1965), p. 279, see also p. 52.

gigantic power that was in military possession of so much of Europe that the remainder lacked the space required for effective defense."[9] This formulation may have been unduly simple; two decades would pass before Soviet military technology and the size of Soviet forces would make this true. However, Kaplan underscored an important point. During the early and mid–1960s, Soviet and Warsaw Pact forces, through modernization, became armored forces configures for a Sovietized "blitzkrieg." Those were the years in which Western defense analysts began to worry that Warsaw Pact forces might sweep Western defenders off the continent—three days to the Rhine and seven to the Channel. America's growing involvement in Vietnam in these same years heightened the fear of Europeans that they would be unable to deal with the increasing threat.

NATO answered the mid-1960s threat to its continental position with a huge deployment of American tactical nuclear weapons in Europe, coupled with a NATO variety of flexible response strategy emphasizing "controlled and deliberate escalation," explicitly including first use of nuclear weapons. American nuclear superiority in the 1960s permitted the further development of "links" between strategic and tactical nuclear weapons, which were supposed to increase both the deterrent effect of this NATO posture and the credibility of a Western threat to employ tactical nuclear devices in the event of adverse conventional battle results. However, there were disbelievers, especially the French who, doubting that the United States had overcome its unwillingness to receive Soviet nuclear attack, also distrusted American promises to risk nuclear engagement for the sake of European territory and interests. Hence, the acrimonious diplomacy concerning the multilateral nuclear force, the modernization of the British nuclear capability, and the impetus for significant French national nuclear programs.

In many ways this second of NATO's strategic epochs gave evidence of more strain within the alliance than had the first. The "troubled partnership," immortalized in Henry A. Kissinger's classic study, stumbled over the many problems inherent in the nuclear legacy of the preceding era; the postwar revival in Europe advanced far enough to permit national rivalries to interrupt the collaboration born of postwar fear and desperation; the United States became so enmeshed in Vietnam that its European allies wondered about both its commitment and its competence. The alliance faced the need for its first major modernization and found that economic costs and technological complexities taxed both the political and the economic institutions of democracies at peace. Trans-Atlantic doubts concerning the extent to which American security might become decoupled from that of Europe were paralleled within the continent by "jockeying to determine which geographic area [would] be

---

[9]Morton A. Kaplan, ed., *Isolation or Interdependence: Today's Choice for Tomorrow's World* (New York: Free Press, 1975), p. 15.

the theater of war if deterrence fails."[10] In one of his few memorable images, President Richard M. Nixon remarked that America could no more disengage from Europe than from Alaska, but nuclear issues continued to promote political divisions.[11]

However, when this strategic era closed sometime between 1972 and 1975, it did so not because of strains within the alliance but because the Soviet Union had acquired nuclear parity with the United States. Like the first era, the second left a troublesome legacy. Out of the strategy of flexible response, NATO retained a propensity, at least in theory and in exercises, to escalate from a position of disadvantage.

THE THIRD DECADE:
STRATEGY OF RAPID REINFORCEMENT

From the early 1970s onward Soviet gains in strategic nuclear status heightened the importance of the balance of conventional forces in Europe. This subject indeed has dominated the literature concerning NATO's military and strategic problems since then. It also became apparent early in the decade that the Soviet and Warsaw Pact forces in Europe were again growing and modernizing at a pace that the nations of Western Europe could not hope to match under ordinary political conditions. During this same time analyses of the potential use of nuclear weapons suggested that neither East nor West could improve its relative position in conflict by first resort to such weapons, unless its adversary unaccountably refrained from replying similarly.

These new circumstances had two important effects. First, they greatly increased NATO's potential difficulty in meeting its second strategic requirement, that of maintaining usable military position on the continent in war. Second, they forced NATO to turn to North America for resupply and reinforcement in the earliest days of any potential war. This at last raised NATO's third strategic requirement, the guaranteeing of sea lines of communication between Europe and North America to the same immediacy as the first two requirements. By 1974 a Brookings Institution study expressed it very bluntly: "The credibility of NATO strategy in the Center rests, in large measure, on the certainty of timely U.S. reinforcement."[12] The same was true for NATO's northern region as well.

---

[10]Henry A. Kissinger, *The Troubled Partnership: A Re-appraisal of the Atlantic Alliance* (New York: Doubleday and Company, 1965), p. 15.

[11]Quoted in Zbigniew Brzezinski, "America and Europe," *Foreign Affairs* 49 (October 1970): 17.

[12]Richard D. Lawrence and Jeffery Record, *U.S. Force Structure in NATO: An Alternative* (Washington, DC: Brookings Institution, 1974), p. 65.

In the mid–1970s, however, just as the Atlantic sea lanes became more important than ever before, NATO recognized that the West no longer possessed the undisputed naval mastery essential to reliable communication between America and Europe. Under way since the late 1950s, by the mid–1970s Soviet naval growth had produced a challenge to American naval power that promised seriously to stretch the capabilities of the alliance for resupply and reinforcement of possible battle zones on the continent in a timely and adequate fashion. To complicate matters, the high intensity of modern war using "smart" weapons, with correspondingly high rates of material consumption, raised the possibility that war in Europe, if it should come, might be so short that sea-borne supplies and reinforcements could not meet NATO's needs even if NATO could defeat the Soviet naval threat.[13]

In view of the foregoing developments, NATO's rapid reinforcement strategy quickly evolved an added element—a parallel strategy of "preinforcement," or as it was more often termed, prepositioning. Heavy equipment and possibly division headquarters were to be placed in Europe well in advance of a need to permit American troops to be flown across the Atlantic in crisis or early in war. Like NATO's preceding strategic eras of massive retaliation and flexible response, its strategy of rapid reinforcement and preinforcement also promised to leave a legacy: reliance on the United States not only for strategic air and nuclear power but for men and supplies to tip the balance of forces in Europe itself.

NATO's original strategic concept, in which the United States was to supply strategic air power and the nations of Europe to provide men and tactical air power, was overturned completely by the late 1970s.[14] Furthermore, NATO's strategic requirements had become much more difficult to meet, for in NATO's early years there had been no serious challenge to its ability to hold on the continent or to use the seas at will.

As the 1970s drew to a close it was unclear whether or when the United States would rebuild the naval power so vital to NATO's trans-Atlantic lines of communication. In classical strategy alliances were designed not only to prevent wars but also to provide a proper balance between land and sea power and to reduce or offset other weaknesses of individual partners. If not ominous, it was far from reassuring that in the late 1970s best seller, *The Third World War: August 1985,* Sir John Hackett has written: "Every nation which without the benefit of sea power had sought to humble others in intercontinental struggles had in the end been humbled itself by sea power. It was a lesson enviously learned by the

---

[13]For the best published discussion of these naval developments, see Paul H. Nitze, Leonard Sullivan, Jr., and the Atlantic Council Working Group on Securing the Seas, *Securing the Seas: The Soviet Naval Challenge and Western Alliance Options* (Boulder, CO: Westview Press, 1979).

[14]Etzold and Gaddis, *Containment,* pp. 335–38.

Soviet Union and carelessly thrown aside by its once greatest exponent—
Great Britain."[15] However, no one nation had ever borne the complete
responsibility for NATO's ability to meet its principal strategic requirements. The failing, if this was the case, would not be that of Great Britain
alone. Certainly, in this one respect NATO's strategic circumstances had
been transformed over twenty years. When Charles de Gaulle withdrew
French naval forces from NATO command in 1959, he did so in part
because he believed that naval power "by definition was designed for use
in areas not protected by NATO commitments."[16] It was a peculiarly
continental view even then, but by the early 1980s the changed balance of
forces in Europe simply had rendered any such conclusion obsolete.

STRATEGIC VERSUS POLITICAL REQUIREMENTS—PART II

For some observers and participants NATO's reactions to changing
circumstances over the years seemed highly encouraging. In NATO's
early years, again to quote Lawrence Kaplan, its "responsiveness to
changing conditions had been a major source of strength."[17] Much later in
1974, NATO's assistant secretary general for Defense Planning and
Policy, D. C. Humphreys, proferred a similarly optimistic assessment of
NATO's adaptations:

> As far as the development of strategy is concerned, NATO's record is
> good. The concept of deterrence is not new; but the way in which
> NATO's resources have been mobilised since 1949 towards pre-
> venting the outbreak of the war rather than towards achieving a
> victory on the enemy battlefield is unprecedented in history, and has
> so far been remarkably successful. As the political aims of the
> Alliance have moved from the policy of containment and the rigours
> of the Cold War towards the pursuit of détente, so has the strategy
> shifted from its base of massive retaliation towards flexible response
> and the sophisticated use of tactical nuclear capabilities.[18]

Such reassurances are only partially true. The evolution of grand strategy
in NATO is, after all, a story of maturation, not of failure. However, the
present analysis of NATO's strategic evolution suggests additional
observations.

---

[15]General Sir John W. Hackett, *The Third World War: August 1985* (New York:
Macmillan, 1978), p. 260.
[16]Kissinger, *Troubled Partnership*, p. 53.
[17]L. Kaplan, "NATO and Its Commentators," p. 455.
[18]D. C. Humphreys, "NATO Defense—The Challenge of Change," *NATO Review*
22 (1974): 8.

First, the parallel dynamics traced here; namely, the increasing difficulty of meeting all three of NATO's strategic requirements and the increasing European reliance on American power, have given rise to all the now familiar debates on NATO strategy—defense versus deterrence and burden sharing, maritime versus continental emphases, nuclear versus conventional stresses, and center versus flanks priorities. Each has its origin, its context, and its significance within the larger strategic setting sketched here. In addition, this means that once problems are created in NATO they do not disappear. In its broadest terms NATO's strategic situation has fully matured. Its strategic requirements are now what they have always been and will remain relatively stable; its political framework has been, and is likely to remain, similarly stable despite possible variations in actual membership; and its circumstances now threaten or stress all of its strategic requirements. Therefore, in the future, NATO's situation may well change quantitatively, but it is less probable to undergo the qualitative change that has been occurring over the past thirty years.

Second, it has become increasingly clear that in spite of alliance rhetoric NATO strategy is largely a function of U.S. strategy, particularly of U.S. capability vis-à-vis the Soviet Union. Over the past thirty years NATO strategy has mirrored U.S. concepts of how to balance or otherwise cope with Soviet military power. Now that NATO has come to rely explicitly on the United States not only for air power and nuclear weapons but also for men, machines, and munitions, the tendency of NATO strategy to reflect American strategy can only grow more accentuated, which places a special responsibility on the United States to shape its defense policy and its force planning with full realization of the implications for and effects on NATO. The Carter administration's emphasis on NATO is, in this context, fully justified and, if anything, still somewhat short of what may be necessary. These same factors, however, impose a parallel responsibility on NATO's European members. They must cease maintaining the useless and dangerous fiction that NATO strategy is independent of U.S. strategy, or that NATO force planning can be independent of the character of American forces and defense policy.

Third, the foregoing analyses suggest that strategy is cumulative in NATO. New strategic concepts do not displace or supersede older ones; they simply augment them. At present NATO has "a strategy" of deterrence, flexible response, controlled and deliberate escalation including first use of nuclear weapons, reinforcement, and prepositioning. This is confusing, inefficient, and possibly unworkable. Until the present tangle is sorted out or otherwise simplified, the alliance cannot afford to take up any new strategic ideas. It would be in NATO's interest to declare an immediate, alliance-wide moratorium on the writings of defense intellectuals, and instead to recycle the vast literature of the last thirty years until some of NATO's superannuated strategies, by some process of natural selection, are relegated to the obscurity of deserved retirement.

The reconsideration of NATO's strategies will indeed tax the men and governments concerned, for NATO strategy and politics are inseparable. Henry Kissinger wrote long ago a testimony to the longevity of NATO's issues:

> If the Atlantic Alliance is to retain any vitality, it requires a common foreign policy—or at least an agreed range of divergence. In its absence, the attempt to devise a common military strategy is likely to prove futile. . . . There is something incongruous about NATO's absorption in technicalities . . . while it lacks a common policy toward the Communist world [it] flounders dividedly in the former colonial areas and has yet to concert a strategic doctrine.[19]

Today the NATO nations still lack a concerted policy toward the Communist world; they are divided over policy in central Asia and Africa. Rather than concert a strategic doctrine they have assembled a collection of such doctrines, from among which the members pick and choose according to the turns of domestic and budgetary politics.

According to classical teaching, because strategy derives from policy, the first desideratum of a war plan is that the means adopted must conflict as little as possible with the political conditions from which the war springs. NATO's experience with strategic evolution, however, has made it clear that alliance strategies are likely to be selected not with a view to the political conditions giving rise to war but with those giving rise to elections and budgets.

CONCLUSIONS

What is to be finally concluded concerning NATO's military roles over its thirty-one years to date? First, NATO's military nature has stood as a monument memorializing the essential tie between Europe and North America, especially the revolution in American foreign policy after World War II that permitted this relationship. In the great twentieth-century historical trend encompassing the diffusion of European power outward into other continents, the NATO alliance has become a landmark on the way to a constructive reordering of a world thrown into disorder by war, revolution, and the end of colonialism. Without an explicit military character and military activities to confirm it, NATO would have meant much less. American participation in NATO's military activities is the most tangible existing evidence of the end of American isolation, the reversal of traditional American foreign policy. It remains a constant and

---

[19]Kissinger, *Troubled Partnership*, pp. 245, 155.

necessary reminder to the American people of their changed traditions, interests, and circumstances.

Second, NATO's military roles remind all its member governments that they have security problems none can solve alone even though it is not exactly clear how they can solve them together. It is frustrating especially for Americans to be reminded of problems that will not admit to solution. In certain U.S. business and government circles, it is virtually a breach of decorum to bring up problems to which there are no ready solutions. However, in one of its most important effects NATO recalls to its members not only the problems but also the conditions in their external circumstances, which by definition are not likely to be ameliorable and with which once must therefore contend over the long term. NATO thus stands as a daily reminder of a point made many years ago by the great French diplomatist, Jules Cambon: "An improvement in political morality does not necessarily alter the very conditions of national existence." NATO's military roles should emphasize that neither détente, interdependence, nor any other new policy of international affairs is likely to relieve the Western democracies of the responsibility to safeguard their institutions.

Finally, NATO's military role, with its difficulties and shortcomings, may lead to rediscovery of the truth in Kennan's observation late in 1948, as NATO's founding was bruited within the American government. "This pact," as Kennan summarized his position in his memoirs, "should not be regarded as the main answer to the Russian effort to achieve domination over Western Europe, nor as a replacement for other needed steps."[20] He feared then that creation of NATO would "not appreciably modify the nature or danger of Soviet policies ... basic Russian intent still runs to the conquest of Western Europe by political means ... and, if there should not be a shooting war, it is this political war which will be decisive." He also warned against "a general preoccupation with military affairs, to the detriment of economic recovery and of the necessity for seeking a peaceful solution to Europe's difficulties."[21]

In 1948, Kennan's words reflected concern over a Western Europe prostrated by colossal war. It would be inappropriate even to intimate that NATO members today approach anything like the fragility of economic, political, and military conditions of those dreadful years. However, in a time of oil-fired inflation, public pessimism over the future, and little confidence in government, it would be a mistake not to recall Kennan's warning against the perennial danger of overreliance on military answers to profound human and political problems. As the literature of the last

---

[20]Kennan, *Memoirs*, pp. 410–11.

[21]George F. Kennan, "Consideration Affecting the Conclusion of a North Atlantic Security Pact," *FRUS, 1948*, 3:284–85. Republished with Analysis and Commentary in Etzold and Gaddis, *Containment*, pp. 153–58.

fifteen years has so often suggested, if NATO is ever to become more than a military alliance or a vehicle for the Atlantic Community or for wider contribution to political and economic progress in the Western World, it will be because a military alliance—however essential—could not suffice by itself either to abate the threats of Marxist revolution and Stalinist brutality or to incorporate the highest aspirations and interests of liberal democracies in a politically awakened world.

INDEX

251